M000233172

WITHDRAWN
TIPTON COUNTY
PUBLIC LIBRARY

TIPTON CO. LIBRARY
TIPTON, INDIANA

The Best American Short Plays

2018–2019

The Best American Short Plays

2018–2019

Edited with an Introduction
by John Patrick Bray

APPLAUSE THEATRE & CINEMA BOOKS
Guilford, Connecticut

Applause Theatre & Cinema Books
An imprint of The Rowman & Littlefield Publishing Group, Inc.
4501 Forbes Blvd., Ste. 200
Lanham, MD 20706
www.rowman.com

Distributed by NATIONAL BOOK NETWORK

Copyright © 2021 by Applause Theatre & Cinema Books (An imprint of The Rowman & Littlefield Publishing Group, Inc.)

All rights reserved. No part of this book may be reproduced in any form or by any electronic or mechanical means, including information storage and retrieval systems, without written permission from the publisher, except by a reviewer who may quote passages in a review.

British Library Cataloguing in Publication Information available

Library of Congress Cataloging-in-Publication Data available

ISBN 978-1-4930-5592-0 (hardcover)
ISBN 978-1-4930-5593-7 (e-book)
ISSN 0067-6284

♾™ The paper used in this publication meets the minimum requirements of American National Standard for Information Sciences—Permanence of Paper for Printed Library Materials, ANSI/NISO Z39.48-1992

Printed in the United States of America

contents

Introduction

This Is Who We Are

John P. Bray

When life itself seems lunatic, who knows where madness lies? Perhaps to be too practical is madness. To surrender dreams—this may be madness. Too much sanity may be madness—and maddest of all: to see life as it is, and not as it should be!

—Miguel de Cervantes, *Don Quixote*

We must all do theatre, to find out who we are, and to discover who we could become.

—Augusto Boal

The last four years have been marked by a great divide among our citizens. With "insta-culture" becoming our new marketplace for the exchange of ideas, there is a sense that whatever our politics or personal convictions, any news story that crosses our feed requires precious little of us: we have a reaction, we scroll past. We nod to the headlines that support our convictions, we shake our heads at the stories that do not (and often, adjust our feed so we will no longer see posts that push against our experiences). In many ways, social media has improved our lives by virtually connecting people from all over the world. On the other hand, there is a sense that we are isolated from human experiences that require *presence*. Theater is one of the few spaces that require *presence* from both performer and audience as they are in a very active, present tense conversation with one another.

The theme of this collection is "This Is Who We Are." Each of the plays demonstrates the thoughtful ways in which playwrights are wrestling to make sense out of the world by providing a clear reflection of not just who we are but also, to borrow from both Cervantes and Boal, who we aspire to become as a nation and as a community. The styles of the plays also reflect different approaches to writing for live, presence-based performance: the rich and compelling characters try to work out their differences with honest moments of human connection. This is who we are: people who are grappling with the desire to be understood, the hope to be loved and accepted, and allowing that hope to shape a larger sense of who we could become if we learn to listen.

We start our journey with two realistic plays, followed by one that is a bit more surreal. In *The Eye of the Wake* by Chima Chikazunga, Elaine calls upon her late father's intern to accompany her to his wake. Once there, she is forced to confront a secret that her father took to the grave about life. *Picket Fence People* by Estelle Olivia, tells the story of Rachel and Eliza, who are building the perfect life. But when Eliza backs out of her artificial insemination they are forced to grapple with what it means to be modern women, mothers, and lesbians trying to live the American dream. In Laura King's lovely, absurd-yet-too-real *Autour du Lit*, Addison and Ever go round and round the bed as they journey through the stages of love. Can romantic love be sustained through the realities of life or are we destined to love and lose over and over again? *Fault Lines* by David Adam Gill is a hard-hitting piece that asks tough questions: How far would you go to protect a child that's different? What if the threat came from the child's parents?

In the science fiction play *Guardians of the Field* by Liz Amadio, a woman arrives at an Energy Transfer Station "somewhere in the universe," expecting to be reunited with her sister, and is, instead, greeted by an official who enthusiastically appoints her Guardian of Field 6832. But what is this field, what are her duties, and why was she chosen? Scott C. Sickles's *Badger and Frame* is a more reflective piece, presenting different time periods in one space: During the summer of 1978, Bobby "Badger" McCandless and Ephraim "Frame" Siebert were best friends. Today, after Bobby's funeral, Ephraim meets his childhood bestie's widow Mary Kate, and, over the course of their conversation, he relives his friendship with "Badger" and their summer of exploration and adventure, from its humble beginnings to its abrupt end.

The next three plays deal with characters trying to bring a loved one to an understanding. In Mathilde Dratwa's *Escape from Garden Grove*, we are introduced to Sophie, a fifteen-year-old who hates home. So she's kidnapping her grandma from the assisted living facility, and they're running away to Belgium. If only the bus would come. If only Grandma knew where Belgium was. Bella Poynton's *Eleven Things That Almost Happened to Rick and Hannah, and One Thing That Actually Did* tells the story of Hannah and Rick, who have been friends for a long time, despite Rick being a difficult person to deal with. He can't be trusted or counted on, and quite honestly, he might be from another dimension! *The Play About the Squirrel or Infestation* by Mia McCullough is one of the most beautiful and heartbreaking plays I have read. When married couple Tom and Sarah discover a squirrel trapped in the attic of their new home they have very different responses to this unplanned . . . situation. *The Play About the Squirrel* is a tragicomic look at unplanned pregnancy and abortion through metaphor.

The origins of theater are said to be routed in myth, and the next two plays have elements of the mythic yet still feel very modern. *The Artist Electric* by Judah Skoff, inspired by the myth of Electra, is a story of sex and madness. Told in dueling poetic monologues, the daughter and second wife of a famed theater director recount the mysterious circumstances of his death at a massive beach house during a wild summer party. Through their divergent perspectives, we wonder how well we can truly know our families, our lovers, and ourselves. *CouchFullaLuv* by Kato McNickle is a magical farce about love, commitment, and the stress experienced by new couples agreeing on large pieces of furniture. But this is no ordinary day in the Furniture Showroom. Feathers from the wings of love fall from the sky, promising romance to those that hold them, and the act of sitting upon one fantastic couch can unleash their passions.

The next two plays have a focus on objects. In *Chocolate* by Judd Lear Silverman, the object is indeed chocolate. Warding off unwanted advances, Rose rides shotgun, surveying land and sea—but still is unsure how to handle a young stranger, Beau, a man with a piece of chocolate. Despite our past experiences, do we risk hurt to find a new adventure? Set in a possible alternate universe, *Unabridged* by Sean Abley shows us a world in which humanity has lost its language, and words are drugs, hoarded and sold by dealers. Barker, a dealer of high quality operating out of an old library, learns a rival dealer is revealed to possess the ultimate stash—the unabridged dictionary.

Lacrimosa by Christopher R. Marshall and *Be Yourself* by Daniel Guyton both deal with characters that are attempting to break free of outside suppositions in order to fully realize who they are. In *Lacrimosa* we meet Joanne, who, after tiring from the monotony of a lifeless marriage, decides to take the initiative and kill her husband so she can be free of him. Each day she attempts a different method of murder, and she gets more and more frustrated because each day she fails until . . . but let's not give the story away. *Be Yourself* by Daniel Guyton focuses on three teenagers that struggle with their own self-image and self-worth. Everyone tells them to "be themselves," but none of them really know what that means.

The next two plays deal with the value of human life—one presented as an absurdist comedy and the other as heartbreaking reality. *Blessed Are the Dead at the Department of Life and Longevity* by John Yarbrough is the tale of a man who attempts to sell his life to the highest bidder. Following is Crystal Skillman's haunting piece *SEEN*: a woman faces herself in mirrors over time as she struggles to reconcile her journeys as she is sex-trafficked across the country.

The last three plays in a way are a look back at the aesthetic journey that we have just taken as we meet characters in both realistic and decidedly unrealistic settings. George Sapio's *The Bottle* introduces us to Sage, who is terminally ill and has a master plan to end her life on her own terms. However, she faces two difficulties: finding the worst play in the world and getting her magic potion back from a purse snatcher. In *Saving Grace* by Bara Swain, underemployed Grace is discovered trying out a new skill—balancing a tennis racket on her finger—when her divorced mother makes a surprise visit. The play explores responsibility, disappointment, and mother/daughter relationships, when Grace's Uncle Lenny ends up in a nearby hospital. Ending our anthology is *Amulets for Garthenon* by Jake Hunsbusher. The play is an example of "geek theater," a genre-blending approach to theater-making introduced by the Vampire Cowboys in NYC. *Amulets* is a hybrid of two distinct television and film genres: the buddy sitcom (think *Perfect Strangers* or *The Odd Couple*) and science fiction (*Star Trek* or *Flash Gordon*). It is a highly theatrical and hilarious piece.

With the title *Best of,* do keep in mind that the choices for inclusion are subjective and, of course, very difficult to make. I do believe there is something in here for everyone, and that each piece, regardless of style, speaks to the theme "This Is Who We Are," as we journey via representational realism through speculative considerations of possible futures, for better and for worse—the better serving as possibilities for who we aspire to be; the worse serving as a warning of what lies ahead if we stay the present course. Thank you for purchasing this anthology.

Note: This edition was completed prior to the pandemic.

The Eye of the Wake

Chima Chikazunga

The Eye of the Wake by Chima Chikazunga. Copyright © 2018 by Chima Chikazunga. All rights reserved. Reprinted by permission of the author.

CAUTION/ADVICE: Professionals and amateurs are hereby warned that performance of *The Eye of the Wake* is subject to a royalty. It is fully protected under the copyright laws of the United States of America, and of all countries covered by the International Copyright Union (including the Dominion of Canada and the rest of the British Commonwealth), and of all countries covered by the Pan-American Copyright Convention and the Universal Copyright Convention, the Berne Convention, and of all countries with which the United States has reciprocal copyright relations. All rights, including professional and amateur stage performing rights, motion picture, recitation, lecturing, public reading, radio broadcasting, television, video or sound recording, all other forms of mechanical or electronic reproduction, such as CD-ROM, DVD-ROM, information storage and retrieval systems, and photocopying, and the rights of translation into foreign languages, are strictly reserved. Particular emphasis is placed upon the matter of readings, permission for which must be secured from Chima Chikazunga in writing in advance. Inquiries concerning rights should be addressed to Chima Chikazunga at chikazungaplays@gmail.com.

Chima Chikazunga

CHIMA CHIKAZUNGA: actor/writer/director. FSU graduate. Select Plays: *3 the Hard Way* (11th Annual DUTF, semi-finalist 2014 Mentor Project, MITF 2016), *Sophie's Sweet 16*, *For Chance*, *The Accidental Kiss* (TFNC DREAM UP FESTIVAL 13,14,15), *Touch My Heart Masterpiece* (CTH Future Classics), *A Thing Called Balance* (INTAR), *Not Just You* (AND Theatre Co. & New City, New Blood Series (TFNC), *Echoes of a Lost Son* (DREAM UP FESTIVAL 18, 2019 PATV WINNER, AWOW), *The Eye of the Wake* (Eclectics Festival, MITF 2016), 3 ECHOES (Short Play Festival, NYC), *For Chance* (DUAF 2020), *Fallen Soldiers* (CTH Icons), *Chantel's Dilemma* (Negro Ensemble Company), *Me or You* (The Breath Project) https://newplayexchange.org/users/9921/chima-chikazunga.

···production history···

The Eye of the Wake was produced as part of the 2019 Artistic New Directions (AND) Eclectics Festival. The production was directed by Chima Chikazunga and featured the following cast:

ELAINE, Sara Parcesepe

CHAUNCEY, Chima Chikazunga

characters

ELAINE AUSTIN, forty-two, Caucasian. Painters' daughter. Bipolar. Lonely, a writer.

CHAUNCEY, twenty-five, African American. Painter's intern. College senior. Hides feelings well, difficulty with grief.

setting

NYC.

time

The present.

···

[At rise: Living room. One week after PAINTER *has passed.* CHAUNCEY *is alone, next to the door to the room. Hesitant, he goes to knock. Then stops. Checks door again, it's locked.* ELAINE *is on the other side of the door, offstage. Finally he knocks.]*

CHAUNCEY Everything OK? [*No response.*] Hey, Elaine, you OK?

ELAINE [*Offstage.*] I'm not going.

CHAUNCEY [*A moment.*] OK, can you open up.

ELAINE [*Offstage.*] I'm not going, Chauncey. I can't.

CHAUNCEY Whatever you want.

ELAINE [*Offstage.*] That's what I want. I can't go.

CHAUNCEY OK but you've been in there almost forty minutes you know. And the door's locked.

ELAINE   [*Offstage.*] I know.

CHAUNCEY   Can you open it?

ELAINE   [*Offstage.*] I can.

CHAUNCEY   Will you open it?

ELAINE   [*Offstage.*] Nope.

CHAUNCEY   Why not?

ELAINE   [*Offstage.*] I don't want to.

CHAUNCEY   OK I think I know the answer to this but "why not?"

ELAINE   [*Offstage.*] Because you're going to try and get me to go.

CHAUNCEY   I don't want you doing anything you don't want to do.

ELAINE   [*Offstage.*] You're just saying that so I'll come out.

CHAUNCEY   No, I'm not.

ELAINE   [*Offstage.*] Yes, you are

CHAUNCEY   . . . I'm serious. If you don't want to go, you don't have to. [*No response.*] "Ships don't sink because of the water around them. Ships sink because of the water that gets in them. Don't let what's happening around you get inside you and weight you down."

[*Suddenly* ELAINE *slowly emerges from room. A moment. They hug.*]

ELAINE   You sound like my dad. [*Beat.*] My father's mother survived the holocaust. And she never let me forget it.

CHAUNCEY   He told me.

ELAINE   He told you?

CHAUNCEY   Yeah, it's why he enlisted isn't it?

ELAINE   Yeah . . . so he told you how he went to Nam?

CHAUNCEY   Yeah. And how him going was a deeper connection to his company's mission statement . . .

ELAINE "We seek to represent voices of those who are afraid for their life to speak up."

CHAUNCEY I told him how I couldn't even believe your grandmother survived. I think I said something like if she ever went back I guess it'd be like going to a plantation down South.

ELAINE Oh please. Don't compare slavery to the Holocaust.

CHAUNCEY Funny, he said the same thing.

ELAINE I'm just saying, don't compare the two. My people suffered enough as I'm sure did theirs.

[*Moment. Lights shift as* ELAINE *has finished looking at a painting on cell phone. A moment. She hands it back to* CHAUNCEY.]

CHAUNCEY It came in the mail. In like this big box.

ELAINE In a box?

CHAUNCEY Yeah.

ELAINE And he shared this with you?

CHAUNCEY Everyday . . . it helped with his process.

ELAINE Process?

CHAUNCEY Yeah, it was like he trusted me. My vision. It was trippy.

ELAINE He liked you.

CHAUNCEY Yeah I guess but this was different. This was his masterpiece.

ELAINE Then you should keep it.

CHAUNCEY I don't need to. He wanted you to have it.

ELAINE Keep it. He mailed it to you

CHAUNCEY Obviously, for safekeeping. I mean—to make sure you got it.

ELAINE You didn't know him like me. Look, I know I called you but you shouldn't have come today. You have no idea the—[*Stops.*] What do you think it was about? Do you think this was about us?

CHAUNCEY No. We spoke about it after. He said he was in a dark place back then.

ELAINE A dark place? No he wasn't.

CHAUNCEY That's what he said. I really didn't get into it too much but—

ELAINE I don't get it. It's been a week. I don't think I can do this.

CHAUNCEY Yes you can.

ELAINE I can't!!

CHAUNCEY Why not, Elaine?

ELAINE He looked at me. When I found him.

CHAUNCEY How could he look at you if he was—

ELAINE He looked at me . . . his eyes were open. It was as if I could read his lips. He was saying "I'm sorry." [*Stops.*] Why would he—

CHAUNCEY I don't know but this was his place of sanctuary. Where he'd come to find peace and get away from everything in front of that easel—

ELAINE Did he though? Find peace? [*Stops.*] I'm glad you're here.

CHAUNCEY I'm glad I'm here too.

ELAINE It's been a week Chauncey. The funeral is today. What are we doing here? I mean with life. What are we doing it for?

CHAUNCEY That's a good question.

ELAINE I know. It's just hard not knowing.

CHAUNCEY Not knowing what?

ELAINE Knowing why. There weren't any signs.

CHAUNCEY Signs? Like what?

ELAINE   Was I a good daughter?

CHAUNCEY   Of course you were. You can't blame yourself for him dying.

ELAINE   Why can't I? He knew what he was doing. He drank. A diabetic who lost his sight, still drank. [*Beat.*] I haven't cried all week. The pain is just—it's just—

CHAUNCEY   Don't talk like that.

ELAINE   I spoke with the guy from the *Times*. The guy from the last review. He called me to give his condolences.

CHAUNCEY   That's nice.

ELAINE   He hated him.

CHAUNCEY   And he reached out to you? That's odd. Especially if he hated him.

ELAINE   No, he apparently went to see him recently to apologize. [*A moment. No response.*] What? What's that look for?

CHAUNCEY   Nothing. I just . . . did he give a reason?

ELAINE   No. They were actually going to meet the night—[*Stops.*]

CHAUNCEY   What is it?

ELAINE   Nothing.

CHAUNCEY   Elaine, it's me, you can tell me anything.

ELAINE   Why do I to have to bury my dad?

CHAUNCEY   Would you prefer the other way around?

ELAINE   That's the way it's supposed to be.

CHAUNCEY   Says who?

ELAINE   Says me. "It's no use."

CHAUNCEY   What's not? [*No response.*] What's no use, Elaine?

ELAINE   I'm sorry my mind is—I just I can't look at so many things that—

CHAUNCEY Remind you of him? It's OK. There's no need to explain. Come on. Let's go.

[*A moment.*]

ELAINE Daddy? Do you think I'll be OK?

CHAUNCEY What'd you say?

ELAINE I said do you think I'll be OK?

CHAUNCEY I heard you . . . but you called me Daddy?

ELAINE No I didn't. Did I?

CHAUNCEY It doesn't matter. I know today's not going to be easy . . . but we should go. Don't wanna be late.

[*As he starts out . . . lights shift to A spotlight on* ELAINE. CHAUNCEY *lingers.*]

ELAINE Thank you all for coming. I know he would be proud to see you all here. Part of me sees him truly in a better place, holding my mother's hand watching over me as I speak to you all today.

My gosh I can't believe I'm doing this. I told myself, when I agreed to give the closing remarks, that I wouldn't cry.

And seeing you all here, knowing how much he loved and admired you all, means a great deal to me.

Life.

"Life isn't about living. Life is about what you do before you die."

My father used to say that. And I guess deep down my mother loved him for it. He always spoke his mind, even before he lost his sight. Which is ironic—[*Stops. Collects herself again.*]

If you know my father, you would know his appreciation he had for Shakespeare but . . .

When I was young, about eight or nine, I used to think my father was playing a game. To me, it was fun. But for my mother, it wasn't.

My father drank. In fact, one of my mother's last wishes was for me to keep it out of the household when she passed on. To which, I did a pretty good job.

Anyway, back to this game. My father would lay down on the floor and pretend to be dead to the world. No matter what I tried, nothing seemed to work. My mother would always say, "it's no use."

Like I mentioned, I was young. I thought we were just playing, but as I got older and as my mother began to share with me certain things, I began to come to know this game wasn't a game at all. See, he would be passed out drunk on the floor, pretty much dead to the world, and I guess I would encourage it because every time he woke up, he would see my face, smile, and say . . . "Sweet Shakes . . . That face . . . My Elaine," and then give me a hug.

To which I would call off to my mother and say, "See told you I could wake him. You said it's no use. You underestimate my daddy."

And every time after "See told you I could wake him. You said it's no use. You underestimate my daddy."

Then at my Sweet Sixteen, when we had our dance it was magical. I'd never seen him so happy, and some of you in this room can vouch for what I'm about to say. My dress looked amazing and I had never seen the Old Man so happy . . . And as the song is winding down, he puked down my back as I had my head on his shoulder.

And I'll never forget my mother's reaction, she ran out on the dance floor in tears hitting him and cursing. I didn't understand it at first . . . Why would she do that . . . see I didn't know what it was until she said one word. She called him many names in the past when she was upset but never this one. This time, she called him a "drunk" . . . My eyes and his eyes locked as he must have felt the ultimate embarrassment because there wasn't disgust or disappointment, only shame.

And so as I stand here before you attempting to hold back my tears, knowing they've been running down my cheeks, I say to you, in the words of my late mother . . . "It's no use."

[*Lights begin to dim/fade*]

ELAINE [*In darkness.*] That's how I want to remember him? "It's no use?" In front of all those people? Hope you're proud of yourself Old Man.

[*Lights full in living room. Hours after funeral service. Enter* CHAUNCEY.]

ELAINE Why . . .

CHAUNCEY I know.

ELAINE But why.

CHAUNCEY It's life . . . like you said.

ELAINE "Life?" He said that.

CHAUNCEY I know.

ELAINE It doesn't even feel like it has been a week.

CHAUNCEY I know.

ELAINE CAN YOU STOP FREAKIN SAYING "YOU KNOW?"!! I know you know!

CHAUNCEY [*A moment.*] How are you holding up? I'm sorry. [*Stops.*] It was a nice service. He lived a good life.

ELAINE It was a bit depressing. I just feel so lost without him.

CHAUNCEY It was the same way with my brother.

ELAINE No offense, Chauncey, but the death of a sibling is probably easier than that of a parent.

CHAUNCEY I wouldn't know. My mother died giving birth to me, remember? [*No response.*] Never mind. We all grieve differently.

ELAINE He left a letter. Well, a recording actually. Nothing planned or anything like that. Kind of . . . like he knew it was his time. Someone from his theatre dropped it off.

CHAUNCEY I was surprised you spoke at the service. It was peaceful and about life. I would've been so—

ELAINE   Actually, I kind of don't want to think about what I said earlier.

CHAUNCEY   I understand.

ELAINE   Thanks for sticking around to help clean up.

CHAUNCEY   Not a problem. This summer with your dad meant a lot to me.

ELAINE   I know he knew about us. It's a father's intuition. But did he find out about you . . . I mean, he never called you—the N WORD did he?

CHAUNCEY   No. Why would you ask that?

ELAINE   No, I DIDN'T MEAN . . . it's not like that.

CHAUNCEY   Then what's it like?

ELAINE   There's a reason why I don't sleep. [*Sigh.*] I failed him.

CHAUNCEY   Failed who? Your dad? No you didn't.

ELAINE   Yeah I did. And it's twice now. Twice the night before my parents funeral, I had a dream about them. Dying.

CHAUNCEY   You had a dream about your dad? Dying? Wait, I'm confused . . . What about your mom, same way? I mean dealing with her death?

ELAINE   My mom was different. [*Collects herself.*] She told me a lot about his past. Mainly during the war. I was never proud of it, and I spent a lot of my child hood growing to resent him. [*Beat.*] It's hard to explain. When I woke up that day, after he died, I was naked. Like naked in his wheelchair. I was still out of it but I felt free. [*Stops.*] . . . Who am I kidding, I called him this morning. I'm sorry but I don't think I can cut off his phone. And now . . . I finally . . . I finally have the guts to say, "Daddy I love you" and I can't. Why, Chauncey? I left like seventeen messages alone today on his phone. It's full now, no one can leave a message.

CHAUNCEY   You need rest, I should go.

ELAINE Hey, would you mind sticking around for a little while longer? I really don't feel like being left alone. We could just talk.

CHAUNCEY I guess . . . Yeah, talking is good.

ELAINE That's not what I meant. You were his intern. You got to know him.

CHAUNCEY I don't understand.

ELAINE Of course not. Sometimes the most boring place in the world can be paradise with the right person.

CHAUNCEY Poetic. You sound like him.

ELAINE Where do you think I got it from? . . . Stay.

[*She takes out* PAINTER'S *flask.*]

CHAUNCEY What's that supposed to be?

ELAINE Come on, it's in our blood.

CHAUNCEY Listen, Elaine, I know what you're implying so don't treat me like I'm an idiot.

ELAINE [*She explodes.*] How long were you buying him booze?

CHAUNCEY He tell you that?

ELAINE He didn't have to. I smelled it on him every day over the last month after you left. And we don't keep alcohol here. So drink with me. I've been at it since this morning. Unless you too good to drink with me? [*She drinks.*]

CHAUNCEY I never said that but I'm not drinking from a dead man's flask.

ELAINE You too good to celebrate his life? [*She drinks.*]

[*Suddenly she licks the side of his face.*]

CHAUNCEY What the fuck are you doing?

ELAINE [*Laughs hysterically.*] Relax. I'm just curious if you have any addictions. Like your brother. [*She takes off her shirt.*]

CHAUNCEY That's not funny. What are you doing?

ELAINE Tell me I'm still beautiful. I just need to hear it.

CHAUNCEY You know you are.

[*She sits him down. undoes his belt. He allows it, as it continues for a while. Suddenly she stops. A moment.*]

ELAINE What's wrong with me! [*No response.*] What's wrong with me!

[*Suddenly she begins hitting herself repeatedly in the head.*]

CHAUNCEY What are you doing?

ELAINE Don't act like this is the first time we—

CHAUNCEY Doesn't matter! We just laid him to rest not more than a few hours ago.

ELAINE Fuck my father!! Look you got me to cry so what's the problem? You know we both needed this. You're only making excuses because you know you liked it. Be happy my father's not here.

CHAUNCEY How can you say this? Do you even know why he was drinking with me?

ELAINE Enlighten me, Chauncey, because I could blame you for his death, condoning his drinking behind my back, but I won't. He made his own bed a long time ago.

CHAUNCEY The man was drinking because he missed your mother.

ELAINE And it killed him. My father is dead and left me a painting that I will never be able to explain. FUCKING HEART WITH TWO SEPARATE INFANTS' HANDS TOUCHING IT . . . one just a little darker than the other. Do you think I want to deal with any of this?! Had my father not been an alcoholic diabetic and lost his sight, we wouldn't be having this conversation. I don't even know who I am anymore. [*Hiccup.*] Do you think I'm gonna end up like him? I'm so empty inside.

CHAUNCEY We're all empty inside. I should go.

ELAINE If you really wanted my child, you shouldn't have done it.

CHAUNCEY Elaine, you're drunk. I never said I wanted you to have my child.

ELAINE You're weak. That's why I'm drinking. I fucked a weak man. Now get your weak ass out of my house

CHAUNCEY I think I should go before something bad happens.

[Suddenly, she pulls out a flask, unscrews it, stops. Suddenly she drinks.]

ELAINE You're the reason I finished it.

CHAUNCEY Finished what? The flask?

ELAINE No, my novel. Synopsis and all . . . You got me to write. I thought of you and I finished my novel. Aren't you happy? It's about a woman in pain who was forced to love Shakespeare and live in her father's footsteps.

CHAUNCEY Don't do this, Elaine.

ELAINE Don't do what? I'm writing again. So soon after his death. And it's because of you. See I dreamed about him discovering you were black just before he died. *[Sigh.]* Did he . . . I mean, my father. Did he ever call you . . . well you know—

CHAUNCEY What? A nigger? *[Sigh.]* You know, it's funny. That's the second time you asked me that. Like it's some sort of problem or I'm some sort of idiot. Why? See, when I first got here I couldn't believe where I was. I felt as if I had arrived. I mean, literally, it was a summer internship that I truly earned; it was all mine. I beat so many others for this opportunity. And then, there he was. Someone I had admired for as long as I could remember. As long as I even began reading plays. And I was going to learn from him. Me . . . and no one else. And then you told me he was racist . . . and for some reason, I felt hurt. I mean, I wasn't hurt because I felt let down by a man whom I idolized and befriended me or even bonded with over a course of a summer. I felt let down because of you. See, at the time, me and you, we never really spoken . . . until that moment. We did other things. Physically, but never mental. I didn't want that with you. Not saying it was just sex. But I often wondered how it would be if he knew I was sleeping with his daughter; would it matter if I was black. Even though he was blind and my mentor . . . "it's not like your name is Jamal or Kareem." Right?

ELAINE That's not what I meant.

CHAUNCEY Those are your words.

ELAINE It's not like that. I swear.

CHAUNCEY Shut the fuck up and listen!!! It's my turn to talk! Sorry, that was rude of me. [*Sigh. Let's go.*] See, when I was a kid I used to go to day camp in the suburbs and I had this friend. We had to be about seven or so and we were riding our bikes over to his house that day after camp. My friend was half Asian but what did I care, we were just kids. We didn't know anything about race like that; all we knew was about friends. And I suddenly forgot where I was going with this. [*Stops.*] Oh yeah . . . So we are riding our bikes over to his house after camp because he's got a hoop in his driveway and his parents weren't there, so we could play. I used to always beat him at camp, so that day we decided to play at his court because "he never loses there." So whatever, I don't care, and we're riding and I begin to notice that the houses are getting nicer. Like they are changing, from what my neighborhood houses look like to his. But I guess that's the norm because we crossed the tracks and seem to be heading towards the water. So anyway, we come across this guy sitting on the stoop of this church drinking a can of beer, but we really don't pay him any mind. Suddenly we hear . . . "Hey get that nigger out of here!" And I stop and I'm like "who?" So I say, "Hey Tommy, I think that guy called you a nickel. You know him? Nickel is half a dime right? He know you are half Chinese? I don't get it and Tommy says, " No keep riding. He wasn't talking to me, he was talking to you. He said nigger, not nickel." Not sure I even let it register but next thing I know, a beer can exploded in between us and I stopped. [*Pause.*] Long story short, Tommy's dad wasn't too far away and spotted us. He was a cop and Tommy was shaken up afterwards. Tommy's dad went back by the church and arrested the guy. [*Beat.*] I hadn't thought about that story until after that day you mentioned your father being racist. So . . .

yeah . . . Fuck him, and fuck your raggety bipolar ass too!!! Who the fuck are you to tell me if someone is racist or not huh? You fuck some black dude and all of a sudden you are now some kind of expert on black people? Bitch, you don't know dick about black people or what a racist is. All you know is after you suck my dick if I taste good or not. Nothing else, so don't get it twisted. You want to tell me your father is racist? I don't give a fuck. I fucked his daughter. He had a black man inside his house, screwing his only child, And she loved this nigga's Mandingo. Ain't that right? [*Laughs.*] Here, you asked me if he ever called me nigger, right? NO . . . BUT HIS DAUGHTER DID.

ELAINE [*A moment.*] I'm really sorry. I said a lot of terrible things today and I—Can you come back tomorrow?

CHAUNCEY Can I what? What are you, insane?

ELAINE [*Crying.*] No I just . . . This whole summer having you here. There's a connection.

CHAUNCEY Just stop.

ELAINE [*Crying.*] I'm sorry for what I said . . . for what I did. Don't leave me. We have something. We're connected. You have to feel it.

CHAUNCEY You don't understand—[*Sigh.*] You need help.

ELAINE So you won't come back tomorrow? [*A moment.*] FUCK YOU THEN!!!! Guess we never had a connection anyway!

CHAUNCEY Fuck you, Elaine.

[*He starts off, stops, doubles back.*]

ELAINE [*Crying.*] "The itsy bitsy spider went up the water spout . . . down came the rain and wiped the spider out. Out came the sun and washed up all the rain and the itsy bitsy spider went up the spout again . . . "

CHAUNCEY Why did you say we had a connection . . .

ELAINE I never said that.

CHAUNCEY Yes you did. Why?

ELAINE I don't know what happened . . . You don't know when these things happen. It was when I was vulnerable not when I was strong, I guess.

CHAUNCEY I never said I didn't think you were strong.

ELAINE I think you did. Yeah maybe you should go.

CHAUNCEY What's wrong with you? Your father's dead but if he could see you—

ELAINE Like it's ever a convenient time to die . . . Look, I'm glad you came back but I think you should go.

CHAUNCEY Really?

ELAINE I don't know . . . maybe.

CHAUNCEY You don't mean that. You need help?

ELAINE I need a lot of help but I'm not right for you. You have your whole life ahead of you.

CHAUNCEY I'm talking about this place. He's gone. Who do you have now to help?

ELAINE I'm a big girl, Chauncey.

CHAUNCEY That's not what I asked, so answer the question, Elaine.

ELAINE Don't do this, Chauncey. Not today. He wasn't your family.

CHAUNCEY Elaine, you need to go through his things. Let me help!

ELAINE After what just happened . . . you wanna help? I don't even know where to start.

CHAUNCEY I've been there before. That's how I felt. Going through my brother's room . . . You feel numb inside, don't you?

ELAINE How'd you know? I'm so numb inside, Chauncey. I think you may be the only person who I can really talk to.

[*He notices she too is fighting tears. A standstill. He crosses to sit next to her. Blackout.*]

• • •

Picket Fence People

Estelle Olivia

Picket Fence People by Estelle Olivia. Copyright © 2018 by Estelle Olivia. All rights reserved. Reprinted by permission of the author.

CAUTION/ADVICE: Professionals and amateurs are hereby warned that performance of *Picket Fence People* is subject to a royalty. It is fully protected under the copyright laws of the United States of America, and all of countries covered by the International Copyright Union (including the Dominion of Canada and the rest of the British Commonwealth), and of all countries covered by the Pan-American Copyright Convention and the United States Copyright Convention, the Berne Convention, and all of the countries with which the United States has reciprocal copyright relations. All rights, including professional and amateur stage performing rights, motion picture, recitation, lecturing, public reading, radio broadcasting, television, video or sound picture recording, all other forms of mechanical or electronic reproduction, such as CD-ROM, DVD-ROM, information storage and retrieval systems, and photocopying, and the rights of translation into foreign language are strictly reserved. Particular emphasis is placed upon the matter of readings, permission for which must be secured by Estelle Oliva in writing in advance. Inquiries concerning rights should be addressed to Estelle Oliva: Estelle.Oliva@gmail.com.

Estelle Olivia

ESTELLE OLIVIA is a Brooklyn-based writer and actor. Their writing includes plays: *Picket Fence People*, *Cross Match*, *Bitter Sweet*, *Tender*, and *Fond at Best*; and screenplays: *Changeling* and *Lobster Queen*. Their work has been written, produced, or developed at The Cell Theatre, Joe's Pub at The Public Theatre, The Actors Studio Drama School, and The CRY HAVOC company. They received their BA in Theatre Arts from Mount Holyoke College, their MFA from The Actors Studio Drama School, and have studied at The Upright Citizens Brigade, The British American Drama Academy, and Atlantic Acting School. EstelleOlivia.com.

··· production history ···

Picket Fence People was originally produced by The Actors Studio Drama School Repertory Season (Andreas Manolikakis, Artistic Director; Shawn Lewis, Executive Director), New York City, on May 8, 2019. It was directed by Sarah Brausch, the set designer was Shawn Lewis, the costume designer was Jennifer Paar, the lighting designer was Ethan Steimel, the sound designer was Sean Hagerty, the production stage manager was Patrick David Egan, and the assistant stage managers were Matthew Luppino and Katie Barnhard. The cast was as follows:

RACHEL, Kendra Mittermeyer

ELIZA, Kat Witschen

characters

RACHEL, early to late thirties. ELIZA's wife. A landscape architect.

ELIZA, mid-twenties to early thirties. RACHEL's wife. A divorce mediator.

setting

Rachel and Eliza's refurbished farmhouse on the outskirts of a liberal university town in an otherwise conservative state.

time

The present day.

···

[A Spring Saturday. Evening sun filters through the windows of RACHEL and ELIZA's open dining/sitting room. It has character and feels homey but modern. Pictures of the happy couple are artfully displayed. There is an exit on one side of the stage leading to the front hall, Rachel's home office, and rest of the house. Another on the opposite side leads to the kitchen.

There is a small seating area with the evidence of a celebration. A cluster of many colored pastel balloons floats nearby (purposefully non gender specific). There is some torn wrapping paper and, sitting propped in a place of honor, is a handmade sock monkey with slightly wonky eyes.

RACHEL *enters with a freshly pressed tablecloth and napkins. Her eyes are drawn immediately to the balloons, she looks away quickly. She clears the dining table and lays the tablecloth, glancing up once or twice. Finally she is drawn over to the sitting area, deeply affected by the scene there. Slowly she sits next to the sock monkey, picks it up tenderly, and holds it tight to her chest.*

She hears the sounds of ELIZA *approaching offstage.* RACHEL *quickly but carefully sets down the monkey and exits to the kitchen just in time.*

ELIZA *enters with a fresh-picked bunch of wildflowers. She takes in the beginnings of the table setting, then her eyes too are drawn to the balloons. She goes to them and takes one in her hands. The balloon suddenly pops and* ELIZA *shrieks.* RACHEL *enters carrying a stack of plates, stares at* ELIZA. *They both freeze for a moment, a palpable tension between them.*]

ELIZA   It popped.

[RACHEL *puts the plates down and goes back into the kitchen. She returns a moment later with a vase and puts the flowers in it. She avoids looking at her wife.*]

ELIZA   Are you ready to talk again?

[RACHEL *goes back into the kitchen. She returns with four water glasses and sets them down, ignoring* ELIZA.]

ELIZA   Rach.

[*RACHEL pulls out silverware and begins to set the table to the standards of a magazine spread.*]

ELIZA   Honey, I don't think this dinner is a good idea anymore.

[*RACHEL continues determinedly, eyes down.*]

ELIZA   Hey, will you look at me? Rachel . . . Are you giving me the silent treatment right now?

[ELIZA *waits for a moment.* RACHEL *continues setting the table. She precisely lays down a fork.* ELIZA *grabs it.* RACHEL *holds out a hand in mute demand, still not looking at her.*]

ELIZA   No! I gave you space, now we have to talk. This is childish.

[RACHEL *is brought up short by the word. Quick beat. She turns away and goes back into the kitchen.*]

ELIZA   God damnit.

[ELIZA *puts her fork down.* RACHEL *returns and thrusts a nice bottle of wine and an opener into* ELIZA's *hands. She exits to the rest of the house.* ELIZA *considers the wine for a moment, then opens it. She takes a generous swig just as* RACHEL *reenters the room and stops in horror at the sight.*]

RACHEL   That is a two thousand and twelve Domaine du Pegau! You have to let it breathe!

[*She snatches it out of* ELIZA's *hands and brings it to the hutch.*]

ELIZA   It's delicious.

RACHEL   You didn't even taste it.

ELIZA   Why don't you pour yourself a glass and sit down with me?

RACHEL   My mother is already on her way with her new boyfriend in tow, I have to—

ELIZA   I'll call and say I'm sick.

RACHEL   She would know something's wrong.

ELIZA   Something is wrong.

RACHEL   Which means she'd come rushing over here urging me to confide in her so she'd have something to relate to me about.

ELIZA   You don't have to accommodate her bad behavior.

RACHEL   And what about yours?

ELIZA   Don't compare me to your mother I—

RACHEL   Why not, Eli? You just upended our life completely with zero consideration for me or my plans. Did the two of you compare notes on how to destabilize me?

ELIZA   No! I wasn't—

RACHEL   Goddamn it. I didn't mean that.

ELIZA Rachel.

RACHEL I just want to get through this dinner, OK? I need you on my side for a couple of hours.

ELIZA I'm always on your side. That doesn't change.

RACHEL . . . Good. Because I don't know what I'd do without you. Who else would do drunken impressions to make me feel better when she reminds me my Tarte aux Fraises is never as good as grandmere's.

ELIZA I didn't mean to hurt you, Rach. I'm so sorry.

[*Tense beat.*]

RACHEL But you didn't get it.

ELIZA No.

RACHEL Because you freaked out.

ELIZA Well yes, but there's more to it—

RACHEL So last night, you came home, and . . .

ELIZA I wanted to tell you.

RACHEL Last night. I thought you were pregnant. I baked you a cake. And I sat here like a fool, and I toasted you with fake fucking champagne. And I cried.

ELIZA [*Overlapping.*] You were so lovely.

RACHEL [*Overlapping.*] I hate crying! And I didn't even care. I was so happy. But it was all . . . a lie.

ELIZA No, Rachel, we aren't a lie.

RACHEL How can you say that, Eli? You let me believe our child was inside of you growing eyeballs and a pancreas!

ELIZA In that moment, how could I possibly tell you that I didn't get inseminated? [*Indicating the monkey.*] You sewed! You—

RACHEL I should have gone with you. You never would have—

ELIZA No, the university contract is too important.

RACHEL What happened? We've been planning this for months. We were so close.

ELIZA I was in that clinic with the crinkly paper and the sterile smell and suddenly, it was real. And I just, didn't know what I was doing there, what we're doing here.

RACHEL I thought we were trying to start a family.

ELIZA We are, we were, I—

RACHEL Which one is it?

ELIZA What?

RACHEL Which one is it? We are, or we were?

ELIZA I don't know! [*Beat.*] It's like every little doubt I've had about . . . work schedules, or house rules has somehow become completely insurmountable.

RACHEL Eliza. We've worked all that out. I have the top three daycares lined up, I downloaded the sharing song.

ELIZA I don't know if I'm ready for this.

RACHEL We're ready for this.

ELIZA I don't know if *I* am ready. For what a kid is going to do to my life. Not just in the day to day but the actual arc of my life.

RACHEL It's the life we've always wanted.

ELIZA I don't want to be someone who just settles onto a path and looks up one day to find that 30 years have passed.

RACHEL You think you've settled?

ELIZA No, no. But there is so much wrong in the world. And all these people who've never looked beyond their own little lives, they—

RACHEL We're not people, we're us.

ELIZA And here I am with my steady job, and Ultimate Frisbee on second Saturdays, in the same small town I went to school in, about to start a family.

RACHEL You're trivializing our entire lives.

ELIZA I'm not trying to! But I don't want to spend mine just mediating nasty, petty little divorces for people who have too much money.

RACHEL You like your job! You keep people human under terrible circumstances.

ELIZA OK, sure but what good does it do on the grand scale? What about having a real dream?

RACHEL I'm living out my dream, Eli. I'm living exactly the life I wanted. I thought you were too. Right up until about 1pm this afternoon.

ELIZA I'm sorry. I'm just trying to explain—

RACHEL And I'm listening but—

ELIZA No, you're contradicting everything I say.

[*An oven buzzer goes off in the kitchen.*]

RACHEL Well I don't understand what you're trying to say then! I don't understand how this happened.

[*She goes to check the oven.*]

ELIZA I'm sorry, but I don't have a goddamn thesis for you! It's just this . . . nebulous . . .

[*She trails off, then pulls herself together and tries again.*]

ELIZA Listen, I know I messed up but I'm telling you how I feel.

[RACHEL *reenters carrying a wooden spoon.*]

ELIZA I need you to hear me. Please.

[RACHEL *holds out the spoon, one hand underneath to catch drips.* ELIZA *leans away from it, giving* RACHEL *a look.*]

RACHEL I am trying. But I hope you can see from my perspective that it's difficult. Because I woke up this morning with a pregnant wife. I woke up with a child. And my whole beautiful life stretched out before me.

ELIZA I'm so sorry—

RACHEL And then you told me that you ran out on our baby and lied to my face about it.

ELIZA An embryo is not the same thing as a baby, Rachel. It's not like I left our kid at the supermarket and never went back!

RACHEL I'm trying! OK?

[*She proffers the spoon again.*]

RACHEL Needs more salt?

[ELIZA *tastes it, then nods her head, chewing.* RACHEL *turns to go back into the kitchen.*]

RACHEL They'll be here soon so you'd better keep going.

ELIZA Oh my god.

[*Quick beat,* ELIZA *regroups.*]

ELIZA I don't want to be one of these kids I went to high school with. I don't want to be 'gay' Brad and Christie with the remodeled house and the godforsaken Christmas cards.

RACHEL Who the hell are Brad and Christie?

ELIZA Brad and Christie are a metaphor! They're the homecoming couple.

[RACHEL *comes back to lean in the doorway, she's lost the thread.*]

RACHEL Did you know a Brad and Christie?

ELIZA No.

RACHEL How does this have anything to do with our family?

ELIZA Because we're turning into those people. I'm turning into those people.

RACHEL What people, Eli?

ELIZA The picket fence people!

RACHEL What??

[RACHEL *points her wooden spoon at* ELIZA.]

RACHEL   If you don't start saying something reasonable, I am going to lose my mind.

ELIZA   I'm saying that I feel claustrophobic in the damned . . . normalcy of our lives! We've accidentally become the privileged poster children for gay rights like "We deserve basic civil liberties cause we're just like you, we're not the scary gays!"

[*She strikes a thumbs-up, fake-smile pose.*]

RACHEL   What on earth is a 'Scary Gay?' Do you want to be a Scary Gay?

ELIZA   Sometimes!

RACHEL   Well I don't know how to help you with that.

[*She turns, about to go back into the kitchen.*]

ELIZA   It's not just that Rachel. It's not just me.

RACHEL   What is it then?

ELIZA   How do you think we got to this crisis point?

RACHEL   All the damn hormones we've been on?

ELIZA   Come on, Rach. [*Gently.*] You and I are just very different people. We don't always deal well.

RACHEL   Of course we are! That's what makes us work. We fill in the cracks. It was in your wedding vows.

ELIZA   I know. I know. And I still believe that. But look at us, we can barely have this conversation. What's going to happen when we have a disagreement about how to raise our kid?

RACHEL   This is different. We'll work it out.

ELIZA   It's not that simple.

RACHEL   Yes, it really is.

ELIZA No, OK? Because my version of 'working it out' is muddling through it together. And your version involves you figuring everything out on your own and implementing a solution.

RACHEL Give me an example.

ELIZA Any one of a hundred things! Like when you did all that research in secret and pulled together a binder full of dudes who'd make good sperm donors?!

RACHEL We picked our sperm donor together!

ELIZA Yes, from the options you'd selected before even broaching the subject.

RACHEL Those were great options!

ELIZA One second you're asking me if I might like to have a child with you, and I say yes, and the next second you've done so much of the work it feels like we're halfway pregnant.

RACHEL I expedited a stressful and arduous medical process! I was trying to make things easier.

ELIZA We went from decision to embryo in four months!

RACHEL Great! So I'm a control freak and I dragooned you into having a child with me?!

ELIZA No, Rachel! I'm saying that you moved so fast we didn't get a chance to sit with the decision.

RACHEL This has always been the plan! We've been talking about it for years. God, I should have just cancelled my meeting and gone with you.

ELIZA No, we needed you to land that contract. It was too important.

RACHEL Not as important as this. They could find another landscape architect, I can't—

ELIZA I'm glad you weren't there!

RACHEL What?

ELIZA If you had been, I might not have realized any of this.

RACHEL What are you saying.

ELIZA I love you, but it's overwhelming. When you smooth out all the rough edges before I have a chance to deal with them. You fix things almost before they become a problem.

RACHEL So you're . . . glad you didn't get it.

ELIZA Well, yes. Aren't you? I mean in light of all this?

[*Beat.*]

RACHEL I thought we could still go back on Monday.

ELIZA What?!

RACHEL Your window of fertility is—

ELIZA Rachel, how could you possibly think that after everything I've just said? You and I have to work through our issues before we can even consider—

RACHEL OK. Fine.

[*She goes into the next room and can be heard rummaging around, opening drawers.*]

ELIZA What are you doing?

[RACHEL *returns with a giant paper pad on an easel and a set of different colored markers.*]

RACHEL If we're going to do this, we may as well be organized about it.

ELIZA Oh, no.

RACHEL Oh yes!

[*She sets the easel up where the audience can see it: it has clearly come from her office and contains the remnants of a previous brainstorming session. She turns to a fresh page. All words in bold are written on the page in flowchart style. Shorthand can be used where possible to speed up writing.*]

ELIZA For the love of . . .

[*At the top of the page* RACHEL *writes "R + E > ISSUES" as she speaks.*]

RACHEL   So we have to work through our '**issues.**' Let's figure out what those are.

ELIZA   I'm not going to chart out our issues with you!

RACHEL   [*Slightly manic.*] Oh come on honey, why not? It'll be fun! We have **No Baby** because my wife is having a **1/4 Life Crisis.**

ELIZA   Hey!

RACHEL   Is that not what's happening here?

ELIZA   Oh, OK. I'll show you what's happening here.

[ELIZA *grabs a marker and draws an arrow from the R, starting a list beneath it.*]

ELIZA   We have no baby because *my* wife has to **micromanage** everything—

RACHEL   I'm organized! That doesn't mean—

[ELIZA *draws arrows from "Micromanage" with examples.*]

ELIZA   You scheduled my **gyno** appointment the same day I said yes to a baby. Won't let me eat **sushi** because—

RACHEL   [*Jumping in.*] It has mercury!

ELIZA   [*Continuing.*] Is making us **chart** out our issues. **Critiquing** my contributions to the flowchart.

[*She does a sarcastic Vanna White pose.*]

ELIZA   Ta da!

RACHEL   Lovely. My turn.

[*She draws an arrow from "E" and creates a list on the other side of the page, speaking as she writes.*]

RACHEL   Eliza. **Determined not to be happy. Drama queen. Idealist. Selfish.**

[ELIZA *goes back to writing, interjecting between and overlapping RACHEL's list.*]

ELIZA   **Perfectionist, mommy** issues, in total **denial**!

[*They both run out of steam and step back to take in all that they've written.*]

ELIZA Well great. It looks like we are in fact the perfect couple after all.

RACHEL Perfect. Don't forget that I hog the covers.

ELIZA And I talk in my sleep!

RACHEL You're funny in your sleep.

ELIZA I am?

RACHEL Damn it. How did we get here E?

ELIZA Um, you went into your office and—

RACHEL I'm sorry. I didn't mean for this to . . . devolve. I just . . . If you need us to have this conversation, right now, then I need it to be productive.

ELIZA It isn't something you can put in boxes and organize away with nice color-coded labels. Not this time.

RACHEL Hey, you don't know, I make really good labels.

ELIZA I assure you, I'm intimately familiar with your labels.

RACHEL This is the only way I can wrap my head around it.

ELIZA I know. I know how you are.

RACHEL Or we could set it aside until after my mother—

ELIZA No, let's . . . chart out our issues I guess.

[RACHEL *turns to a fresh page.*]

RACHEL So. We have **No Baby** because my wife got **Cold Feet**.

ELIZA This isn't just cold feet.

RACHEL [*Crossing out cold feet.*] OK, maybe that's a pejorative term. What did you call it, a panic?

ELIZA OK, yes. But that isn't the central issue. I only panicked because I started realizing all of this . . . stuff.

RACHEL Right. So **Panic** leads to **Realization** that I am—

[*She starts to make a list, then stops, questioning.*]

RACHEL   . . . **controlling**, pushy, overwhelming?

[*She looks to* ELIZA *for confirmation.*]

ELIZA   Not . . . OK. I just mean that, sometimes, when I try to talk to you about whatever's bothering me, you offer these logical, perfect little solutions. And then it's all supposed to be figured out but I don't actually feel any better.

RACHEL   [*Beat.*] I don't know how to write that one.

[*She gives the marker to* ELIZA. ELIZA *considers the chart. She turns back to* RACHEL *to try to explain again.* RACHEL *starts nervously refolding napkins at the table.*]

ELIZA   It's like, whenever I can't quite . . . articulate why something doesn't feel right you use it as proof that there's nothing to worry about.

RACHEL   Well, I can't help you if you can't tell me what's wrong.

ELIZA   And when I can articulate it you say "Well, you seem to have a good grasp on where this is coming from." As if that helps.

RACHEL   OK, what would you rather I do?

ELIZA   How about just comforting me? Acknowledging that my fears are valid? [*Beat.*] Expressing whatever you're feeling through words instead of trying to fold it into a fucking dove over there?

RACHEL   It's a sailboat!

ELIZA   Is this subconscious symbolism? You'd like to sail away from it all?

RACHEL   Yes. I would. Preferably to Bermuda.

ELIZA   Great, let's go.

[RACHEL's *phone rings. She looks at the screen. Holds it up for* ELIZA *to see 'mom' calling.*]

RACHEL   Unfortunately I have a dinner to prepare so if we could just—

ELIZA And what do you plan to say to your mother? You want us to sit here and lie? Coo about how excited we are while she urges me to consider a C-section again?

RACHEL No, what I want, what I wanted, was for that not to be a lie. For you to have told me any of this ages ago, even last night. What I want is for us to be able to go back to the clinic on Monday and get our baby.

ELIZA [ELIZA *adds a new item under her initial*] Eliza: **needs time**.

RACHEL What are we talking about here? I mean, do you want any part of our lives?

ELIZA Yes! Yes, of course.

RACHEL But . . . you hate our house.

ELIZA That's not what I said—

RACHEL This house that we've spent every damn Sunday refurbishing since we bought it.

ELIZA I love our house.

RACHEL Well what then?

ELIZA I don't know I—

RACHEL Well I need you to know. I need to know what we're doing Eli.

ELIZA Yes, and I need time to figure that out.

RACHEL How much time? What's the game plan?

ELIZA I don't know! That's the whole point. I've never known. I never had a plan, Rach.

RACHEL I can't live like that.

ELIZA Oh, I know. When I met you . . . you told me your five-year-plan on our second date.

RACHEL I did not . . . Did I?

ELIZA [*Fondly.*] Yes. You did.

RACHEL Oh.

ELIZA But I . . . It's like I was stuck in a thicket, OK? I couldn't tell my ass from my elbow. And you walked up and pulled out a map and said, "Hey, this is where I'm going, maybe you can see where you're headed too." Except I'm the idiot who had never seen a fucking map before.

RACHEL Not an idiot.

ELIZA So I said, "Yes, thank god, someone who knows what the hell they're doing. I'm going wherever you're going, baby."

RACHEL So I just dragged you along with my plan?

ELIZA You swept me off my feet.

RACHEL There's no agency in that!

ELIZA I chose you. I chose to follow your path. And it's been beautiful.

RACHEL But?

ELIZA But now that your endpoint is in reach, now that I know what a goddamned map is, I want a destination of my own. A dream for myself. Not just for us.

RACHEL I don't know what that looks like.

ELIZA Neither do I.

RACHEL But, Eli, now I feel like I've just steamrolled you into this whole life you never wanted. And that's . . . I mean Jesus, that's what my mother does. Are you saying that that's what I've become? Please don't be saying that.

ELIZA Rach, you could never be your mother.

RACHEL Don't let me turn into the fucking villain in your life, God, please don't do that to me. That is never what I want.

ELIZA There are no villains here, that's—

RACHEL —Putting me in a position where I'm hurting you and you don't tell me, you don't give me a chance to stop; that is just about the cruelest thing you could do to me, Eliza.

ELIZA I didn't mean to. But this is the point. We have to be able to talk about this stuff, we have to let it get messy. And right now . . .

[*She turns back to the chart and adds '***Lost***' to the E list.*]

RACHEL I always knew what I wanted. You know that. If you were just going along with me, or if I manipulated you into agreeing to have this baby with me—

ELIZA You didn't—This is my realization, my fuckup. I get to have ownership over that.

RACHEL So what, you want me to change the way I do things but you don't want me to take any blame? Do you—

[*Her phone rings again.*]

RACHEL Goddamn it.

ELIZA You have to cancel.

RACHEL She'd have a conniption.

ELIZA So what?

RACHEL It's not worth it, you know that.

ELIZA I know that she's been almost as excited about this baby as you are. I know that she's called you more in these last four months than she probably has in the last four years.

RACHEL Eli . . .

ELIZA I know that you've finally found something you can talk about without poking at each other. [*Beat.*] I know that lying to her probably feels safer right now, but it won't pay off in nine months when there's no grandchild to hand her.

RACHEL You don't understand what she's like.

ELIZA I do understand. As much as a person on the outside of it possibly can.

RACHEL If I give her a single crack she will start working her spindly fingers into our lives.

ELIZA Is your mother the reason you're so keen to have this baby right now?

RACHEL No! I mean—

ELIZA —Why then?

RACHEL Because, Eli. This baby . . . [RACHEL *goes back to the sock monkey. She breaks down a little as she speaks.*] I was starting to fall in love. Hell, by noon today, as I thought about it more and more I was irrevocably in love with our child. And then, oh, then to find out they didn't exist? That I had made up this whole person in my mind and they were never even . . .

[ELIZA *goes to* RACHEL.]

ELIZA Oh, love. I'm so, so sorry.

RACHEL They're still sitting in some fucking petri dish Eli. Our potential babies . . . And I can't leave them.

[*They take a moment of grief at the life that never was.* RACHEL*'s phone rings again.*]

RACHEL Oh my god!

ELIZA Don't answer it.

RACHEL She'll just keep calling.

ELIZA Rachel, please don't let her—

[RACHEL *answers the phone.*]

RACHEL Hi, Mom. . . . nothing's wrong. . . . I'm sure. . . . No, I don't need—I made dessert, Mom . . . I have it all under control.

ELIZA [*Overlapping in a whisper as she makes "cancel it" gestures.*] Rachel, Rachel, will you just . . .

[*She tries to take the phone away from* RACHEL. RACHEL *resists but* ELIZA *manages it after a moment.*]

ELIZA Hi, Maureen. It's Eliza . . . Yes, so exciting. But, I'm so sorry, I think we'd better reschedule dinner . . . No, I'm fine, it's Rachel . . . She's caught some horrible flu.

RACHEL [*Overlapping in a whisper.*] Oh my god, Eli! What are you—

ELIZA . . . I know. She didn't want to cancel, you know what she's like, but . . . Yes, exactly! [*She laughs.*] Oh, I know!

[RACHEL *pours two glasses of wine.*]

I would never normally . . . No, we'll be fine . . . Will do. Yes, I . . . OK, buh-bye now.

[*She hangs up.* RACHEL *hands her a glass.*]

RACHEL That was . . . easy.

ELIZA Said she could hear it in your voice.

RACHEL Oh.

ELIZA She offered to come help.

RACHEL Please. She always dumped me with my grandparents at the first sneeze.

ELIZA I know. [*Small beat.*] Did you really make Tarte aux Fraises again?

RACHEL It's her favorite.

[ELIZA *gives her a look.* RACHEL *goes to the kitchen.* ELIZA *sits at the table.*]

ELIZA "But dah-ling, I'm sure maman used cardamom in hers. It simply isn't the same."

RACHEL I have Grandmère's handwritten recipe! It is the same. She's ridiculous.

[RACHEL *returns with the tart and sits, setting it between them.* ELIZA *digs in.* RACHEL *toys with her glass. The silence stretches painfully.* ELIZA *sets her fork down reluctantly.*]

RACHEL How did this happen, Eli?

ELIZA I don't know. It was one thing and then another and we just let them slip by.

RACHEL No I mean, what brought this on? This whole realization.

ELIZA [*Beat.*] I've been working with this woman.

RACHEL A client?

ELIZA Yeah . . . It's a nasty case.

RACHEL You haven't mentioned . . .

ELIZA You know I don't like to bring that stuff home, make you deal with it too.

RACHEL [*Small beat.*] You can you know.

ELIZA She got a job with the Peace Corps in Morocco. And she wants to take her daughter.

RACHEL Ah.

ELIZA Of course the father just hates that idea. And I was sort of on his side at first. But then, I finally asked her why, why this was so important when it was causing such turmoil . . . She'd lived her life the way she was supposed to, checked all the boxes without ever asking herself what she really wanted. And that's . . . me. I feel like I've spent most of my life just trying to get through. Get away from my shitty hometown, my miserable parents, whatever. And here was this woman who'd finally realized she still had a chance to live her life. To give her daughter something more than that.

RACHEL But, you must see that all the time.

ELIZA She was just so . . . hopeful. And then yesterday, her sitter cancelled. So she brought in the kid. And this little seven-year-old girl was just sitting in my office, drawing quietly while her parents screamed at each other in the next room. And . . . I can't do that to our kid, Rachel. I can't risk putting our child through that because I never stopped to ask myself what I really want out of life.

RACHEL That is not going to be us.

ELIZA You can't know that. No one ever thought they'd end up in my office.

RACHEL I was that kid, OK?

ELIZA We're going to have this tiny little helpless human being who's completely dependent on us for everything.

RACHEL I feel like you're caught up in some idea of how this is all supposed to go.

ELIZA How can we ever prioritize anything we want for ourselves ever again?

RACHEL You're right. We won't be able to pick up at a moment's notice and . . . move to Morocco. But I was never going to be that person anyway.

ELIZA Well, I know that.

RACHEL And being a parent doesn't mean you give up everything else. I'd like to raise a child whose mothers don't have reason to be resentful of their existence.

ELIZA OK, I mean, yes. Of course, me too.

RACHEL Good. And if you're looking for purpose, or something larger in your life. Eli, I don't know what could be bigger than raising our child.

ELIZA I'm just . . . I'm still not sure.

RACHEL You think I'm sure?

ELIZA You always seem that way.

RACHEL I'll show you how sure I am.

[RACHEL *exits to her office.*]

ELIZA Oh god, what now?

[ELIZA *refills her glass.* RACHEL *returns carrying a box. She plonks it down and lifts out a huge stack of papers and holds it out to show* ELIZA.]

RACHEL Do you see this?

ELIZA Uh, honey, what am I looking at here?

[*She holds the papers in one arm and pulls them out as she names them matter-of-factly. She tosses each one into the air as she moves onto the next, so they go fluttering down all over the dining room. She finally grows more hysterical as she makes her way through them.*]

RACHEL This is a pie chart of monthly baby supply costs, this is a pro and con list of all our schooling options, this is a sample calendar of what an average week will look like at six-months-old, and one-year-old, and once school starts. This, what's this, oh yes, a detailed analysis on sleep training methods, and the statistical probabilities of various congenital health issues, just in case, this is a draft of my new will, and yours, and a list of possible guardians in case we die in a fiery car crash, and all of this crap and hours of 3 a.m. research binges, these are my doubts Eliza. These are all of my fears and neuroticisms and paranoias.

[*She tosses the rest of the stack to float through the room in spectacular fashion.*]

RACHEL I am *sure* of exactly jack shit.

ELIZA Oh my god.

RACHEL But I have to tell you E, I am not going to be one of those couples who throws their hands up at the first bump in the road. I am not going to give in to fear and resentment and destroy everything we've built together. I fucking love you and God at the gates is going to have to pry this marriage out of my cold undead heavenly hands.

ELIZA I love you, too, you know.

RACHEL Good.

ELIZA And I don't want a divorce.

RACHEL So OK then.

ELIZA . . . I don't know if that solves anything though.

RACHEL It does.

ELIZA What exactly does that solve?

[RACHEL *goes to her.*]

RACHEL   It means we're going to figure this out.

[*They have a moment together. Long beat. Then—*]

ELIZA   And . . . the baby?

[RACHEL *pulls back to look at her.*]

• • •

Autour du Lit

Laura King

Autour du Lit by Laura King. Copyright © 2018 by Laura King. All rights reserved. Reprinted by permission of the author.

CAUTION/ADVICE: Professionals and amateurs are hereby warned that performance of PLAY is subject to a royalty. It is fully protected under the copyright laws of the United States of America, and all of countries covered by the International Copyright Union (including the Dominion of Canada and the rest of the British Commonwealth), and of all countries covered by the Pan-American Copyright Convention and the United States Copyright Convention, the Berne Convention, and all of the countries with which the United States has reciprocal copyright relations. All rights, including professional and amateur stage performing rights, motion picture, recitation, lecturing, public reading, radio broadcasting, television, video or sound picture recording, all other forms of mechanical or electronic reproduction, such as CD-ROM, DVD-ROM, information storage and retrieval systems, and photocopying, and the rights of translation into foreign language are strictly reserved. Particular emphasis is placed upon the matter of readings, permission for which must be secured by Laura King, in writing in advance. Inquiries concerning rights should be addressed to Laura King: king-laura@att.net.

Laura King

LAURA KING holds an MFA in playwrighting (with a concentration in dramaturgy) from the Playwright's Lab at Hollins University and a master's in English from Northwestern University. She is a member of the Dramatists Guild (Atlanta Regional Representative), the Southeastern Theater Conference (Playwriting Committee chair and Publications Committee), and Working Title Playwrights (dramaturg). Laura also serves as a Literary Associate for YouthPLAYS, which has published many of her plays for young audiences. Laura's full-length plays *Independence Day at Happy Meadows* and *The Harmony Baptist Church Ladies Auxiliary Christmas Jubilee* are available for licensing through Stage Rights. Her play *The Cayuga Canal Girls* is a winner of the 2020 AACT NewPlayFest. For more information about Laura's work, see laurakingplaywright.com.

···production history···

Get Scene Studios, Atlanta, Georgia, July 19–28, 2018

    Director, Abra Thurmond

    EVER, Candi Vandizandi

    ADDISON, Andrea Laing

BoxFest Detroit, Detroit, Michigan, August 17–25, 2018

    Director, Gabriella S. Csapo

acknowledgments

Special thanks to Daniel Carter Brown, Abra Thurmond, and Jillian Walzer for their work on a workshop production of this play in 2016.

characters

    EVER, a male or female adult.

    ADDISON, a male or female adult.

The characters can be played by any combination of genders (male-female, female-female, or male-male). Because the characters travel through time, they can be played by actors of any age as long as they are adults.

setting

A bedroom with a bed with white linens, two nightstands, and one alarm clock.

···

[Lights up on a large bed with white linens. There is a nightstand on either side of the bed and one alarm clock. ADDISON *and* EVER *are completely underneath the covers. They are in the throes of passion.* EVER *throws off the covers.]*

EVER   I've got to tell you something.

ADDISON   What? Did I do something wrong?

EVER   I love you.

ADDISON   Is that all? You scared the crap out of me.

EVER What do you mean is that all? That is a very big all. I've never said those words before, you know.

ADDISON Never?

EVER I've said them to my Dad and my Mom and my cat Ninny and one time to a double-chocolate almond cupcake with raspberry icing but I've never said them to another human. I've been trying to say them to you for the past six months, ever since our first night together, but I couldn't do it. But I decided that tonight was the night I was going to say them. No matter what. And I did it. I said it. Mission accomplished.

ADDISON Great.

EVER Is that all you're going to say?

ADDISON I love you, too, babe.

EVER You do?

ADDISON Sure.

EVER Why?

ADDISON Huh?

EVER Why do you love me?

ADDISON Are we really going to do this?

EVER Yes, please.

ADDISON OK. I love you because you can dance.

EVER That's it?

ADDISON You're a really good dancer. It comes effortlessly to you.

EVER Nothing is without effort.

ADDISON That's how it seems. And when we dance together, everything else slips away, and the world is perfect, and we're perfect. Now come back to bed.

[ADDISON *and* EVER *retreat back under the covers. They start to get intimate again.* ADDISON *throws off the covers.*]

ADDISON Wait.

EVER What?

ADDISON Why do you love me? You said you love me but you never said why.

EVER Because you're the one.

ADDISON The one?

EVER The capital "O" One.

ADDISON When did you figure that out?

EVER After that first night. We spent the next day together, and then you went to work, and I waited for you to come back. I was trying really hard not to fall asleep, but I must have dozed off. Then I heard the door open, and I saw your reflection in the mirror. I wasn't sure if you were real or if I was still asleep. That's when I knew.

ADDISON What?

EVER That it didn't matter if I was awake or asleep because you were everything I had ever dreamed of. Now come back to bed.

[ADDISON *and* EVER *retreat back under the covers. They start to get intimate again.*]

EVER Addison?

ADDISON What did you say?

EVER Do you think it will always be like this?

[ADDISON *throws off the covers.*]

ADDISON What?

[ADDISON *and* EVER *sit up.*]

EVER Do you think it will always be like this?

ADDISON Like what?

EVER I don't know. Easy.

ADDISON Would you rather it was hard?

EVER No. Easy is always better.

ADDISON Then let's stick with easy.

EVER Deal.

[ADDISON *pulls the covers back over them both. They start to get intimate again.* EVER *sits back up.*]

EVER You've got to promise.

[ADDISON *sits up.*]

ADDISON Anything.

EVER Promise it'll always be like this.

ADDISON I promise.

[ADDISON *tries to kiss* EVER *during the following but* EVER *keeps talking.*]

EVER That we won't let anything get in the way.

ADDISON Nothing will get in the way.

EVER That we'll love each other forever.

ADDISON Forever.

EVER No matter what.

ADDISON No matter what.

[EVER *grabs* ADDISON *and they lock eyes.*]

EVER Swear?

ADDISON Swear.

[EVER *kisses* ADDISON *and they retreat back under the covers. Alarm sounds.*]

EVER Shut that damn thing off.

ADDISON It's on your side.

[EVER *reaches out from under the covers and hits the alarm.*]

EVER Ugh.

ADDISON Rude awakening.

EVER I'm not getting out of this bed.

ADDISON Never?

EVER Never. I'm never getting out of this bed.

ADDISON I see a few flaws with your plan.

[ADDISON *gets out of bed.*]

EVER Why do we have to get up?

ADDISON Work.

EVER Why do we have to go to work?

ADDISON Money.

EVER Why do we need to make money?

ADDISON Food.

EVER I'm hungry.

ADDISON Me, too. Want some breakfast?

EVER Do I have to get out of bed?

ADDISON It wouldn't hurt.

EVER Then no.

ADDISON You still don't see any problems with this plan?

EVER No.

ADDISON Come on, Ever.

[ADDISON *pulls the covers off* EVER, *who immediately pulls them back up.*]

EVER Stop.

ADDISON Life awaits.

EVER I can't.

ADDISON You always do this.

EVER   Do what?

ADDISON   You know what.

EVER   I have no idea what you're talking about.

ADDISON   How long have we been together?

EVER   Five years and three months.

ADDISON   And every Monday you do this.

EVER   I can't help it. I'm afraid.

ADDISON   Of what?

EVER   Of going out there. Everything's harder out there. I like it better in here. With just you.

ADDISON   I like it better in here with just you, too, but we can't hide forever.

[ADDISON *pulls the covers off* EVER *again.*]

EVER   Why not? Come back to bed.

[EVER *takes* ADDISON's *hand and pulls* ADDISON *back into the bed. They kiss.*]

ADDISON   You know what I think?

EVER   That you should kiss me some more?

ADDISON   Yes, but you know what else?

EVER   What?

ADDISON   That it's time to face the world.

[ADDISON *gets out of bed.*]

EVER   Party pooper.

ADDISON   I have never pooped on a party in my life.

EVER   Blatantly untrue.

ADDISON   Supporting evidence?

EVER   Last New Year's Eve. You spent the whole evening grousing about idiots who drink to forget what they're supposed to be celebrating.

ADDISON What can I say, I was drunk. Now stop stalling and get ready.

EVER Just one more hour.

ADDISON Not one more minute.

EVER I have an idea.

ADDISON You're stalling again.

EVER We should take turns.

ADDISON Doing what?

EVER You go to work one day and I'll stay here. And then the next day, I'll go to work and you can wait here. Whoever is home can stay in bed with one eye open waiting until they catch the reflection of the other in the mirror.

ADDISON And why are we doing this?

EVER To protect our fortress of solitude.

ADDISON You've lost it.

EVER No, it'll be great. Look.

[EVER *starts to assemble a fort on top of the bed using the bed linen.*]

EVER We'll build a fort. We won't let anybody else in. It'll be just for us.

ADDISON Don't think anybody else will fit.

[EVER *continues to build the fort.*]

EVER We'll make it safe and cozy and private.

ADDISON And impractical.

EVER It'll be the perfect love nest.

ADDISON How are we gonna eat?

EVER We'll live off love.

ADDISON I'd rather live off double cheeseburgers.

[EVER *sits disgustedly on top of the fort, destroying it.*]

EVER You have no romance.

ADDISON   Blatantly untrue.

EVER   Supporting evidence?

[ADDISON *jumps on top of* EVER *and they kiss passionately.*]

ADDISON   I rest my case. Now up and at 'em, soldier.

[ADDISON *gets out of bed.*]

EVER   Do I have to?

ADDISON   Welcome to reality.

EVER   Reality sucks.

[EVER *gets out of bed. They both prepare to face the day. Alarm sounds. They look at each other.*]

ADDISON   It's your get.

EVER   I got it last time.

ADDISON   *I* got it last time.

EVER   Get the alarm, Addison.

ADDISON   You get the alarm, Ever.

[EVER *shuts off the alarm.*]

EVER   You never do anything I want you to do.

ADDISON   Don't start in.

EVER   Oh, I'm starting in.

ADDISON   Then I'm walking out.

EVER   It won't be the first time.

ADDISON   You're throwing that in my face now?

EVER   It's your habit to walk out on me every ten years, but so far you always come back.

ADDISON   So far.

EVER   Fine. Then go.

ADDISON   I'm going.

EVER   Don't look back.

ADDISON   I won't.

[ADDISON *starts to exit.*]

EVER   Where are you going to go?

ADDISON   I don't know. Someplace where I can do whatever the hell I want.

EVER   Sounds good. Let me know when you get there and I'll join you.

ADDISON   You're not invited.

EVER   You don't think I want a place where I can do anything I want? A place where I'm not tied to you and your moods and your feelings? Jesus, I never knew anyone could have so many feelings. It's unnatural.

ADDISON   At least I feel them. You bottle everything up so tight that every emotion is an explosion. You're like a thermometer with only two temperatures: freezing and boiling.

EVER   You can bet right now I'm boiling.

ADDISON   Oh, I'm so scared. What are you gonna do? Scald me?

[EVER *hits* ADDISON *violently with a pillow.* ADDISON *stares at* EVER *for a moment.*]

ADDISON   I can't believe you did that.

EVER   Believe it.

ADDISON   That was a very loaded move.

EVER   Don't overreact.

ADDISON   That came from someplace dark.

EVER   Don't be stupid.

ADDISON   Someplace deep, down inside you. It came from right there.

[ADDISON *hits* EVER *in the stomach with a pillow.*]

EVER   Ow. Where? My stomach?

ADDISON   Your gut. Deep inside your gut you resent me.

EVER   I do not.

[EVER *hits* ADDISON *with a pillow.*]

ADDISON   You resent me. Admit it.

EVER   Knock it off. I don't resent you.

ADDISON   You do. Just say it.

[ADDISON *and* EVER *have a full-on pillow fight, with* ADDISON *telling* EVER *to confess feelings of resentment and* EVER *denying those feelings.*]

EVER   All right, all right. Enough. Stop. I admit it.

ADDISON   Say it.

EVER   I resent you.

ADDISON   I knew it!

EVER   Happy now?

ADDISON   No, I'm not happy. Why would I be happy?

EVER   Because you won.

[EVER *sits on the floor.*]

ADDISON   This round.

[ADDISON *sits next to* EVER. *They are quiet for a minute.*]

ADDISON   Do you really resent me?

EVER   Sometimes.

ADDISON   I resent you sometimes, too.

EVER   I know.

[ADDISON *and* EVER *are quiet for a minute.*]

ADDISON   You're just always here.

EVER   Even when you're not here, you're here.

ADDISON   It's exhausting.

EVER   I know.

ADDISON   I guess it's good to get it out.

EVER   Not really.

ADDISON   I know.

EVER   So, what happens now? We just go round and round and round?

ADDISON   It seems that way.

EVER   What's the point?

ADDISON   That's life.

EVER   You say that a lot.

ADDISON   What?

EVER   That's life. That's reality.

ADDISON   Well, it is.

EVER   That's not what we promised.

ADDISON   I know.

EVER   We'd promised it'd be easy.

ADDISON   I know.

EVER   It's not.

ADDISON   I know.

EVER   I guess that's life.

[*Alarm sounds again.*]

ADDISON and EVER   It's your get.

[*As the alarm continues to sound, EVER stretches out on the floor. ADDISON starts to strip the bed. Time passes. The alarm stops and EVER sits up. ADDISON does not hear EVER speak.*]

EVER   Addison, I have to tell you something. I've been wanting to tell you for a while now, since the night of our thirtieth anniversary party.

Remember that night? Everybody there to celebrate us, and we barely said a word to each other. Well, now I have something to say. I don't love you anymore.

[EVER *stands up and stretches.*]

EVER   That's a relief. I couldn't keep it in another second. I've been trying not to say it, but it's been there for a long time.

[EVER *crosses to* ADDISON. ADDISON *doesn't notice and keeps stripping the bed.*]

EVER   You always say I keep things bottled up too long. That letting things out would make me feel better. You were right. I feel so much better.

[EVER *lies on the bed.* ADDISON *keeps stripping the bed around EVER.*]

EVER   All those nights lying here in bed next to you, these thoughts would flitter into my mind. I don't love you. Then just as quickly they would flitter away. And we'd go on. And on and on and on. And somewhere along the line I started wanting to say it more often. A couple times a year maybe. Then I started wanting to say it monthly.

[EVER *jumps on the bed.*]

EVER   It's January—I don't love you. It's February—I don't love you. It's March—I don't love you. It's April—well, you get the idea.

[EVER *sits on the bed.*]

EVER   At first I thought it was because of the way you chew your food. Not up and down like a normal person but side to side like a camel. Sometimes we'd be eating breakfast and I'd look across the table, over the scrambled eggs and hash browns, and it took all my focus not to knock the fork out of your hand and scream, "Why can't you be normal?" But instead I'd close my eyes and clamp my jaw. You'd ask if I was all right and I'd nod, afraid to open my mouth because of what might spill out. And we'd go on.

[EVER *gets off the bed and moves closer to* ADDISON, *who still doesn't hear.*]

EVER   Then the feeling came even without an impetus. But still I'd push it down and we'd go on. But I can't go on anymore. I'm done. I don't love you.

[EVER *turns away from* ADDISON.]

EVER   I know you're upset, but it's nothing personal. We can work out the logistics later. It's a lot to process, but I know we can do it if we put our minds to it. And I'm thinking very clearly now. I feel more focused than I've felt in years. I'll take over now. I'm sure you need some time.

[EVER *takes over stripping the bed and handling the linens.* ADDISON *sits on the bed.*]

ADDISON   I don't love you anymore. I *don't* love you anymore. I don't *love* you anymore. I don't love *you* anymore. Who cares how I say it? The truth is I don't fucking love you anymore. I haven't loved you for a long time. Maybe I never loved you. No, that's not true. I loved you once. Just not anymore. Isn't that strange that love can just disappear? Ever?

[ADDISON *looks at* EVER, *who moves away without hearing.*]

ADDISON   Maybe it's fickle. The fickle finger of fate. Who said that? It doesn't matter. What matters is that I don't love you anymore. I know I keep saying it, but maybe if I say it enough I can figure out what happened. Where the love went. Because I don't know.

[ADDISON *watches* EVER *for a moment.*]

ADDISON   I know *when* it happened. It was the underwear. Remember the underwear we used to wear when we were first together? I liked that underwear. Now everything's so normal and bland. I know it seems like a small thing. But one day I looked in our bureau and saw all the normal underwear staring up at me and that's when I knew I didn't love you anymore. And that I didn't want to do this anymore. It was all the underwear's fault.

[*Alarm sounds.* EVER *turns to* ADDISON. *They can hear each other now.*]

EVER   Can you get that?

ADDISON Sure.

EVER Everything OK?

ADDISON Everything's fine.

[*The linen is now completely stripped off the bed.* EVER *and* ADDISON *look at the naked bed.*]

EVER We can't just leave it like this.

ADDISON I kind of like it.

EVER It won't be very comfortable.

ADDISON I'm too tired to remake it.

EVER You're getting old, sweetie.

ADDISON I got old a long time ago.

EVER I guess we could try to sleep on it like this.

[EVER *and* ADDISON *lie down on the naked bed and stare at the ceiling.*]

ADDISON How do you feel?

EVER Exposed.

ADDISON I guess that's why linen was invented.

EVER Should we make the bed now?

ADDISON In a minute. I want to lie here just a little while longer.

EVER OK.

ADDISON There's something intriguing about it.

EVER Inviting.

ADDISON Invigorating.

EVER Intoxicating.

[EVER *and* ADDISON *pause for a moment and then vigorously make out on the bed. Alarm sounds.* EVER *and* ADDISON *rush to remake the bed.*]

ADDISON Make sure you tuck your side in.

EVER   It's tucked.

ADDISON   Fluff up your pillow.

EVER   Got it.

ADDISON   Is the sheet bunched up at the bottom?

EVER   Just a little. No one will notice.

ADDISON   I'll notice.

EVER   Not at first.

ADDISON   But eventually. And it'll bug me.

EVER   You'll get over it.

ADDISON   I'm not so sure.

EVER   It's just a little bunching.

ADDISON   Now it is, but it'll only get worse. Soon it'll be a tangled mess and I won't be able to stand it.

EVER   So, then what?

ADDISON   We'll have to pull it off and start all over again.

EVER   We could just ignore it.

ADDISON   That never works.

EVER   Sure, it does. I know people who go years ignoring stuff.

ADDISON   And it festers in their gut like a diseased worm until their insides are so infected that they explode.

EVER   Or not.

ADDISON   Pull the sheet up.

EVER   Addison, I have to tell you something.

ADDISON   Smooth it out.

EVER   It's important.

ADDISON   Grab the blanket.

EVER   I'm sorry.

ADDISON   For what?

EVER   For the wear and tear along the way.

[ADDISON *looks at* EVER.]

ADDISON   I'm sorry, too.

EVER   I guess that's life.

ADDISON   That's reality.

EVER   But it's been a good life.

ADDISON   A good, long life.

EVER   So, what happens now?

ADDISON   We just keep going round and round and round.

[ADDISON *and* EVER *lean across the bed and kiss.*]

EVER   Toss me a pillow.

[ADDISON *tosses* EVER *a pillow. They put the finishing touches on the made bed.*]

ADDISON   There.

EVER   Good as new.

ADDISON   Better than new.

[*They look at the bed and then at each other. They smile and climb into the bed and get under the covers. They start to get intimate. Alarm sounds.* ADDISON *turns it off.*]

EVER   I'm not getting out of this bed.

ADDISON   Never?

EVER   I'm never getting out of this bed.

ADDISON   Then I'll stay here with you.

EVER   Really?

ADDISON   All day if you want.

EVER   Can we make a fort?

ADDISON We can make a fort and have a pillow fight and stay here safe and warm.

EVER I love you for that.

ADDISON I love you too, babe.

EVER Why do you love me?

ADDISON You haven't asked me that in a long time.

EVER Tell me.

ADDISON I love you because once a long time ago you used to dance.

EVER I haven't danced in years.

ADDISON Life happened. The dancing stopped. The love didn't. Why do you love me?

EVER I once thought you were everything I ever dreamed of. But then life happened. Dreams changed.

ADDISON But the love didn't.

EVER Actually, the love did.

ADDISON It did?

EVER You stopped being the love of my dreams and started being the love of my life. Now when I see your reflection in the mirror, I see the real you.

ADDISON Every flaw.

EVER Every imperfection.

ADDISON Every fallibility.

EVER But the love remains.

ADDISON Sustains.

EVER Do you think it will always be like this?

ADDISON I hope so.

EVER You have to promise that we won't let anything get in the way.

ADDISON   Everything will get in the way.

EVER   I know.

ADDISON   But I still promise.

EVER   That we'll love each other forever.

ADDISON   Forever.

EVER   No matter what.

ADDISON   No matter what.

[ADDISON *and* EVER *bury down under the covers. Alarm sounds. They are still.*]

[*Blackout.*]

• • •

Fault Lines

David Adam Gill

Fault Lines by David Adam Gill. Copyright © 2018 by David Adam Gill. All rights reserved. Reprinted by permission of the author.

CAUTION/ADVICE: Professionals and amateurs are hereby warned that performance of PLAY is subject to a royalty. It is fully protected under the copyright laws of the United States of America, and all of countries covered by the International Copyright Union (including the Dominion of Canada and the rest of the British Commonwealth), and of all countries covered by the Pan-American Copyright Convention and the United States Copyright Convention, the Berne Convention, and all of the countries with which the United States has reciprocal copyright relations. All rights, including professional and amateur stage performing rights, motion picture, recitation, lecturing, public reading, radio broadcasting, television, video or sound picture recording, all other forms of mechanical or electronic reproduction, such as CD-ROM, DVD-ROM, information storage and retrieval systems, and photocopying, and the rights of translation into foreign language are strictly reserved. Particular emphasis is placed upon the matter of readings, permission for which must be secured by David Adam Gill, in writing in advance. Inquiries concerning rights should be addressed to David Adam Gill: david@davidadamgill.com.

David Adam Gill

DAVID ADAM GILL is a Brooklyn-based writer. Full-length plays: *Providence* (Transient Theater, CHI & Roy Arias Stages, NYC); his *F*cked-up Family Trilogy! Experimenting with Katz* (New Ambassadors), *Irregulars*, and *Unfinished*. Short plays: *More Myself Than I Am* (*Shiyr Terror: Terrifyingly Funny*; Axial Theatre's *Twisted Valentines Festival 2018*; The Secret Theatre's *Act One: One Act Festival 2019*—Best Play; *Manhattan Repertory Theatre's Under 15 Play Competition 2019*—Best Play); *Fault Lines* (New Ambassadors' *Blurring Boundaries* & Secret Theatre's *LIC Short Play Festival*—finalist), *Wee Annie's Hold* (NATC octoberFEARfest & Act One: One Act Festival 2020). David is the artistic director and cofounder of New Ambassadors Theatre Company and curator of their play development lab. David is a proud member of the Dramatists Guild of America.

··· production history ···

Fault Lines was produced in 2019 as part of New Ambassadors Theatre Company's Blurring Boundaries: Six Short Plays Festival, and The Secret Theatre's LIC Short Play Festival (finalist)—both directed by Tom Wallace with the following cast (in order of appearance):

EDDIE, Todd Butera*

MARTY, Randall Rodriguez*

JANET, Marie Eléna O'Brien*

*Denotes member of Actors Equity Association

characters

EDDIE
MARTY
JANET

setting

Windsor Terrace, Brooklyn.

time

3 a.m.

···

[*Scuffling in the dark. Stop. Panting. Lights up on the front stoop of a two-family house in Brooklyn. It is late at night. MARTY is on the ground, with EDDIE standing over him holding a handgun. He checks the chamber, which is empty, then puts the gun into his jacket pocket. MARTY is sitting on the lowest step, breathing heavily. He is drunk.*]

EDDIE   Oh, thank God, Marty. I thought you'd gone over the deep end.

MARTY   Where is he?!

EDDIE   Calm down.

MARTY   Don't tell me to calm down, you sonuvabitch.

[MARTY *pauses, catches his breath.*]

Goddamn you! [*Nothing.*] GODDAMN YOU!

EDDIE Would you keep it down, you're gonna wake up Janet.

MARTY I don't give a fuck.

EDDIE Terrific.

MARTY I DON'T GIVE A FLYING FUCK!

EDDIE You want the cops to come? 'Cause that's what she'll do.

MARTY Do you want the cops to come? Kidnapping my son.

EDDIE You're drunk.

MARTY DONNIE!

[MARTY *tries to stand. He can't.*]

EDDIE You're gonna push that kid too far.

MARTY I don't care.

EDDIE After all that's happened with Kenny?

MARTY I'd rather see him dead.

EDDIE You're talking crazy.

MARTY I mean it.

EDDIE Your own son.

MARTY He's not my son.

EDDIE That's terrific, just great.

[JANET, EDDIE'*s wife comes to the door, opening it just enough to see out the window.*]

JANET Eddie, it's three in the morning. What's going on out there?

EDDIE Nothing.

JANET Who's that?

EDDIE Go back inside.

JANET Marty?

MARTY [*Hiding his face.*] Tell her to go away.

JANET [*Stepping out.*] Marty? Is that you?

EDDIE For Godsakes, Janet, go back inside.

JANET [*Stepping onto the top stoop.*] You've got some nerve, Buster!

EDDIE Janet, don't.

JANET Showing up here. You've got some freakin' nerve!

MARTY Tell her to go away.

JANET You go away, Marty. For good. Do us all a favor and jump off the nearest overpass.

EDDIE Jesus, Janet. He lost his son.

JANET Whose fault it that?

EDDIE We're all of us sad about this.

JANET You killed that boy, Marty, sure as if you pulled the trigger yourself.

EDDIE Janet.

JANET And may God never let you forget it.

EDDIE Blaming doesn't help anybody.

JANET It helps me, Eddie! IT HELPS ME! [*She is in* MARTY's *face.*] DO YOU HEAR ME, MARTY?! YOU SONUVABITCH! YOU SON-OF-A-BITCH!

[JANET *starts hitting* MARTY, *smacking him in the face and on his arms and chest.* MARTY *does little to protect himself from the blows.* EDDIE *holds* JANET's *hands to stop her hitting.*]

EDDIE Janet! Janet, come on—quit it! JANET! I SAID GO BACK INSIDE!

MARTY DONNIE!

JANET [*Moving to block the door.*] Oh, no you don't.

EDDIE Come on, Marty. Leave the kid alone.

MARTY I WANT MY SON!

JANET Over my dead body.

EDDIE A minute ago he wasn't your son.

MARTY You have no right!

JANET What right do you have?

MARTY I'm his father!

JANET That's not how a father treats his flesh and blood.

MARTY Stay out of it.

JANET We will not.

EDDIE What do you want to make him play football for? He doesn't like it.

JANET He showed up here—

MARTY It's none of your goddamn business.

EDDIE He's a small guy, he gets beat up, he was all bloody.

JANET With two broken ribs. Enlighten us about that why don't you.

MARTY Fuck you! DONNIE! GET YOUR ASS DOWN HERE NOW!

JANET Sweet talking will get you everywhere.

EDDIE This is how it started with Kenny. Making him do things he didn't want to do.

MARTY Stop sticking your nose where it doesn't belong. You turn my boys against me. You stole Kenny from me.

JANET How dare you.

MARTY You stole Kenny, and now you're trying to steal Donnie.

EDDIE Marty, come on. You kicked Kenny out of the house. What'd you expect us to do?

MARTY Let him be.

JANET That wasn't an option.

EDDIE We gave him a place to sleep so's he wasn't out on the streets.

MARTY I was teaching him a lesson.

JANET And how'd that work out for you, Marty? Huh? How'd that lesson land?

EDDIE You're living in the stone age, man.

JANET What you put that boy through was nothing short of abuse. And now Donnie? Keep it up and I'll have Child Services on your ass faster than you can say Dunkin' Donuts.

EDDIE Janet, stop. She doesn't mean it.

JANET Just watch me. You think I don't know? A lot of these kids, they turn to drugs and much worse when they're shut out of their homes. What I see in that Emergency Room, it'd make your skin crawl.

MARTY I should have been harder on that kid. He wasn't tough enough.

JANET Not tough enough? Because he didn't go around thumping his chest like his macho father?

MARTY I'm not gonna make the same mistake with Donnie.

JANET You're out of your mind, Mister.

EDDIE Donnie doesn't want to play football. I don't understand why you make him.

JANET He's interested in art. And music. He's gifted.

MARTY Pussy stuff. Girl stuff. Football—that's a man's game.

JANET Did football make a man out of you, Marty? On the contrary, it made you a bully and a coward.

MARTY It builds character. Ain't nothing wrong with it. Nothing.

JANET Character? Is that what you call it?

MARTY Then you come along, and coddle him, and make a sissy out of him. Just like his brother.

JANET That's your takeaway?

EDDIE He showed up here, Marty. It looked like he'd been beaten to a bloody pulp.

MARTY Everybody gets roughed up, it's part of the game. So you get up and get back out there and try harder. Hit back harder! Bruise for bruise! I wasn't no bigger than either of those boys when I played.

EDDIE But he's not you.

JANET Thank God.

MARTY And I wasn't my dad, but I saw that it meant something to him so I did it. No questions. And it shaped me. Made me strong.

JANET Your definition of strong is skewed, Buster.

MARTY You have no idea.

JANET How about the strength of trying to be who you are in the face of an abusive father? Don't kid yourself, Marty. Kenny was stronger than you'll ever be. Weak pitiful man.

EDDIE Janet! This isn't helping!

JANET Weak pitiful man! And if I remember rightly, you weren't such a hot shot on the field back in high school either.

MARTY I didn't go crying home like a goddamn baby the first time I landed at the bottom of the pile. These kids, they got no thick skin like we used to.

JANET Thick skin. He's a little boy for Christ's sake.

EDDIE Marty, you're too hard.

MARTY Not half enough.

JANET Ooh! You disappointed fathers boil my blood. You can't make a go of your own life, so you cram it all down your sons' throats—God knows any of them have the strength to crawl out from under it!

MARTY Mind your own goddamn business.

JANET It is our business. We know those kids since they were born.

EDDIE We're Kenny's godparents.

MARTY Were.

JANET [*Sting; beat.*] And let me tell you something, Martin Delgado. I see someone suffering—a child suffering—I'm not just going to stand idly by!

EDDIE At the hands of anyone.

JANET Let alone his own father and mother.

MARTY Easy for you to talk.

JANET We'd do the same for any stranger.

MARTY It's easy for you. You had girls. It's easier.

EDDIE That's not fair.

JANET How is it easier?

EDDIE You know we had a tough time with Becca.

MARTY I'd rather have a son who's an addict than a faggot.

JANET Well, you got both.

EDDIE That's just stupid, Marty.

JANET And if either of my girls came to me and told me they were gay, I would love them, no questions asked.

MARTY Easier said than done.

JANET No, it's not. That's just plain ignorant. You're given a kid that's different, there's no manual, I get that. But to force them into some cookie cutter idea of something that goes against the very grain of who they are?

EDDIE What were you trying to accomplish, turning Kenny out onto the streets like that? Cutting him off from his mother and from Donnie?

MARTY [*Angry.*] He should have fought me harder.

JANET   So this is all his fault? Because he didn't turn around and slug you back?

MARTY   [*Almost losing it.*] Yes. Because he gave up. The minute he started in with the drugs he gave up.

JANET   You think he would have even touched any drugs if he wasn't needing an escape from his life? From you.

EDDIE   Think about it, Marty.

MARTY   I know what I know.

JANET   You call yourself a father? You're no father. You're a terrorist. You terrorized that boy, plain and simple.

MARTY   Fuck you. Fuck you both.

JANET   And you can tell Estelle to stop calling me. I don't want to hear her excuses. She has no right to cry over the loss of that boy, when she sat by and did nothing to stop you. I'll never forgive either of you for the pain and suffering you caused. Big man! Big macho man!

MARTY   Eddie, I'm warning you! Tell her to go away!

JANET   Or what? Or you're gonna do what? Huh? Murderer!

MARTY   SHUT UP!

JANET   MURDERER! MURDERER!

MARTY   TOLD YOU TO SHUT THE FUCK UP!

[MARTY *lunges at* JANET *who screams and steps back. He grabs her throat and pushes her till she falls to the ground.* EDDIE *grabs* MARTY *by the hair and pulls him away.* JANET *is kicking and punching at* MARTY.]

JANET   LET GO! LET GO OF MY LEG YOU SONUVABITCH!

EDDIE   Jesus Christ, Marty! What the hell was that?!

JANET   Get the Hell out of here! EDDIE, TELL HIM TO LEAVE!

EDDIE   I know you all my life, and I've never been more ashamed of you. [*Beat.*] Marty, you'd better go home.

JANET NOW!

MARTY I want my son.

JANET He doesn't want you!

MARTY He's my son.

JANET He's afraid of you.

EDDIE Can you blame him?

MARTY DONNIE! I'M GONNA COUNT TO THREE—ONE!

JANET [*In* MARTY's *face.*] You gonna teach Donnie a lesson too? Huh, Big Man?! It's not bad enough you lost one son, you wanna make it two!

MARTY TWO! GET YOUR ASS OUT HERE NOW!

JANET You're not manly, you're a coward. You're a bully, and in my book, a bully is a coward.

MARTY THREE! I'M NOT GONNA SAY IT AGAIN, DONNIE! DONNNNNIE! [*He punches the front door violently.*]

JANET I'm calling the cops.

MARTY [*Almost spent.*] Give me my son!

EDDIE Janet, don't. I'll get him to leave. Just go inside. Come on, Marty. Up.

[EDDIE *tries to help* MARTY *to his feet which proves difficult. The gun falls out of his pocket.*]

JANET What's that?

EDDIE It's not loaded.

JANET Holy Jesus, Eddie!

EDDIE It's not loaded.

JANET Is that the one? IS THAT THE ONE, MARTY?!

EDDIE I'll put it inside.

JANET   No, wait. [*Pause.*] I want to see it.

EDDIE   Janet, come on. Don't be stupid.

JANET   GIVE IT HERE, EDDIE!

[EDDIE *carefully hands* JANET *the gun. She turns it around in her hands, mesmerized by it.*]

JANET   I can't—[*She shivers.*] To feel you're all alone in the world, and have it come to this. To think this is the only solution. I can't wrap my mind around it.

EDDIE   How could you do it, Marty? You were his father.

JANET   Oh, the worst bullies are the parents. The very worst. I see it all the time. Fathers and mothers, pretending they're the victims, and all the while destroying their kids lives. It couldn't have been easy for him. To come out to you. Mr. Macho. You wanna talk about guts? Talk about being a man? And what did you do? You took away the one place he should feel safe, had the right to be safe. For fuck's sake, Marty! You yanked that out from under him, you and Estelle. With your "tough love." We gave it back to him, Eddie and me and the girls, as best we could. But Thanksgiving . . . He told me what you did. How you forbade anyone to speak him, to even recognize his existence. He showed up here—It broke his heart. Christ, Marty, it broke mine. [*Deep sigh.*] I loved that kid. And now that boy upstairs has no brother, and is scared of his own parents. He's terrified he's going to end up like Kenny. You're pushing him to the same thing, and I swear to God, Marty, I'll point this gun at you myself before I let that happen.

EDDIE   Janet.

JANET   No, Eddie. This selfish sonuvabitch does everything in his power to push his son into an early grave, and he has the nerve to come here and point the finger at us.

EDDIE   Let's . . . let's just all—

JANET   WHAT, EDDIE? LET'S JUST ALL WHAT?

EDDIE Christ, Janet. He lost his son.

JANET [*Beside herself with anger.*] Stop being the good guy, Eddie! We lost Kenny too! We lost him too! NOW, YOU! GET THE HELL OFF MY PROPERTY!

[*After an intense moment* MARTY *crumbles to the ground, letting out a gut wrenching wail.*]

MARTY Ahhhhhhhhhhhhhhhh! Kenny! My boy! My boy is gone! My boy . . .

[*He shakes his head, and cries.* JANET *stands with one foot inside the door, deciding what she should do, then steps back out onto the stoop and sits on the top step next to* MARTY, *crying with him.*]

EDDIE Thanksgiving. All he wanted was to be with you guys. Why'd you do it?

MARTY I couldn't look at him. I thought . . . if I took away his family, he would—

JANET Change? [*Beat.*] That sweet, beautiful, perfect boy?

MARTY [*Stares blankly into* JANET'*s face.*]

JANET Jesus, Marty.

[MARTY *shakes his head as if he has no answer, then he starts to tremble, and letting his head drop, sobs violently.* JANET *puts her arm around his shoulder, trying to calm him as if he were a child.* EDDIE *stands looking on, as the lights fade to black.*]

• • •

Guardian
of the Field
A One-Act Journey
Through Timelessness

Liz Amadio

Guardian of the Field by Liz Amadio. Copyright © 2018 by Liz Amadio. All rights reserved. Reprinted by permission of the author.

CAUTION/ADVICE: Professionals and amateurs are hereby warned that performance of *Guardian of the Field* is subject to a royalty. It is fully protected under the copyright laws of the United States of America, and all of countries covered by the International Copyright Union (including the Dominion of Canada and the rest of the British Commonwealth), and of all countries covered by the Pan-American Copyright Convention and the United States Copyright Convention, the Berne Convention, and all of the countries with which the United States has reciprocal copyright relations. All rights, including professional and amateur stage performing rights, motion picture, recitation, lecturing, public reading, radio broadcasting, television, video or sound picture recording, all other forms of mechanical or electronic reproduction, such as CD-ROM, DVD-ROM, information storage and retrieval systems, and photocopying, and the rights of translation into foreign language are strictly reserved. Particular emphasis is placed upon the matter of readings, permission for which must be secured by Liz Amadio in writing in advance. Inquiries concerning rights should be addressed to Liz Amadio: liz.amadio@gmail.com.

Liz Amadio

LIZ AMADIO has produced and/or directed staged readings and workshop productions of 75+ works showcasing 300+ artists. As DAPLab Moderator (2008–2018), she produced seasons including her full-length plays, *Evolution: Among Statues, Skeletons,* and *Millennium Mom,* which premiered at Theater for the New City's 2016 *Dream Up Festival.* Liz played Militant Mom. As Cosmic Orchid's Artistic Director, Liz curates Integrative Theatre, a synergy of performing and visual arts. *The Hoodie Play* (BASP 2015–2016) recently had four university productions and a NJ Thespian Festival presentation. *The Voire Dire Project's* 2019 *Photography Cycle,* a Puffin Foundation Grant recipient, featured twenty-five artists, four one-acts, and four artworks at The Medicine Show Theatre. Liz helms *iPower Theatre Collective*—NYC high school students integrating arts and social justice—a past Citizens Committee Grant recipient and a 2020 Chelsea and Hudson Yards Grant recipient. Lincoln Center Education Leadership Lab, 2019. MFA, Actors Studio Drama School. Member: Dramatists Guild; League of Professional Theatre Women; National League of American Pen Women.

···production history···

Guardian of the Field was developed as part of Cosmic Orchid's *The Voire Dire Project 4.0: The Photography Cycle* with the collective creativity of the cast, inspired by "Birds," a photograph by Carol Martinez.

It premiered at The Medicine Show Theater as an AEA Showcase production and was directed by Shellen Lubin.

The cast was as follows:

LIASIA, Lori Sinclair Minor*

JENNIFER, Amy Fulgham*

*Member Actors' Equity Association.

characters

LIASIA, a beautiful woman, African American.

JENNIFER, another beautiful woman, Caucasian.

time

The present.

setting

An Energy Transfer Station, somewhere in the universe.

note

Permission for reproduction of the adaptation of the poem "Bare Trees" was graciously provided by the author, Shellen Lubin.

•••

[LIASIA *is sitting behind a desk. She is, at first, calmly waiting. As she waits, she gets increasingly more anxious; she retrieves some papers from an envelope, alternately reading them then folding them to place them back in. After what feels like quite a long time,* JENNIFER *enters carrying what looks like a hot pink, old-fashioned computer punch card.*]

JENNIFER [*Giggling.*] Hi. I'm Jen. You are?

LIASIA Liasia. Pleased to meet you.

[*They shake hands.*]

JENNIFER [*Still giggling.*] I guess I'm supposed to give you this . . . but . . . what is it? I mean—are you serious—or what?

LIASIA Yes, I'll take that. Why is that funny? It's your ID—your processing card. Lots of folks coming through. We need to keep a system.

JENNIFER I get that. But what I mean is it's a batch card . . . or a punch card, isn't it? Like from the olden-days computers. Please don't tell me you people are running that far behind with technology up here. I don't mean to be disrespectful.

LIASIA I hardly think we're running on an antiquated system. As a matter of fact, we're very organized.

JENNIFER OK, great. If you say so. Then you'll know where my sister is. Did they tell you where to send me to reunite with her? I'm pretty sure she's expecting me. She's been up here for quite some time now.

LIASIA No. There's nothing about your sister in your dossier.

JENNIFER You have a dossier on me?

LIASIA Of course! I told you—it's all very organized. Organized and orchestrated. [*Consults her directions*] Well, it's not a dossier, exactly. But I have instructions. And I've been expecting . . . You. [*Stands*] Now, Jennifer. It is my pleasure to inform you that you have the honor of being appointed the Guardian of Field 6832. [*Shakes her hand.*] Congratulations!

JENNIFER You're giving me a job? I just got here! I worked all my life. I've been working since I was thirteen years old. I would have thought I'd have some sort of extended vacation.

LIASIA I should think you'd be honored.

JENNIFER Honored? I don't even know what this field is—I'm supposed to be honored to be in charge of it?

LIASIA Ah, my bad. I got my speech out of order. This building is surrounded by fields—energy transfer stations, really. And each energy transfer station has a Guardian. And right outside that window is Field 6832. And you are its new Guardian. Congratulations, again.

JENNIFER I respectfully decline the position.

LIASIA Pardon?

JENNIFER You heard me. I respectfully decline. Look, you seem like a nice woman. I'm not trying to give you a hard time. How about I just go down the hall to that receptionist that sent me to you, and I'll clear it up with her? I'm supposed to be meeting my sister so I'll just—

[*Starts to leave.*]

LIASIA —Please don't leave.

JENNIFER Why not?

LIASIA At least, let me show you the field. I mean that's part of my job. Is that fair?

JENNIFER It's not going to make any—

LIASIA —Please. You might be surprised.

JENNIFER Fine. Look, I'm sorry. I don't mean to be rude. I guess I'm still just a little disoriented. Of course, I'll look at the field.

LIASIA Right this way.

[*Lighting shift represents change of location.*]

[*LIASIA escorts JENNIFER downstage center to the window. They look out toward the fourth wall, as they speak.*]

LIASIA [*Continued.*] This is Field 6832.

JENNIFER How many are there?

LIASIA I'm not sure. I just know this one is yours.

JENNIFER It looks the lemon of the bunch.

LIASIA Why do you say that?

JENNIFER If this is supposed to be about new life, it hardly qualifies.

LIASIA I think it's beautiful.

JENNIFER But it looks like Autumn—the end to life. There's nothing Spring-like about it. Spring is about rebirth.

LIASIA Really? Look at all those myriad points of light.

JENNIFER It looks like where all the dead spirits go to rot.

LIASIA There's no such thing as a dead spirit.

JENNIFER There isn't? It certainly looks like a spiritual wasteland—

LIASIA —Well, one could argue that all spirits are dead, then.

JENNIFER Maybe they are.

LIASIA That is a magnificent field with a thousand points of light.

JENNIFER OK, George Bush. I'll bite. But the vegetation still looks like it's dying.

[LIASIA *takes a long look at* JENNIFER, *as if she's not sure of what she said, pondering the viability of what she just heard.*]

LIASIA Lots of vegetation looks orange during the spring. Anyway, that's not the point. It's about the spirits—they're all convening here.

JENNIFER Are each of those lights separate souls?

LIASIA I'm not sure. I just assume each of them are—

JENNIFER —Looks to me like this places splinters spirits.

LIASIA Has anyone ever accused you of being a naysayer?

JENNIFER No! Actually, yes—maybe. But you've got to admit it looks kind of desolate.

LIASIA I'm sorry. I just don't see that. I see beauty. I see a collection of life.

JENNIFER Then why don't you keep guard on it—Field six-thousand . . .

LIASIA . . . Six-thousand, eight-hundred, thirty-two.

JENNIFER Yeah, whatever.

LIASIA Well, it doesn't matter what I see. You're the one they chose to be the Guardian—which I don't think means keeping guard, by the way.

JENNIFER Well, what does it mean?

LIASIA I'm not sure.

JENNIFER So why do you—

LIASIA —Keeping guard sounds like you're a prison guard on the cell block of the state pen. Being a Guardian is much more . . . nurturing—like tending to young children.

JENNIFER Well, maybe they should call it a Rancher because I'm pretty sure they're going to want me to corral those spirits back into a formed soul.

LIASIA I wouldn't know. I only know what's on the instruction sheet. [*Consults her directions.*] And it says that to be Guardian of one of the fields of this vast network of energy transfer stations is a great honor. And I wholeheartedly believe that!

[*They look quietly for a moment, inspecting aspects of the field.*]

JENNIFER Are those buildings back there? I think I see buildings! Are they other Human Resources offices?

LIASIA Is that what you think I am—a Human Resource Administrator?

JENNIFER Aren't you? You tell me you've got a "job" for me. And yet, you haven't given me a written list of duties.

LIASIA How can you turn something so beautiful into something—

JENNIFER —Look! Excuse me if I came here with some preconceptions, ok? We spend our whole lives imagining what happens when . . . And here I am—and this is totally nothing like I imagined. [*Pause.*] And I still say I have a right to see my sister.

LIASIA I understand how you feel. And I'm not saying you'll never get reunited with your sister. I'm just saying that's not why you were sent to me.

JENNIFER Why was I sent to you?

LIASIA To be appointed—

JENNIFER and LIASIA —Guardian of the Field.

[*Silence, as they both gaze.*]

JENNIFER Hey! You see that window? I see a window. I bet she's in there. I think I can even see a woman in the window. Can we go there?

LIASIA [*A bit flustered, consults her directions.*] Well, that's the next thing on the agenda. We're supposed to visit the field—take a walk around so you get a feel for the place.

JENNIFER I'm game. Let's go.

[*They start to walk toward the door. Suddenly,* JENNIFER *stops.*]

JENNIFER [*Continued.*] Hey! Do we stop somewhere to get hard hats? I would think we need hard hats, don't we?

LIASIA You really have a vivid imagination, don't you?

JENNIFER Well, you're the one who called it an energy transfer station. I hear that and I'm thinking Con Ed.

LIASIA Con Ed? I don't think I—

JENNIFER —Con Ed. Consolidated Edison. I guess you didn't live in New York, then.

LIASIA No, I wasn't even American.

[*Opens an imaginary door—light shift.*]

JENNIFER Oh. What . . .

[*Pauses for explanation but doesn't want to pry.*]

JENNIFER [*Continued.*] Well, Con Ed is the electric company—the power company. And they have these huge power stations in different parts of the city and every now and then—

LIASIA [*Holds the door for* JENNIFER.]—We're not going to a construction site.

[*Lighting shift represents change of location.* LIASIA *slides open an up and down sliding door.*]

[LIASIA *and* JENNIFER *traverse the stage to represent travel toward Field 6832, talking as they go.*]

LIASIA [*Continued.*] So, I think once we get there, you'll see the brilliant lights like I do when looking out the window. I suppose my eyes are accustomed to the view.

JENNIFER It did seem like we were looking at two entirely different scenes. Do you know how long it's going to take?

LIASIA I think it's just up here a ways. We have to go through a tunnel.

[*Light shift:* LIASIA *and* JENNIFER *come to a dead stop at the juncture of multiple 'tunnels.'*]

JENNIFER Which one? There's a lot of tunnels here.

LIASIA [*Consults her directions, then points to the ground toward their tunnel.*] They have numbers—down here—see?

JENNIFER And which—

LIASIA —6832—This way.

[*Lighting shift represents tunnel, as they enter.*]

JENNIFER That's an odd number. I mean, it doesn't mean anything to me. It's just random. If I'm supposed to guard—

LIASIA —You're not guarding. You are the guardian.

JENNIFER If I'm supposed to be the guardian of 6832 [*Proud of herself for remembering the number.*] You'd think it would have some meaning for me.

LIASIA [*Reflective.*] Although . . . 6832 does mean something to me.

JENNIFER What does it mean?

LIASIA [*Realization.*] It's the address of my childhood home.

JENNIFER Your childhood home?

[*Lighting shift represents the end of the tunnel.* LIASIA *and* JENNIFER *exit the tunnel downstage right into the field. They are in awe of where they are and what they see.*]

JENNIFER [*Continued.*] Wow! I take it back. I take it all back. This is absolutely beautiful. These lights—they're stunning. They're shimmering and vibrant. Everything looks alive with spirit.

LIASIA I agree. I hadn't been down here yet to see it in person.

JENNIFER Really? All this time you're—

LIASIA [*Seems in a trance.*]—I'm kind of envious. I'd love to be the keeper of this energy field.

JENNIFER Guardian.

LIASIA Whatever. You're really lucky. You know that?

JENNIFER I guess so. So, what am I supposed to do? Do you think I'm supposed to collect the separate energy lights and put them together to make a new spirit?

LIASIA I don't know. Look! There's birds up in that tree. Birds.

JENNIFER Are they little mini-guardians—my assistants?

LIASIA I don't know.

JENNIFER You don't know much. How did you get this job anyway?

LIASIA The birds—maybe *they're* integrating the spirit lights. Or maybe they're manifestations of the integrated spirit!

JENNIFER So, I guess you're not going to do my orientation.

LIASIA What orientation? There is no orientation. At least, I don't think so. [*Scans through her directions.*]

JENNIFER Where's *my* directions? If you don't have them, what am I supposed to do—just wait for someone else to show up with them?

LIASIA I don't know.

JENNIFER Look, I don't really mind playing guessing games with you because I don't have much else on my plate, seeing as I just got here. I mean, at first, it was a little annoying but now, I'm feeling safer, more at home. But really, you're not being very helpful—at all. Isn't there someone else they could have tasked with escorting me to my field? Maybe someone with a little more prowess? Ok, forget prowess. How about someone with just a tad more experience. I mean if I counted the times you said: "I don't know" so far—

LIASIA —Stop badgering me!

JENNIFER I'm just trying to—

LIASIA —I don't know anything about energy transfer stations or Field 6832! Nothing. Nada!

JENNIFER Wow. Relax. I didn't mean to stress you out. I just naturally assumed—

LIASIA —I just got here myself!

JENNIFER What do you mean: "You just got here"?

LIASIA I just got here, as in, I just arrived. They sent me directly to that interview room, handed me these directions, and told me I was to give you instructions—that you were to be Guardian of Field 6832. I'd only been here about ten minutes when you—

JENNIFER —Ten minutes!

LIASIA Well, it felt like ten minutes. It's not like we're in time here, or anything. That's about as accurate as I can get. It *felt* like I was only here about ten minutes.

JENNIFER Jesus! You have no idea what you're doing.

LIASIA Exactly. We both seem to be in some sort of orientation.

JENNIFER But you sounded all official with that bit: "Lots of folks coming through. We need to keep a system." My "dossier"?

LIASIA I was winging it! I thought I was supposed to act like I knew what I was doing—like I've been doing the job for an eternity—or quite some time . . . for a while, anyway.

JENNIFER So, you don't really know why they gave me that pink card to give to you.

LIASIA [*Lightbulb.*] That pink punch card was for my benefit. Pink was my mother's favorite color. And when I was a young girl, she worked as a computer tech. We had those punch cards all over the house. Matter of fact, we used them to leave notes for one another. None of them were pink, though. They were all beige.

JENNIFER Well, everything here seems a lot more vibrant. [*Pause.*] So, I gave you a lot of signs. That's fine for you but what about me?

[JENNIFER *and* LIASIA *gaze out again, silence between them.*]

JENNIFER [*Continued.*] Wait! What number is this field again?

LIASIA Six, eight—

JENNIFER —No! Not six, eight or six-thousand eight-hundred—sixty-eight *dollars* and thirty-two cents. That's the paycheck!

LIASIA What paycheck? I told you it's the address of the home I grew up in. Sixty-eight, thirty-two Eglinton—

JENNIFER —The one my sister got for her first job. She had an index card on her vanity mirror with a big $68.32 and tons of dollar signs circling it. It was fuchsia—the index card. Well, she called it fuchsia. It was *pink*! [*Giraffe neck.*] Where *is* that building?

LIASIA Building?

JENNIFER The building with the window—the one with my sister in it. At least, I think it's my sister. It looked like my sister.

LIASIA I don't see any window. I don't even see any buildings.

JENNIFER [*Points.*] You don't see that building?

LIASIA I don't see it now and I didn't see it when we were looking out that window.

JENNIFER Maybe we don't see the same thing. Maybe we're not
supposed—

LIASIA —Look over there. A stream.

JENNIFER I don't see a stream. Now I'm sure we're not seeing—

LIASIA —I think I'll . . .

[*Just as* LIASIA *starts to meander downstage left toward the stream,* JENNIFER *sees
an envelope on the ground.*]

JENNIFER [*Picks up envelope.*] Hey! Look at this. It says: "Jennifer" on
this envelope. It must be my instructions.

[JENNIFER *doesn't notice that LIASIA has walked away. Opens the envelope, but
pauses, as if she hears LIASIA's words.*]

LIASIA A deep connection to the sacred value of life.

[JENNIFER *now reads its contents.*]

JENNIFER [*A poetic tone.*] I love winter. I love the trees bare. They are
graceful skeletons outside my picture window—black dancers against
the white field—in harmony and counterpoint to the stream. Beating
at the ice around their pointed toes . . .

[LIASIA, *now by the stream, dances as she follows its path.*]

LIASIA . . . Purification, protection, healing . . .

JENNIFER . . . Their backs are arched, their heads flung to the side—
only their arm/branches sway in the violent wind and rushes of snow
and music.

[LIASIA *has now settled by the stream, swaying her arms.*]

LIASIA Suffering and redemption. Do you remember?

JENNIFER [*Stops the poem and speaks to herself.*] I know this poem. I
remember . . . [*Recites on.*] . . . To see the trees budding and flowering
is just one step of the process. To see them fully clothed and shiny is
but a moment.

[LIASIA, *dancing, has transformed into a tree by the stream.*]

LIASIA Not solely a physical being. It is but a moment.

JENNIFER [*To* LIASIA.] Hey, this is mine. This is for me.

[*Looks around. Only now realizes that* LIASIA *is gone. Runs toward the tree that is* LIASIA].

JENNIFER [*Continued.*] It was written by my sister—sent to me her first year away at college. She *is* here.

LIASIA Ancestors and descendants, connection to spirit.

JENNIFER [*Recites with renewed passion.*] I love winter. I need to see things through the evolution—the stripping away of pale Spring greens and lush Autumn golds, trusting in the surety of their return.

LIASIA Just a moment to commune before transition.

[*Slow, slow fade through last two lines of dialogue/movement.*]

JENNIFER Do you think we're supposed to stay here . . . until we eventually turn into spirit lights ourselves?

LIASIA Maybe we already are . . .

[JENNIFER *looks downstage into the horizon and clearly sees the window where her sister is.*]

[*Blackout.*]

• • •

Badger and Frame

Scott C. Sickles

Badger and Frame by Scott C. Sickles. Copyright © 2018 by Scott C. Sickles. All rights reserved. Reprinted by permission of the author.

CAUTION/ADVICE: Professionals and amateurs are hereby warned that performance of *Badger and Frame* is subject to a royalty. It is fully protected under the copyright laws of the United States of America, and all of countries covered by the International Copyright Union (including the Dominion of Canada and the rest of the British Commonwealth), and of all countries covered by the Pan-American Copyright Convention and the United States Copyright Convention, the Berne Convention, and all of the countries with which the United States has reciprocal copyright relations. All rights, including professional and amateur stage performing rights, motion picture, recitation, lecturing, public reading, radio broadcasting, television, video or sound picture recording, all other forms of mechanical or electronic reproduction, such as CD-ROM, DVD-ROM, information storage and retrieval systems, and photocopying, and the rights of translation into foreign language are strictly reserved. Particular emphasis is placed upon the matter of readings, permission for which must be secured in writing in advance. Inquiries concerning rights should be addressed to:

Barbara Hogenson
The Barbara Hogenson Agency, Inc.
165 West End Avenue, Suite 19-C
New York, NY 10023
[212] 874-8084
BHogenson@aol.com

Scott C. Sickles

SCOTT C. SICKLES is an LGBTQ/biracial Korean American writer. His plays have been performed in New York City, across the US, and internationally in Canada, Australia, the UK, Hungary, Singapore, Indonesia, and Lebanon. He is the author of *Playing on the Periphery: Monologues and Scenes for and About Queer Kids.* Plays include: *Nonsense and Beauty* (Repertory Theatre of St. Louis; Edgerton New Play Award; ATCA Steinberg Award Finalist), *Marianas Trench* (O'Neill Finalist), *Pangea* (O'Neill Semifinalist), *Composure* (Winner, New York Innovative Theatre Award; Lambda Literary Award Finalist), *Intellectuals* (Smith & Kraus's New Playwrights: Best Plays of 2007), *Moonlight & Love Songs* (GayFestNYC), *Lightning From Heaven* (Beverly Hills Theater Guild/Julie Harris Playwriting Award), *Beautiful Noises* (Smith & Kraus), *murmurs* (Samuel French), and *Turtles and Bulldogs* (Applause). Five consecutive Writers Guild of America Awards for the daytime drama *General Hospital*, eight Emmy nominations. Member, Dramatists Guild, New Play Exchange. www.ScottCSickles.com.

··· production history ···

Badger and Frame was presented as part of Emerging Artists Theatre's New Works Series at TADA! Theater in New York City in October 2018. Produced by the playwright, it was directed by Susan Izatt with the following cast:

EPHRAIM SIEBERT / SHERIFF, Jason Howard

MARY KATE MCCANDLESS / BADGER'S MOM, Sara Thigpen

BADGER, Andreas Casso

FRAME, Jeremy Cohen

characters

EHRAIM SIEBERT, almost fifty. Bobby's best friend from when they were kids. A speech therapist living in Chicago.

MARY KATE McCANDLESS, just over fifty. Bobby McCandless's widow. They were together since Junior High. They never lived anywhere else but their hometown. Mother of two teenage boys.

BADGER, eleven and one-half years old. Athletic, energetic, handsome. Sweet but not necessarily bright. A "normal" boy.

FRAME, ten and three-quarters years old, actually almost eleven. Bookish. Smart. Shy. Profoundly average.

BADGER'S MOM, late thirties. A highly frustrated offstage voice. Can be played by same actor as MARY KATE.

SHERIFF, a stern offstage voice. Can be played by same actor as **EPHRAIM.**

setting

The present: the McCandless's backyard.

The past: the backyard, a treehouse, a small boat, an island beach, an island cave.

time

The present day: 2017.

The past: 1978.

note

While not explicit, this play deals with sexuality in preadolescent boys and the discovery of attraction at a young age. As such, BADGER and FRAME should probably be played by teens or even adults. Their behavior and speech should reflect the ages of the characters without resorting to caricature.

• • •

[*The McCandless Backyard. Two chairs. The present day scenes take place in 2017. The flashbacks take place in the summer of 1978: in the backyard, in a treehouse in that backyard, in a boat on the water, and in a cave, all represented on bare parts of the stage. At rise:* MARY KATE McCANDLESS—*early fifties maybe looks older, recently widowed and dressed in black; a decent working-class woman—stands in the backyard, staring slightly upwards (at the offstage treehouse).* EPHRAIM SIEBERT—*late forties maybe looks younger, well-dressed for a funeral but not ostentatious—enters.*]

EPHRAIM   Sorry. Is it okay . . . to come out here?

MARY KATE   Did you come out here to smoke?

EPHRAIM   Oh, God no. Did you?

MARY KATE   No. Bobby made me quit. A long time ago . . . I just needed a break from . . . all that.

EPHRAIM   If you need to be alone . . .

MARY KATE   Please, stay.

EPHRAIM   You're sure?

MARY KATE   We're not related so it's fine. Sorry, your name again?

EPHRAIM   Ephraim. Siebert. We met at the funeral home.

MARY KATE   Right. [*Extends her hand.*] I'm the Widow McCandless. But you may call me Mary Kate.

[*They shake hands.*]

MARY KATE   [*Contiued.*] Refresh my memory. You came in from . . .

EPHRAIM Chicago.

MARY KATE Right . . . And how did you know my husband? Sorry, I know I should remember—

EPHRAIM Not at all. You've got more important things . . . Anyway, I, uh . . . I used to live next door. Right there.

MARY KATE Your father was Ralph?

EPHRAIM He was.

MARY KATE He was a nice man. Cranky . . . But nice.

EPHRAIM That's him. Was. Anyway, thanks for letting me come.

MARY KATE Any friend of Bobby's . . . You said you reconnected on Facebook?

EPHRAIM About six months ago.

MARY KATE After how long?

EPHRAIM A while . . . We were inseparable the summer before he went to junior high but...

MARY KATE Then he went to junior high.

EPHRAIM And I was still stuck in the sixth grade. I was very surprised to get his friend request.

MARY KATE He reached out to you?

EPHRAIM Yes. Why?

MARY KATE He hated Facebook. Signed up for it. Swore he would never use it. Then of course, Mr. Popular . . .

EPHRAIM Yeah. I noticed he had a lot of friends but—

MARY KATE and EPHRAIM Never posted anything.

MARY KATE When I got your message, I was surprised he was still even using it.

EPHRAIM He and I . . . we messaged back and forth a bit. I was hoping to come visit but . . .

MARY KATE Life?

EPHRAIM Life. Should've done it anyway.

MARY KATE I don't know. Why the hell would anybody come back here?

EPHRAIM I've got to say, it's weird being back. Someone else is living in my father's house. Now I'm standing in Badger's backyard for the first time since . . .

MARY KATE Badger . . . I forgot about that. [*Pause.*] Yeah, I know what you mean. I never thought I'd end up living here. In this house. I keep telling my kids, never marry your high school sweetheart. Especially never marry your junior high sweetheart. Don't get me wrong, I loved Bobby. Still do. But we never went anywhere. Never saw the world. Never even been to Chicago. No, when you marry your junior high sweetheart, there's a good chance you end up where he started . . . in the house your husband grew up in.

[MARY KATE *and* EPHRAIM *look around. Cross fade to: the backyard, 1978. FRAME enters. He's a bookish boy around eleven years old. Something about his clothes don't match, a minor but noticeable detail. He reads a book. BADGER bursts in, locked in the midst of an imaginary lightsaber battle which he fights with gusto, making sound effects with his mouth as he swings. He's a little older than FRAME, energetic and athletic, in jeans and a t-shirt. He stops when he sees FRAME.*]

BADGER Intruder alert! Intruder alert!

[FRAME *looks up from his book.*]

BADGER [*Continued.*] Identify yourself, stranger, or become a prisoner or the Rebel Alliance!

[FRAME *just stares.*]

BADGER [*Continued.*] Maybe you think you can keep your identity a secret! But no one can keep a secret from . . . The Force! [*Waves his hand like Obi-Wan Kenobi in front of* FRAME's *face.*] Tell me your name, stranger . . .

FRAME Ephraim Siebert.

BADGER Wow! That worked?!

FRAME I guess.

BADGER What's your name again?

FRAME Ephraim.

BADGER That doesn't make any sense.

FRAME It does if you're Jewish.

BADGER I'm Scotch Irish, so I'm going to call you Frame.

FRAME Okay.

BADGER My name's Badger.

FRAME Why did your parents name you Badger?

BADGER They named me Robert, but my mother says I have a face like a badger and I'm always bothering her, so she started calling me Badger to make me feel bad.

FRAME That's not nice.

BADGER I know. So I started calling myself Badger like I was proud of it. I told her badgers are cool and nobody messes with them. So now she calls me Robert again. You don't mind if I call you Frame, do you?

FRAME I don't think so.

BADGER Cool. What are you reading?

FRAME *The White Mountains.*

BADGER Is that, like, a nature book?

FRAME It's science fiction. About a society where—

BADGER Science fiction like *Star Wars*?

FRAME No. It's different from that.

BADGER That's too bad.

[BADGER'S MOM *calls from offstage.*]

BADGER'S MOM Robert! Stop talking to that boy and come in and eat your lunch!

BADGER Can he come in with me?

BADGER'S MOM Is his mother going to feed you tomorrow?

BADGER I don't know! I'll go ask!

BADGER'S MOM Say goodbye and get in here or I'll throw it out!

BADGER I have to go.

FRAME Okay.

BADGER I'll be back in fifteen minutes! If I'm not, I need you to get the plans for the Death Star to the Rebels. Can I trust you to do that for me? Can I trust you to guard these plans with your life? The galaxy is depending on you!

FRAME Yes! I'll hide them in the R2 unit and get them to Obi-Wan Kenobi and he'll help me get them back to the Princess and on to the Rebel Base! [*Pause.*] Right?

BADGER You're weird. [*As he runs off.*] I'll meet you in the Cantina at Mos Eisley Spaceport!

[BADGER *exits.*]

FRAME Bye.

[*Cross fade to* MARY KATE *and* EPHRAIM *in the backyard.*]

MARY KATE When you marry your junior high sweetheart, there's a good chance you end up where he started . . . in the house your husband grew up in. And every day is pretty much like the rest of them. [*Pause.*] Sorry.

EPHRAIM It's fine. It's a sad day.

MARY KATE Thanks but . . . I buried my husband an hour ago. Maybe I can wait a day to start bitching about him.

EPHRAIM Are you saying anything you didn't say to his face when he was alive?

MARY KATE   No. He heard it all. The son of a bitch loved arguing with me. That fuckin' smile of his . . .

[EPHRAIM *remembers the smile. He looks up at the point where* MARY KATE *was staring at the top of the play, i.e., the "treehouse."*]

EPHRAIM   Is the treehouse still . . . That's not the same . . . one?

MARY KATE   Bobby built that for the boys. They loved it . . . for a week. Then he made it his own. Which, let's be honest, was his plan all along.

EPHRAIM   What happened to the old one?

MARY KATE   It wasn't safe anymore so we had to tear it down. The supports were crumbling. They couldn't hold the weight of two growing boys, let alone one full-grown man.

[*Cross fade to the treehouse, 1978. Night. There is a duffel bag and a lit electric lantern next to the boys (both of which will be used in their next scenes).* BADGER *and* FRAME *are arm wrestling.* FRAME *struggles mightily using both hands while* BADGER *is using only one. With some effort but not too much,* BADGER *wins.*]

FRAME   Why are you so strong?

BADGER   I don't know. I climb stuff. And my dad taught me how to chop wood at our cabin.

FRAME   You have a cabin?

BADGER   We did until he left.

FRAME   Did your parents get a divorce?

BADGER   Yeah.

FRAME   I'm sorry.

BADGER   I'm not. Other kids at school are always complaining about their parents getting divorced. I don't get it. I couldn't wait! I just wish my dad took me with him.

FRAME   Oh?

BADGER Yeah, he was cool! He lives in Ohio now. He sends me postcards sometimes. I found the first one in the garbage, so when I get home from school now I always check the mail first. I usually get them before she throws them away.

[BADGER *pulls some postcards and a photo from the duffel and shows them to* FRAME.]

BADGER [*Continued.*] See? He lives in Sandusky.

FRAME Where Cedar Point is?

BADGER Yeah. We went there once. It was cool.

[FRAME *picks out a photograph.*]

FRAME Is this him?

BADGER Yeah.

FRAME He's really handsome.

BADGER My mom tells me I look just like him. It's why she hates me. [*Holds the picture up next to his face.*] What do you think?

FRAME I, uh . . .

[FRAME *gets lost in* BADGER'*s face for a moment before* BADGER'S MOM *calls from off stage.*]

BADGER'S MOM Robert! Who are you talking to?

[BADGER *puts his arm around* FRAME *and covers* FRAME'*s mouth with his hand.* FRAME *freezes, less afraid of getting caught at this point and more because he's not used to being touched, especially not by another boy.*]

BADGER Nobody! I'm just playing Star Wars!

BADGER'S MOM I'm not going to find that boy from next door up there with you, am I?

BADGER No!

BADGER'S MOM I don't want him hanging around here! I'm going to see about getting a fence to keep him out!

BADGER Okay! I'm going to go to bed now!

BADGER'S MOM Don't make me come out here again! [*Lower as she goes away.*] I should get rid of that damn treehouse. What have you done to deserve a treehouse anyway . . . ?

[BADGER *listens a moment. They whisper throughout the rest of this scene.*]

BADGER Okay, she's gone.

[BADGER *lets* FRAME *go. He turns to* FRAME *who is flustered beyond speech and movement, except to tentatively touch his lips where* BADGER's *hand just was.*]

BADGER [*Continued.*] You okay?

[FRAME *gulps and nods.*]

BADGER [*Continued.*] Then say so. Say something! Anything! Tell me you're alive!

FRAME Uuuuuhhhh . . .

BADGER You are weird.

[BADGER *smiles at* FRAME *and gives him a playful nudge.*]

BADGER [*Continued.*] We better go to sleep.

[BADGER *turns out the lantern, lies down, and closes his eyes.* FRAME *looks at* BADGER, *then lies down next to him, his eyes wide open. Cross fade to* EPHRAIM *and* MARY KATE *in the backyard.*]

MARY KATE The supports were crumbling. They couldn't hold the weight of two growing boys, let alone one full-grown man. I tell you it broke his heart to take that thing down.

EPHRAIM I'm surprised his mother didn't tear it down.

MARY KATE She tried! She climbed up there on a ladder once, screaming her head off, took one swing at it with a hatchet, missed, and fell right on her ass.

EPHRAIM I wish I were surprised.

MARY KATE You're thinking she was drunk, aren't you? That's what we all thought. When she was in the hospital, we tried to get them to detox her . . . Turns out, she didn't have a drop of alcohol in her system. No booze, no drugs, nothing. Everything about that woman would have made sense if she was under the influence but no. She was just that unhappy.

EPHRAIM I didn't realize.

MARY KATE Don't feel too sorry for her. She was still a miserable, hateful woman. Even on antidepressants, she was horrible. She was just a little happier about it!

EPHRAIM I just thought she hated me.

MARY KATE Look at you, thinking you were special. No, she hated everybody. Especially Bobby. Did that stop him from moving in and taking care of her? Nope. And what could I do? I wasn't working. I was busy raising his children. Then I had to take care of that battle-axe on top of everything else. I felt like those priests in *The Exorcist*. I swear, her room was ten degrees colder and stank. She made our lives hell. The boys didn't know if they were coming or going. And Mama McCandless took forever to die. *Forever.* And when she finally did, don't you know . . . Bobby cried like a baby. I asked him "Why? Why would you shed one tear over that terrible woman?" And he just said, "Other boys get to miss their mothers and I'm not going to."

EPHRAIM I'm sorry.

MARY KATE Thanks. Sounds like you got a taste of it.

EPHRAIM An *amuse bouche*.

MARY KATE [*Laughs.*] I know what that is from *Top Chef.*

EPHRAIM That's where I learned it too.

MARY KATE Yeah . . . Sometimes she would be so mean to me and the boys, when the nurse came over, I'd take them out to the lake. I'd put them in the rowboat and we'd just sit there for hours. The nurse understood, even encouraged us. "Take your time, honey. Come back when she's sleeping." Didn't even charge us for the extra time.

EPHRAIM The boat . . . Was is called The Tallulah?

MARY KATE Actually . . . it was called *The Tulia* . . . after Bobby's grandmother on his father's side. But Bobby *never pronounced it correctly*. After a while, it was too much to fight and we all just called it Tallulah.

EPHRAIM You don't still have it, do you?

MARY KATE Right there. In the shed. The boys treat it like gold. They could have given a damn about the treehouse but that boat . . . It's in better shape now than it ever was.

EPHRAIM Bobby and I went out in it once. [*Looks at her. Pointedly.*] *Once.*

MARY KATE [*Nods, understanding.*] Fuckin' bitch . . . What did she do?

[*Cross fade to:* BADGER *and* FRAME *sitting, facing each other in a rowboat (which can be the stage floor), wearing life jackets over their clothes (if they're in the budget).* BADGER *has the oars (which are mimed). The duffel bag is with them. Sound effects of heavy wind and rain. They shout over it.*]

BADGER Don't be scared!

FRAME Why not???

BADGER Because The Force Is With Us!

FRAME Well, I'd rather live long and prosper!

BADGER I'm going to forget you said that!

FRAME Can you use the Force to get us home?

BADGER Damn right I can! And in under twelve parsecs!

FRAME Parsecs are a unit of distance!

BADGER What?

FRAME Parsecs! They measure distance not time! So if the Millennium Falcon made the Kessel Run in under twelve parsecs, that means it shortened the distance!

BADGER Of course it did! Because it was going so fast!

FRAME I can't argue with that!

BADGER   That's because I'm a genius!

FRAME   That's not the reason!

[*A bright flash and loud crack!*]

FRAME and BADGER   HOLY SHIT!

FRAME   That almost hit us!

BADGER   We're not going to make it back to the dock!

FRAME   What do you mean, we're not going to make it back?!?

BADGER   I've got a Plan B! Here, come sit next to me!

FRAME   I don't want to fall in!

BADGER   Then slide!

FRAME   What?!?

BADGER   Here, wait!

[BADGER *brings the oars in to the boat.*]

BADGER   [*Continued.*] Now, crouch! Like you're going to do a cannonball!

[FRAME *does.*]

BADGER   Now hold out your hand!

[FRAME *holds out his hand.* BADGER *reaches out and takes it, pulling* FRAME *over to his side of the boat.* BADGER *guides him so they're sitting next to each other. He gives* FRAME *one of the oars and takes the other.*]

FRAME   I don't want to drop it in the water!

BADGER   You can't. It's got a thingy on it that keeps it from going through the loop! Now remember how I showed you?

FRAME   Uh-huh!

BADGER   Okay! Now, row!

[*As they row, lightning flashes again, then the lights cross fade to: a low blue light representing a cave.* BADGER *and* FRAME *drag "the boat" and the duffel into this light.* FRAME *breathes heavily. Sound effects: the storm can be heard raging outside but they don't have to shout over it now.*]

BADGER [*Continued.*] You okay?

FRAME I'm . . . fine . . .

[*They sit as* BADGER *pulls the lantern out of the duffel, sets it down, and turns it on.*]

BADGER You hungry?

FRAME Starving.

[BADGER *gets two sandwiches out of the duffel. They start to eat.*]

BADGER We may be here for days. Weeks even. We'll have to ration our food.

FRAME We will?!

BADGER No, we'll be back home tonight. Unless the rain doesn't stop. Then, we'll just go back in the morning.

FRAME Won't your mom be mad?

BADGER She's always mad. What about your parents?

FRAME They're probably really worried.

BADGER You're not going to get into trouble?

FRAME Maybe a little. My mom'll probably ground me forever but thank God I'm alive. And my dad'll yell a little about "hoping I learned my lesson." Then he'll tell my mom it's good for me to get into a little trouble now and then. Like normal boys.

BADGER Your parents don't think you're normal?

FRAME They tell me normal is boring.

BADGER That means they think you're weird but they love you anyway.

FRAME I know.

BADGER Do your parents ever hit you?

FRAME Not in a long time and never that hard. Just a little whack on the fanny.

BADGER "Fanny"?

FRAME You know. The butt.

BADGER I know what a "fanny" is. I just can't believe you said it. You sound like a granny. Like you have a little Tweetie bird that Sylvester the Cat is always trying to eat.

FRAME [*Imitates Granny as accurately as possible.*] "Nothing like this has happened to me since the boys got back from Gettysburg!"

[BADGER *just stares at* FRAME *mouth agape. Then he starts laughing uncontrollably, falling to the ground.* FRAME *laughs too, but tentatively.* BADGER *composes himself.*]

BADGER I can't believe you just did that!

FRAME Why? Was it—(weird)?

BADGER That was the funniest thing I've ever seen! Do it again!

FRAME Maybe later. I'm really cold.

BADGER Oh. No problem. Take off your clothes and spread them out.

FRAME Why?

BADGER So they can get warm and you can dry off.

[BADGER *starts to undress but* FRAME *just stands there trying not to watch him.*]

BADGER [*Continued.*] What, are you shy all of a sudden?

FRAME No! Not all of a sudden . . .

[BADGER *is now in just his swim trunks. He goes over to* FRAME, *still clothed and shivering.*]

BADGER Do you want me to help you?

FRAME No, I can do it.

BADGER Clothes are harder to take off when they're wet. Here.

[BADGER *helps pull* FRAME*'s shirt off.* FRAME *looks up at him.*]

FRAME Thanks . . . I've got the rest . . .

[BADGER *spreads their clothes out while* FRAME *takes off his shoes, socks, and pants.*]

FRAME [*Continued.*] Are you sure it's safe in here?

BADGER Oh yeah. Nothing lives in here. It shouldn't anyway.

FRAME Why not? It's a cave. How do we know there aren't any bears or snakes . . .

BADGER This is a man-made lake.

FRAME It is?

[*When* FRAME *is in his swimming trunks,* BADGER *grabs a towel from the duffel and tosses it to* FRAME *to dry off.*]

BADGER Yeah. It used to be a rock quarry or something. They filled it in with water and in the middle of it, there was still this island with a cave.

FRAME Is the cave man-made?

BADGER Kind of. From when they dug the rocks, I guess. At least I think so. Anyway, we'll sleep in the boat.

FRAME We're going to sleep here?

BADGER Just until the storm dies down. I'm really tired from all that rowing. Aren't you?

FRAME Now that you mention it.

BADGER Why don't we catch some z's now? We'll see how the weather is when we wake up?

FRAME Okay.

[BADGER *pulls out a worn beach towel from the backpack and spreads it out.*]

FRAME Wow. You're really prepared.

BADGER I used to be a Cub Scout.

[*As they sit on the beach towel,* BADGER *turns off the lantern. They are seen in the low, blue glow.*]

FRAME What are you doing?

BADGER Saving the batteries.

FRAME You didn't bring extras?

BADGER Of course I did but . . . We shouldn't waste them.

FRAME Right.

BADGER Don't worry. You're safe. [*Finally noticing.*] You're shivering.

FRAME I'll be fine.

BADGER Come here. We'll use our body heat to keep warm.

FRAME Oh . . . Okay . . .

[*As* FRAME *sits still,* BADGER *gets behind him, pressing his chest against* FRAME*'s back. He reaches around and rubs* FRAME*'s arms to warm him up. Then,* BADGER *just stops and holds* FRAME. *It's a hug they both need.* FRAME *leans against him. They slowly, calmly, breathe together.*]

BADGER How's that?

FRAME Better.

[*Lights fade to black. The sounds of the storm gently subside. Time has passed. They boys lie next to each other:* BADGER *on his back,* FRAME *upstage of him.* FRAME *props himself up and leans over* BADGER *to turn the lantern back on. He looks down at* BADGER.]

FRAME Badger? Badger, the storm stopped.

[FRAME *lifts his hand to nudge* BADGER *but hesitates, nervous to touch* BADGER*'s bare skin. He looks down at his friend in the light of the lantern. Then nudges him.*]

FRAME Badger, the storm stopped. We can go home now. Badger?

[FRAME *looks at* BADGER *some more in the light. Unable to stop himself, despite an Herculean attempt to do so, he slowly, hesitantly, and without breathing, leans down and gently kisses* BADGER *on the cheek. The kiss lasts a full second or two.* FRAME *lifts his head back up.* BADGER *stirs, looking up at him. Then . . .* BADGER *smiles.*]

BADGER You're so weird.

[BADGER *puts his arm around* FRAME *pulling him close,* FRAME's *face on his shoulder, as he turns out the light.*]

[*In black. Hear offstage voices.*]

SHERIFF   Maybe they're in here.

[*Morning light fades up on* BADGER *and* FRAME *lying together,* FRAME *still resting his head on* BADGER's *shoulder, their clothes still spread out on the ground. A flashlight beam finds them.*]

SHERIFF   Uh, Ma'am. I think you should take a look at this.

BADGER'S MOM   Why, what have you . . . [*Pause.*] BADGER!!!

[BADGER *and* FRAME *jolt awake.* FRAME *looks terrified, about to bolt.* BADGER *opens his eyes and stares calmly, defiantly, even hatefully into the beam of light . . . and puts his arm around his friend.*]

BADGER'S MOM   GET . . . DRESSED!!!

[*Cross fade to* MARY KATE *and* EPHRAIM *in the backyard.*]

EPHRAIM   Bobby and I went out in it once. [*Looks at her. Pointedly.*] Once.

MARY KATE   [*Nods, understanding.*] Fucking bitch . . . What did she do?

[EPHRAIM *looks at her. He takes a moment, smiles, and explains . . .*]

EPHRAIM   What else? She blamed me for the whole thing.

MARY KATE   Never mind it was Bobby's boat. And probably Bobby's idea.

EPHRAIM   Well, we were out on the water a long time and my parents were worried.

MARY KATE   Oh no, did they call her?

EPHRAIM   They rang the doorbell.

MARY KATE   Well, that did it! All because you two went on a little boat ride?

EPHRAIM   What can I say?

[*As* MARY KATE *and* EPHRAIM *talk,* BADGER *and* FRAME *get dressed and put all the stuff into the duffel.*]

MARY KATE [*Shakes her head.*] So, I guess you were grounded?

EPHRAIM My parents grounded me for a week but . . .

MARY KATE Bobby's mother wouldn't let you hang out with him anymore.

EPHRAIM Summer was almost over anyway. Then . . .

MARY KATE Junior high.

EPHRAIM Junior high.

MARY KATE Still. You were right next door.

EPHRAIM So was he. [*Pause.*] Life.

MARY KATE Life.

[*Silence. Without looking at each other,* BADGER, *duffel in hand, and* FRAME *exit in different directions. Once they're off . . .*]

MARY KATE I'm glad you got away.

EPHRAIM Not until college but . . . Me, too.

MARY KATE You know, some days there's nothing I'd like more than to sell this house . . . or burn it to the ground . . . anything to get rid of the stench and memory of that woman. But she's been gone a while now and . . . We managed to make a lot of happy memories here. And now that Bobby's gone . . . this is what we've got left. So, we're kind of stuck.

[EPHRAIM *fishes out his wallet and gives her his card.*]

EPHRAIM If you're ever in Chicago.

MARY KATE Seriously? Thanks. [*Reads the card.*] Speech therapist? Maybe you could get my boys to stop cussing like the Devil.

EPHRAIM I wonder where they get it . . .

MARY KATE From their fucking father. Obviously.

EPHRAIM   Obviously.

MARY KATE   I read there's some kind of boat tour in Chicago that's supposed to be a big deal . . .

EPHRAIM   Yes! The Architectural Boat Tour!

MARY KATE   Is it really all that?

EPHRAIM   It so is.

MARY KATE   Then it's on the list! [*Up to the treehouse.*] You hear that, Bobby?! I'm blowing your insurance money on a trip to Chicago! [*Looks back at* EPHRAIM.] Part of me thinks he's up there hiding in that treehouse. And once these people leave, he's going to climb back down . . . and we're gonna live happily ever after. Which of course means we'll be arguing all the fucking time. But . . . happiness is different for everybody, isn't it?

EPHRAIM   I guess it is.

MARY KATE   You want climb up? Have a look around?

EPHRAIM   Thanks but . . . it's not the same.

MARY KATE   I guess not.

EPHRAIM   I should be going anyway. It was great talking to you.

MARY KATE   Yeah, you too.

EPHRAIM   Sorry again for your loss.

MARY KATE   Yeah. You too.

[*They share a warm look. (Note: It should not be implied that she knows the nature of his feelings for her husband. They're both people who lost someone in common.) As* EPHRAIM *starts inside,* MARY KATE *takes a few steps toward the treehouse. She stops and looks up at it. Behind her,* EPHRAIM *does the same.*]

[*Lights fade.*]

• • •

Escape from
Garden Grove

Mathilde Dratwa

Escape from Garden Grove by Mathilde Dratwa. Copyright © 2018 by Mathilde Dratwa. All rights reserved. Reprinted by permission of the author.

CAUTION/ADVICE: Professionals and amateurs are hereby warned that performance of *Escape from Garden Grove* is subject to a royalty. It is fully protected under the copyright laws of the United States of America, and all of countries covered by the International Copyright Union (including the Dominion of Canada and the rest of the British Commonwealth), and of all countries covered by the Pan-American Copyright Convention and the United States Copyright Convention, the Berne Convention, and all of the countries with which the United States has reciprocal copyright relations. All rights, including professional and amateur stage performing rights, motion picture, recitation, lecturing, public reading, radio broadcasting, television, video or sound picture recording, all other forms of mechanical or electronic reproduction, such as CD-ROM, DVD-ROM, information storage and retrieval systems, and photocopying, and the rights of translation into foreign language are strictly reserved. Particular emphasis is placed upon the matter of readings, permission for which must be secured, in writing in advance. Inquiries concerning rights should be addressed to:

Ally Shuster & Chris Till, CAA
Ally.Shuster@caa.com
Chris.Till@caa.com

Mathilde Dratwa

MATHILDE DRATWA's plays include *Milk and Gall,* which will be produced at Theatre503 in London in 2021, *Dirty Laundry,* and *A Play about David Mamet Writing a Play about Harvey Weinstein.* Her work has been developed and presented by the Ground Floor at Berkeley Rep, Rattlestick, LAByrinth Theater Company, the Great Plains Theater Conference, the Playwrights' Center, and in London at the Young Vic. Mathilde is a member of Dorset Theater Festival's Women Artists Writing Group, a member of the Orchard Project's Greenhouse, and a two-time Pulitzer Center grant recipient. Recently, she was a Dramatist Guild Foundation Playwriting Fellow, a member of New York Foundation for the Arts' Immigrant Artist Program, and a co-leader of the FilmShop collective. A seasoned educator, Mathilde is a Master Teaching Artist for the New Victory and Roundabout Theatre Company. She is also the cofounder of Moms-in-Film, which, among other things, provided free childcare to filmmaker-parents at SXSW and Sundance.

··· **production history** ···

Escape from Garden Grove was produced by Ingenue Theatre at Public Assembly in Brooklyn. It was directed by Brian Roff, and the cast was as follows:

FAYE, Vicki Blankenship

SOPHIE, Martine Moore

characters

FAYE, a woman in her seventies.

SOPHIE, her granddaughter. fifteen.

setting

A bus stop.

··· • • • ···

[*A bus stop.* SOPHIE, *a teenager, sits on a bench next to* FAYE, *her grandmother, in her seventies.* SOPHIE *has a backpack.* FAYE *holds a large handbag. Both* SOPHIE *and* FAYE *are wearing wigs.*]

FAYE   Can I take it off yet?

SOPHIE   Not yet.

FAYE   When?

SOPHIE   Soon.

FAYE   It's itchy.

SOPHIE   I know. As soon as we get on the bus.

FAYE   It's wet.

SOPHIE   I know.

FAYE   I hate the rain.

SOPHIE   I know. I'm sorry.

FAYE   I wish you got me a red one.

SOPHIE   These are from the school play. They're the only ones I had.

FAYE They didn't have any red ones?

SOPHIE It's West Side Story. They're trying to make us look Puerto Rican.

FAYE Well, get me a red one next time. Really red, like Lucille Ball. All the most beautiful women have red hair. Maureen O'Hara, Rita Hayworth . . .

SOPHIE Lindsay Lohan.

FAYE Who?

SOPHIE Nevermind.

FAYE Annie Walsh who lives in the room next door to mine has red hair. Bet she dyes it.

SOPHIE She dyes her hair? But isn't she old?

FAYE She enjoys male attention. I know—I hear it all through the wall. The walls at Garden Grove are too thin. I'm not even going to tell you what I hear when Annie Walsh entertains her gentlemen friends.

SOPHIE Gentlemen friends?

FAYE She's on her fifth boyfriend since I moved in. It's the red hair.

SOPHIE Wow.

FAYE Though to be fair to Annie, she likes older men, so it's not really her fault she has so many boyfriends: they keep dying.

SOPHIE Oh! I—uh . . . I'm sorry?

FAYE They were really old.

SOPHIE Oh my God! Stop!

FAYE When the Garden Grove nurse found out about Annie Walsh, she gave this big talk about SDTs and taught us how to—

SOPHIE Grandma, stop. Please . . . And I think it's STDs. I wish the bus would get here.

FAYE Me too. The rain makes my / hip ache

SOPHIE [*Overlapping.*] Hip ache, I know.

[*She unfolds a bus schedule.*]

SOPHIE [*Continued.*] The schedule says every ten minutes. Uh oh!

FAYE What?

SOPHIE It says exact change. I only have a twenty. I forgot. Do you have any change?

FAYE Change? No. I have my check book . . .

SOPHIE The bus driver's never going to take a check.

FAYE Sorry. I never carry cash.

SOPHIE How do you buy food and stuff?

FAYE I don't—Garden Grove takes care of all that.

SOPHIE But—you always give me money! Every time I come see you!

FAYE Your mother slips it to me when she comes in and hugs me, and I give it right back to you.

SOPHIE Really?

FAYE I'm surprised you haven't noticed.

SOPHIE What's in your bag, then? No money, no phone . . . You carry around that big bag just for your checkbook?

FAYE Well . . . let's see . . . tissues . . . jelly beans . . .

SOPHIE Jelly beans?

FAYE I take them from the bowl at reception.

SOPHIE You have a handbag full of jelly beans?

FAYE They're free.

SOPHIE Wait, I know what I forgot! Do you have your passport?

FAYE What?

SOPHIE Your passport.

FAYE I don't have a passport.

SOPHIE You don't?

FAYE I've never had a passport.

SOPHIE How could you not have a passport? That's a big problem. We have to get you one.

FAYE What would I need with a passport?

SOPHIE Oh. Yeah. I'm kidnapping you.

FAYE You're kidnapping me?

SOPHIE Yes.

FAYE You're kidnapping me.

SOPHIE I said, yes.

FAYE You can't kidnap me.

SOPHIE Why not?

FAYE Because I'm seventy-five years old.

SOPHIE No you're not.

FAYE Okay. Seventy-seven.

SOPHIE Grandma, you're seventy-nine.

FAYE I thought we were going to your friend Courtney's house to watch the Oscars.

SOPHIE We are. I mean—we're going to her house. We're not watching the Oscars, they're not till Sunday.

FAYE I knew it!

SOPHIE But we are going to Courtney's house.

FAYE Honey . . . We should call your mom. She'll worry.

SOPHIE No. I hate her. I'm never going home ever again.

FAYE What happened?

SOPHIE She's just a—she's the worst. I hate her so much. She's selfish and she controls everything. Like . . . My stupid curfew. And she flips out if I drink even a drop of alcohol, but Dad would let me drink wine at dinner all the time!

FAYE I think that's a European thing.

SOPHIE Courtney's parents said they're cool with us crashing at their place for a few nights while we get organized. They're hippies. I told them we were running away to Belgium and do you know what they said?

FAYE We're running away to Belgium?

SOPHIE Yeah. And guess what Courtney's parents said?

FAYE You're trying to take me all the way to Belgium?

SOPHIE Yes. They said, "Belgium? Is that in Germany?"

FAYE Honey, are you in some sort of trouble?

SOPHIE I'm fine! I'm not in trouble. I'm trying to tell you Courtney's parents thought Belgium was in Germany.

FAYE I didn't know where it was either, before your mom met your dad. She said she met a man from Belgium and I thought she was talking about the place where he worked. His company.

SOPHIE It's the capital of Europe you know.

FAYE It is?

SOPHIE Yes. And it's pretty. You'll like it. You can go to the beach. The beach is good for you right? The air?

FAYE Mmmm.

SOPHIE And it's really flat. So you can go on walks, you won't get tired. You know, if it's not raining.

FAYE Does it rain a lot in Belgium?

SOPHIE I'm pretty sure it rains everywhere.

FAYE I don't like the rain. It makes my / hip—

SOPHIE [*Overlapping.*] Hip ache. I know. But I looked it up. It rains 135 days a year in Belgium which sounds like a lot, I know, especially considering that Seattle gets 140—I checked—and apparently Seattle's considered the rain capital, even though I've never been there so I don't know if that's true and my friend Sam—she's a girl, Samantha, you met her, remember her?

FAYE She the black one?

SOPHIE No, that's Courtney. She's the one we're staying with. Sam's got short blond hair and freckles . . .

FAYE Oh. The fat one.

SOPHIE Yeah. No! She's from Portland and she says it's not true what they say about Seattle. So it might not be true about Belgium either. Plus it's probably all changing now anyway with global warming. Belgium's probably going to be the best place to live, weather-wise.

FAYE I didn't know you knew so much about the weather, Ellie.

SOPHIE Sophie. Mom's Ellie. I'm Sophie.

FAYE I'm sorry sweetheart.

SOPHIE That's okay.

FAYE You should be a weather girl.

SOPHIE Yeah, well, I did some research. I knew you'd worry. And yes it does rain kind of a lot in Belgium when I'm there, but that's because I usually only go for the holidays, in the winter, so it's obviously colder then. Last time I went in the summer, for my grandfather's funeral—not Grandpa's obviously I mean Dad's dad, grand-père—it was pretty awesome. I mean—the weather, not the funeral. Although actually . . . it was kind of fun. I'm sure Grandpa's funeral was fun too. I mean—obviously it was sad, I didn't mean—

FAYE It's okay. It was a long time ago.

SOPHIE Do you still miss him?

FAYE Sometimes. It's not really missing him anymore. It's more just . . . remembering him.

SOPHIE Oh. I can't really remember him.

FAYE Sometimes even I can't. Fifty years he wouldn't shut up, and now I can't even remember his voice. You'd think I'd appreciate the peace and quiet. But sometimes I close my eyes and try to imagine him saying something, and I can't. It's gone.

SOPHIE I'm sorry. Maybe it'll come back.

FAYE Maybe.

[*They look out at the rain in silence.* SOPHIE *can't think of what to say.* FAYE *coughs.*]

SOPHIE Are you cold?

FAYE Not cold, just wet. I'm going to take this wig off now.

SOPHIE No! Grandma! What if someone sees us?

FAYE Trust me, nobody from Garden Grove is going to be out in this weather.

[*She takes off her wig.*]

SOPHIE Are you sure?

FAYE Positive.

[SOPHIE *takes off her wig,* FAYE *coughs again.*]

SOPHIE What time do you take your pills?

FAYE Dinner time, with food.

SOPHIE If I'd had more time, I'd have brought food. I'd have made pumpkin cookies like you taught me. Or a meatloaf sandwich. But . . . I came straight from school. I'm sorry. Are you hungry?

[FAYE *shakes her head, coughs again.*]

SOPHIE [*Continued.*] Are you sick?

FAYE Just old.

SOPHIE But your pills . . . they're prescription pills?

FAYE Mm-hmm.

SOPHIE We'll have to find you a doctor then. Over there. I think my other grandfather's doctor speaks a little bit of English. He came to the funeral.

FAYE That's nice of him.

SOPHIE Yeah. My dad bought him a case of wine when my grandfather died, which I thought was kind of weird. I think my dad should have given it to him when my grandfather was still alive, when the doctor was actually successful at his job of keeping him alive, instead of afterwards when he'd let us all down.

FAYE Doctors can only do so much, Ellie.

SOPHIE Sophie.

FAYE Sophie. They're not magicians.

SOPHIE No, I know. I'm just saying.

FAYE Is he handsome?

SOPHIE The doctor?

FAYE Handsome doctors are always more expensive.

SOPHIE What?

FAYE Trust me. I've seen my fair share of doctors, so I should know. I can't afford the handsome ones.

SOPHIE It's Belgium, Grandma. Doctors are basically free.

FAYE You sound like Obama.

SOPHIE Obama's the best.

FAYE Oh. Well . . . Does Belgium have a president?

SOPHIE Belgium's weird. There's a king, but he doesn't really do anything . . . And then there's a prime minister, and the government, but they don't really do anything either. There was no government for almost two years, and the country was fine.

FAYE That's impossible.

SOPHIE It's true. I remember because the whole time my dad didn't shave. Some famous actor there started this protest. (Well, as famous as you can be in Belgium.) He said he wouldn't shave until they elected a new government. I think the only other person who did it was my dad. And he was in America. That's why he had such a long beard for a while, remember? It was insane. Multicolored. It had brown, grey, white, even red—

FAYE No wonder your mother left him.

SOPHIE Grandma!

FAYE Sorry, sweetie, I didn't mean that.

SOPHIE You can't—Don't. And if we're going to stay over there, you're going to have to be nice to him.

FAYE Honey, he's definitely not going to want his ex-mother-in-law around.

SOPHIE I'm sure he'll be fine. I'll call him from Courtney's house.

FAYE He doesn't know we're coming?

SOPHIE Not technically.

FAYE What does that mean? Not technically?

SOPHIE It means not yet.

FAYE Eleanor Kay Anderson!

SOPHIE Will you stop calling me that? I'm nothing like her. My name is Sophie. Sophie Marie De Smet, if you want to do the whole angry thing.

[*A loud beeping noise.*]

SOPHIE [*Continued.*] What's that?

FAYE Nothing.

SOPHIE Grandma? What's happening?

FAYE My incontinence alarm.

SOPHIE What—I—what does that mean?

FAYE I had an accident.

SOPHIE What—oh—what should I do? What do I need to do?

FAYE You need to get me back home.

SOPHIE No, it's okay, we can figure this out—

FAYE Sweetie, listen to me. You need to bring me home.

SOPHIE That's not your home.

FAYE It's where I live.

SOPHIE Why? Why would you want to go back there—ever?

FAYE Because I can't change my underpants out here. And because . . . I can't control my bladder and I have a bad hip.

SOPHIE So?

FAYE I don't want my family to have to deal with any of that. I told your mother years ago, the second I start getting old, put me in a home.

SOPHIE Nobody told me that. Nobody tells me anything.

FAYE You're still young.

SOPHIE I'm not that young!

FAYE When you get older, you—

SOPHIE When I get older I'll leave this place and these people and make my own decisions about my own life! I am sick of people making decisions for me. Mom, Dad, everybody. You're the only one who doesn't try to hide stuff from me.

FAYE Nobody is trying to hide anything from you.

SOPHIE That's a lie. Nobody tells me what's really going on. They think I'm too young and that I don't know anything. But I know stuff. I know about sex.

FAYE Sophie? Did something happen to you? With a boy?

SOPHIE   Not with a boy! Yesterday after school I got on Mom's computer and I found . . . a video. Of her. She's on the kitchen table having—Oh God. I can't even say it. I can't—I don't want to talk about it.

FAYE   All right.

SOPHIE   They're on the kitchen table. And she's naked, and he's so hairy, Grandma. Why would she make a video? And they keep talking. All through it. They never shut up. They say—they—they say—

[SOPHIE *is getting really upset.* FAYE *has taken her into her arms.*]

FAYE   Shhhhh. Shhhhh. It's okay. It's okay.

SOPHIE   I can't even—I can't go back, I can't ever look at her, after all the things she did—I can't—

FAYE   Shhh . . . Shhh. OK. OK.

SOPHIE   She cheated, Grandma! She's just a cheater! A cheater and a slut and—

FAYE   Honey. They're divorced, sweetie.

SOPHIE   No! The divorce hasn't even come through yet. They're not even really divorced. I hate her! I hate her!

FAYE   Oh, honey.

SOPHIE   It's all her fault!

FAYE   It's never one person's fault. Never.

SOPHIE   Marriage is supposed to be forever!

FAYE   It's so complicated.

SOPHIE   It's a promise. How is it complicated? I don't understand.

FAYE   Want to know a secret?

SOPHIE   What?

FAYE   Your grandpa cheated on me.

SOPHIE   Oh God. I'm so sorry. I can't believe Grandpa would—

FAYE   I don't want you to blame him. That's not why I'm telling you. It's the opposite.

SOPHIE   That makes no sense.

FAYE   Listen. When I was younger, especially when your mother was born, I . . . I'd yell at your grandpa all the time. I'd yell at him for . . . Little things. For taking his shoes off in the living room and leaving them there. It felt like he was doing it on purpose to make me mad.

SOPHIE   I do that! I take off my shoes when I watch TV. Mom flips out, every time.

FAYE   Must run in the family. The crazy thing is, I didn't even care so much about the shoes.

SOPHIE   So why did you yell at him?

FAYE   It's complicated. I don't really know. Marriage is hard. Your grandpa and I were lucky.

SOPHIE   That's not lucky! What he did, it's—it's mean and . . . and horrible . . . and awful. Why didn't you leave him?

FAYE   Wasn't anywhere to go. Some of my friends had been through the same thing. Most of them stayed.

SOPHIE   That's so terrible. I'm sorry, Grandma.

FAYE   Don't be. I'm glad I stayed. Your grandpa was a wonderful husband, a wonderful father.

SOPHIE   But—

FAYE   Nobody tells you what it's like after five years, or after ten years, or after thirty years. When you're young you fall in love and you think that's enough.

SOPHIE   It is enough! Love is . . . Love is the most amazing, the most—

FAYE   You need so much more than love. Perseverance. Intelligence. And a sense of humor. We had a good life together.

SOPHIE But . . . He cheated on you! With another woman!

FAYE I bet at the end of his life, he couldn't even remember that woman's name.

SOPHIE Really?

FAYE Really.

[*She opens her purse.*]

FAYE [*Continued.*] Jelly bean?

[*They eat jelly beans.*]

SOPHIE Okay. I guess I'll take you back now. Here—put your wig back on.

FAYE Not necessary. It's not a prison, you know.

SOPHIE You mean we could just have walked right out the front door?

FAYE Yes.

SOPHIE Fuck!

[*A beat.*]

SOPHIE [*Continued.*] Sorry.

FAYE That's okay.

[*A pause. Then* FAYE *giggles.*]

FAYE Fuck!

[*She's delighted. She enjoys saying it.*]

SOPHIE Grandma!

FAYE Fuck fuck fuck!

[SOPHIE *laughs.*]

FAYE [*Conttinued.*] Come on! Swear with me! Fuck!

SOPHIE Fuck!

FAYE What's another one?

SOPHIE Shit!

FAYE Shit! Fuck!

SOPHIE Motherfucker!

FAYE Oooh that's a good one! And fitting, too . . .

SOPHIE Grandma!

FAYE Say that one again, with me. It'll make you feel better. Ready? One, two, three:

FAYE and SOPHIE Motherfucker!!!

SOPHIE I still hate Mom.

FAYE It's okay to hate your mother sometimes.

SOPHIE And I'm never going to let anyone get away with cheating on me. I'll bash his brains in.

FAYE Okay, Honey.

SOPHIE Grandma? When I gave you the wig . . . Why did you put it on? If you can just walk out whenever you want?

FAYE You looked like you . . .

SOPHIE What?

FAYE It was fun.

SOPHIE I wish I could stay with you for a while.

FAYE At Garden Grove? You'd steal all of Annie's boyfriends.

SOPHIE Ewww! Grandma, gross!

• • •

Eleven Things That Almost Happened to Rick and Hannah, and One Thing That Actually Did

Bella Poynton

Eleven Things That Almost Happened to Rick and Hannah, and One Thing That Actually Did. by Bella Poynton. Copyright © 2019 by Bella Poynton. All rights reserved. Reprinted by permission of the author.

CAUTION/ADVICE: Professionals and amateurs are hereby warned that performance of *Eleven Things That Almost Happened to Rick and Hannah, and One Thing That Actually Did.* is subject to a royalty. It is fully protected under the copyright laws of the United States of America, and all of countries covered by the International Copyright Union (including the Dominion of Canada and the rest of the British Commonwealth), and of all countries covered by the Pan-American Copyright Convention and the United States Copyright Convention, the Berne Convention, and all of the countries with which the United States has reciprocal copyright relations. All rights, including professional and amateur stage performing rights, motion picture, recitation, lecturing, public reading, radio broadcasting, television, video or sound picture recording, all other forms of mechanical or electronic reproduction, such as CD-ROM, DVD-ROM, information storage and retrieval systems, and photocopying, and the rights of translation into foreign language are strictly reserved. Particular emphasis is placed upon the matter of readings, permission for which must be secured, in writing in advance from Bella Poynton. Inquiries concerning rights should be addressed to Bella Poynton: bdpoynton@gmail.com.

Bella Poynton

BELLA POYNTON is a playwright, director, and instructor of theatre studies. Her playwriting often focuses on science fiction and speculative themes. Her short play *A Rare Bird* was recently published in *The Weirdest Plays of 2020* (Kindle Unlimited), and her play *The Offer* was included in *The Best Ten Minute Plays of 2019* (Smith & Krauss). Bella's plays have been produced and developed at the Great Plains Theater Festival, New Perspectives Theater, the Science Fiction Theater Company, Otherworld Theatre, the Pittsburgh New Play Festival, Alleyway Theatre, the Antaeus Company, Road Less Traveled Productions, Quantum Dragon Theatre, and many more. Bella has been a finalist for the Woodward/Newman Drama Award, the Heideman Prize, the Christopher Brian Wolk Award, the Samuel French OOB Festival, and, most recently, the Maxim Mazumdar Playwriting Competition. She is the Literary Manager of Post-Industrial Productions in Buffalo, NY, a co-editor of Interventions at *Contemporary Theatre Review*, program director of Queen City Playwrights in Buffalo, NY, an instructor of playwriting at Alleyway Theatre, and the Graduate Liaison of the Playwriting Symposium at the Mid America Theatre Conference. Bella holds an MFA in Playwriting from the University of Iowa and is currently a PhD candidate at the University at Buffalo.

···production history···

Eleven Things That Almost Happened to Rick and Hannah, and One Thing That Actually Did was produced as part of the 40th Annual Buffalo Quickies at Alleyway Theatre in Buffalo, NY. The production was directed by Joyce Stilson and featured the following cast:

HANNAH, Stephanie Bax

RICK, Dylan Brozyna

characters

HANNA, female, thirty, studious, neurotic, smart, and anxious.

RICK, male, forty, a nerdy, low-maintenance, drifter type. That friend who disappears for a year at a time and you come to find out they moved to Lisbon, Portugal, and had a great time . . . but they're back now.

time

Now.

setting

Here.

···

[*At rise.* RICK *sits with a coffee and a book. He reads intently. He glances at his watch—no big rush. After a long few seconds,* HANNAH *enters. She pauses. There is a DING—like a bell ringing. Only after the DING does* HANNAH *go to* RICK.]

RICK Heyyy!

HANNAH Heyyy! Gosh, how are you??? I haven't seen you in like four months!

RICK Good, good! Hey, listen thanks for making it out on such short notice.

HANNAH What?

RICK Thanks for making it out.

HANNAH What are you talking about, making it out? We just—ran into each other. Just now.

I didn't . . . 'make it out.'

RICK Wait, what? Are you kidding? I texted you like twenty minutes ago and asked if you wanted to meet up.

HANNAH You're making this up.

RICK No, look.

[RICK *shows her his phone.*]

HANNAH Holy shit.

[*She looks at her phone and sees his text.*]

HANNAH What the—

RICK I was in the neighborhood because there's this fantastic lemon farmer down the street—

HANNAH A lemon farmer?

RICK Yeah.

HANNAH We're in upstate New York.

RICK I know, she grows them in her backyard.

HANNAH It's the middle of winter.

RICK Crazy, right?

HANNAH How do you find out about this stuff?

RICK Well see, my friend Jordan's husband works at the Tesla plant and apparently, he has an uncle who wrote a grant and apparently got like ten grand from Tesla to build a greenhouse on the back of this abandoned building on the corner of—

HANNAH No, no, no. Never—never mind. You—you don't have to tell me anymore.

RICK Anyway—this is such an insane coincidence. You just happened to come in here? That's wild, right? . . . Right? Hey—are you okay?

HANNAH Yeah . . . I'm just kinda shocked that this happened. It's like bizarre. Like the kind of thing that probably won't ever happen to me again my whole life. Running into someone who thought you were meeting up on purpose. I wonder if it's ever happened to anyone else. Like ever . . . in history.

RICK Ha! What are you talking about? This kind of stuff happens to me all the time.

[*There is a loud DING. The actors go back to where they were at the start of the scene.* HANNAH *goes back to her starting place. There is another DING. She walks in.*]

RICK Heyyy!

HANNAH Heyyy!

RICK How've you been?

HANNAH I'm really stressed, actually. Grad school is pretty horrible.

RICK That sucks. Listen, let me get you something. Do you want a coffee? A sandwich?

HANNAH Maybe a tea . . . Don't worry I'll get it.

[*She gets out her wallet.*]

RICK No, I'll get it.

HANNAH No, Rick, it's okay, I can pay for a tea. I know we're both struggling.

RICK Oh no, I'm not anymore.

HANNAH Wait, really?

RICK Yeah—I just got a new job.

HANNAH That's fantastic! Congrats! Doing what?

RICK Assistant to the vice chair at Tesla. It's really great so far.

HANNAH Assistant to the—oh my god! How?

RICK I know. It's wild. A friend of mine has this sister who works there and she's constantly well—there, you know? Like they work her to the bone. Like she literally. Never. Leaves. I think they even have like a makeshift room for her to take naps in when she gets too tired? So anyway, my friend just so happened to need her to sign some paperwork for some family medical stuff that's going on and I happened to be hanging out with him that day, so I went along, and when we got there—

HANNAH No—no—its okay. I believe you. You don't—you don't have to tell me—But —Wow. I didn't even know you had an engineering background.

RICK I don't.

HANNAH Or, you know, an administrative background.

RICK Don't have that either.

[HANNAH *stares at* RICK.]

HANNAH Wait then how—How did—*Who ARE you?*

[*We hear the DING. The actors reset. DING.* HANNAH *enters.*]

HANNAH Rick!

RICK Hannah! It's so great to see you.

HANNAH It's great to see you, too. It's been like four months.

RICK I know, we have to see each other more. I'm sorry I was MIA. I lost my phone again and the time just slipped away, you know? But anyway, I gotta tell you, I need to leave in fifteen minutes.

HANNAH Wait, like, leave the coffee shop?

RICK Yeaaah, I know. I'm sorry. But it's almost eight and I gotta be back in home by nine to be in bed by ten so I can get up at seven.

HANNAH Are you kidding?

RICK No? Why would I be kidding? I have a new job now.

HANNAH That one at Tesla?

RICK What? Oh, no. That's ancient history. I'm a mourner now.

HANNAH A mourner?

RICK Yeah at one of the local funeral homes. I go to funerals and wakes for people who don't have many friends and mourn with them.

HANNAH . . . Why am I somehow not surprised? And anyway, who has a funeral at 7 a.m.?

RICK I don't know, but someone is! Maybe the deceased was a morning person. Makes sense in a way, right?

HANNAH Rick, I literally just drove forty-five minutes to come out and see you.

[RICK *shrugs with a guilty look on his face. The bell DINGS. The actors reset. Another DING. HANNAH enters. Sound of birds and camping wildlife.*]

HANNAH Wait. Where are we this time? The scene changed.

RICK We're on the trail.

HANNAH What trail?

RICK You know. The trail. The proverbial trail.

HANNAH No, Rick. This is an actual trail. Like a hiking trail. The proverbial trail would mean that we were chasing someone.

RICK Oh yeah no, we're not doing that.

HANNAH So, why? Why are we on a trail?

RICK Jesus, Hannah. Just for fun, okay? Some people like to walk! Not everything has to happen at a coffee shop!

[*The bell DINGS. The actors reset. They are still on the trail. Another DING. This time, it's night. The sound of crickets can be heard.*]

HANNAH Wait we're still here?

RICK Yeah! This is kinda great, right? I love the outdoors. Makes you feel good, you know? At one with nature. Peaceful. Calms the soul. It can heal depression, you know?

HANNAH Oh my god—*OH MY GOD!*—Holy crap—is that a bat!?

RICK Yes, that does appear to be a bat.

HANNAH What the hell! Get me out of here!

RICK It's just a bat—

HANNAH Do you have any idea how dangerous bats are?!

RICK In fact, I do. A friend of mine was once attacked by a bat who had been living in a small tree in an island inside a strip mall and the poor guy had to get the rabies vaccine—

HANNAH Rick—

RICK And he had a terrible reaction to it because apparently some people don't do well with the vaccine, but of course you have to have it, but anyway—

HANNAH Rick!—

RICK After he had the vaccine, he seemed to develop this strange aversion to—

HANNAH *Rick!!!*

RICK What is it? I'm trying to tell a story.

HANNAH I don't care! Get me out of here!

[*The bell DINGS. The actors reset. They are back at the coffee shop. DING.*]

HANNAH Oh, thank God.

RICK What?

HANNAH We're back at the coffee shop.

RICK Hannah you're being kind of insensitive, here. We were talking about something really important and I really need your advice.

HANNAH Oh! I'm sorry. Go on. I'm listening.

RICK Well . . . I think the guy I work for may be a Nazi.

HANNAH What! Holy crap, that's horrible. How do you know?

RICK Well, he invited me over for dinner at his house, and I went. You know—to be polite. Make friends. Anyway, I asked where the bathroom was, but I still got lost on the way and wound up in his basement.

HANNAH What? How does someone—

RICK And so, I turned on the light as I went down there and there was just . . . tons and tons and tons of Nazi paraphernalia. Like it was everywhere. Flags and uniforms and plaques . . .

HANNAH I'm sorry, did you say you only THINK your boss might be a Nazi?

RICK Yeah. Do you think that assumption is well founded? Or do you think he might just be a big history buff?

[*The bell DINGS. The actors reset. They are on the trail again. DING.*]

HANNAH OH GOD NO, THE TRAIL AGAIN. WHY ARE WE ON THE TRAIL AGAIN? HOW DID WE GET HERE?

RICK I don't know but its kind of nice, isn't it?

HANNAH NO, RICK. WE'RE RUNNING. WHY ARE WE RUNNING?

RICK People go running, Hannah.

HANNAH Wait . . . hold on! WHERE ARE MY SHOES??

[RICK *stops.*]

RICK What?

HANNAH Why am I not wearing any shoes? You're wearing shoes! Why am I shoeless?

RICK I don't know but you really shouldn't do that, Hannah. Running without shoes isn't good for your arches.

HANNAH I am aware, Rick. But I don't remember how this happened!

RICK Well sheesh, how would I know? Maybe they were hurting you?

HANNAH Who runs without shoes??

[*The bell DINGS. HANNAH is out of breath. RICK resets. DING. HANNAH doesn't move. DING. HANNAH is out of breath. DING.*]

RICK Come on we've gotta do the next bit.

HANNAH Wait a sec—

RICK Hannah—

HANNAH Hold on.

RICK Hannah—

HANNAH Hold on, I'm catching my breath.

RICK Hannah—

HANNAH Rick, I swear to God . . . just give me a second here, I—

RICK No, no it's something else.

HANNAH What?

RICK You have a bug in your hair.

HANNAH Oh my god, get it out!!!

RICK There. Got it. Huh. It's a tick.

HANNAH WHAT?

RICK Must have fallen on you when we were running on the trail.

[*The bell DINGS. HANNAH goes back to the coffee shop. She sits reading a book. Another DING.*]

HANNAH I'll pay you twenty dollars an hour to study for this test with me.

RICK Seriously?

HANNAH Yes. All you have to do is come here and sit with me and make sure I don't use social media and just do my work.

RICK Holy cow, really?

HANNAH Yep. I need someone to make me accountable.

RICK Well yeah, sure! That sounds fantastic. When would it be?

HANNAH I'd say about—three times a week for the next four months?

RICK Wait like—I would have to be here? Three times a week? At the same time? Consistently?

HANNAH Well, yeah. That's how grad school is. You have to study consistently. But, I'd be paying you a lot. And you don't have to actually do any of the studying.

RICK Hahahahaha. That's hilarious. I've never been anywhere at the same time and place three times in one week since I was in elementary school. No freaking way.

[*The bell DINGS. HANNAH and RICK switch places. Another DING.*]

RICK Heyyy!

[*Pause.*]

RICK Heyyy? . . . Hey? What, no warm welcome?

HANNAH You haven't returned a text of mine in three months.

RICK I know, I know. I'm sorry, I lost my phone.

HANNAH You always lose your phone!

RICK Well I lost it again. Got a new one with a new number. Let me give it to you.

[*He goes to get his phone out.*]

HANNAH How do you lose that many phones? How many phones have you lost in the past year? Three? Four? Five? Where do they go? Where could they possibly go?

RICK I don't know. I think about that sometimes. All my lost phones. And where they are . . .

HANNAH But wait a minute, I don't understand. If you lost your phone and you no longer have the same number, then . . . . how are we both here now? How did we even get in contact and decide to meet up? How is even happening?

[RICK *shrugs*.]

HANNAH Your life is so weird. Are you like . . . clairvoyant, Rick? Are you some kind of medium? Are you a spiritualist mind reader? A mentalist? A wandering guru who once visited the east and found enlightenment and is so in touch with the universe that you literally know where exactly people are going to be at certain moments in time and space?

RICK No. I'm just a guy who loses his phone a lot.

[*The bell DINGS. HANNAH and RICK change their outfits. HANNAH puts on heels. RICK puts on a suit coat. They are holding champagne flutes. The bell DINGS.*]

HANNAH Oh, thank goodness. This is better.

RICK Where are we?

HANNAH We're at the theatre.

RICK Oh wow. I never get out to the theatre! I mean I do sometimes. I used to do some acting. But I just kinda lost my motivation. Oh look! There's Matt!

[*He waves.*]

HANNAH You know Matt?

RICK Of course I do! Matt and I go way back. Hey, there's Jon!

[*He waves.*]

RICK And that's Stephanie! Hey!

[*He waves.*]

RICK And there's Becky!

[*He waves.*]

RICK And that's Brett and Emily and Katie and Bob and Joyce! Hey—hey! Hey guys!

HANNAH Rick, how do you know all these people?

RICK I don't remember. They're just old friends, I guess.

[*He continues to smile and wave at people he knows.* HANNAH *is dumbfounded.*]

HANNAH How in the name of God is it possible for you—and all of your *youness* to possibly know more people than I do at the premiere of a play that *I wrote*???

[RICK *turns to her, shocked.*]

RICK *You* wrote this play!?

[*The bell DINGS. It's later in the evening.* HANNAH *is wearing Rick's suit coat. Her heels are off. Neither have champagne flutes anymore. DING.*]

RICK Wow. That was a great play.

HANNAH Thanks.

RICK You really wrote that play?

HANNAH Yeah.

RICK No, but like really?

HANNAH Like really.

RICK Wow, that's wild.

[*Pause.*]

RICK But I didn't understand that one part where the girl was talking to herself and then all of a sudden there was were two of her, but the other one was a man and she was trying to communicate with—

HANNAH Not—not—not right now, okay? I'm just a little tired. Another time, okay, bud?

RICK Okay. So, hey what are you doing tomorrow?

HANNAH Not much. It's Saturday. Don't you work?

RICK No. Not tomorrow. I was promoted.

HANNAH Really? At the funeral home?

RICK Yeah, they said I was doing a really good job. They even gave me an office of my own. With a desk, and a phone, and everything.

HANNAH Wow, like a real office phone? That can't get lost?

RICK Heh. Yeah. Its connected to the wall with cords and everything. I'll give you the number.

HANNAH That's kind of big deal, Rick. I'm proud of you. Congrats.

RICK Thank you. So, should we go to the trail tomorrow?

HANNAH Errrm, no.

RICK Coffee, then?

HANNAH Sure. What time?

RICK Hmm. Hadn't thought of that yet. I'm not sure. So . . . I'll text you, okay?

[*DING. Blackout.*]

• • •

The Play About the Squirrel, or Infestation

Mia McCullough

The Play About the Squirrel, or Infestation by Mia McCullough. Copyright © 2018 by Mia Mc-Cullough. All rights reserved. Reprinted by permission of the author.

CAUTION/ADVICE Professionals and amateurs are hereby warned that performance of *The Play About the Squirrel, or Infestation* is subject to a royalty. It is fully protected under the copyright laws of the United States of America, and of all countries covered by the International Copyright Union (including the Dominion of Canada and the rest of the British Commonwealth), and of all countries covered by the Pan-American Copyright Convention and the Universal Copyright Convention, the Berne Convention, and of all countries with which the United States has reciprocal copyright relations. All rights, including professional and amateur stage performing rights, motion picture, recitation, lecturing, public reading, radio broadcasting, television, video or sound recording, all other forms of mechanical or electronic reproduction, such as CD-ROM, DVD-ROM, information storage and retrieval systems, and photocopying, and the rights of translation into foreign languages, are strictly reserved. Particular emphasis is placed upon the matter of readings, permission for which must be secured from the playwright's agent in writing in advance. Inquiries concerning rights should be addressed to:

Samara Harris
Samara Harris Literary Agency
samaraharris.com
sharris@samaraharris.com
(773) 852-2262

MIA MCCULLOUGH

MIA MCCULLOUGH is a writer, filmmaker, teacher, and comedian. She is the author of numerous plays, most of which have been seen at theaters around the country, including Steppenwolf, the Goodman Theatre, Chicago Dramatists, and Stage Left (Chicago), The Old Globe and Mo'olelo Performing Arts Company (San Diego), Red Fern and Ensemble Studio Theatre (NYC), and the Victory Theater and the Road Theatre (Los Angeles). In 2016 McCullough wrote and published a book on the creative writing process called *Transforming Reality*. She has taught playwriting and/or screenwriting at Northwestern University, Chicago Dramatists, and Carthage College. McCullough wrote and coproduced a web series called *The Haven*, inspired by her experiences working at a domestic violence shelter. You can learn more about *The Haven* at www.thehavenweb.com. *The Play About the Squirrel, or Infestation* is the first in a series of three *Squirrel Plays*. Two of *The Squirrel Plays* were presented at the Edinburgh Fringe Festival in 2018.

···production history···

The Play About the Squirrel, or Infestation, in its current iteration, was presented alongside *Compensation* by Part of the Main Theatre Company at the Edinburgh Fringe Festival in August 2018. An earlier version received four performances produced by Stage Left Theatre at the Chicago RhinoFest in 2007.

characters

> **MAN,** thirties or forties, white.
>
> **WIFE,** thirties or early forties, white.
>
> **REALTOR,** man or woman of color, but preferably a woman, any ethnicity.
>
> **EXTERMINATOR,** man or woman of color. Can be played by same actor as REALTOR.

setting

Suburbia, a pleasant house.

time

Now.

···

scene 1

[REALTOR *and* WIFE *stand in bare room, looking. Window in fourth wall.*]

WIFE It's a nice house.

REALTOR Yes. Very nice house.

WIFE So pleasant.

REALTOR The nicest on the street, I think.

WIFE And the garden.

REALTOR Maybe the nicest on the market.

WIFE But not the cheapest.

REALTOR No. Well . . .

WIFE Well.

MAN [*Entering.*] This is a nice house.

WIFE and REALTOR Yes.

MAN Well maintained. Perfect size. Attractive neighborhood. I need to ask—

WIFE Dear . . .

MAN I *need* to ask.

REALTOR Anything.

[*Pause.*]

MAN Are there squirrels?

REALTOR Locally?

MAN On the property.

REALTOR I don't think . . .

MAN We don't want squirrels.

REALTOR Well, you should have an exterminator check before/ signing anything.

MAN /But is there a history of squirrels? Getting into the house? Is there a way to know if the house is prone to squirrels?

REALTOR Prone?

MAN Susceptible.

WIFE Easy penetrated.

REALTOR Penetrated?

MAN Infested.

WIFE Is there a way to know if this is the sort of house that squirrels are drawn to, feel welcome in.

MAN Because we don't want that.

[*Beat.*]

REALTOR Is there a reason you're asking about this house in particular? It hasn't come up—

MAN This is the first house we really like. I mean, we like this house, right?

WIFE I love this house.

MAN There's no point in asking if you don't like the house.

REALTOR I see, well, I— There's no documentation on squirrels, infestations, and the like. You could ask the neighbors.

MAN That's a fantastic idea. I'll ask the neighbors.

WIFE Dear . . .

[MAN *exits. Pause.*]

WIFE [*Continued.*] He doesn't want squirrels.

REALTOR Some people don't. [*Awkward beat.*] And you don't . . . want them either?

WIFE Oh, well, you know, they're cute and all. But they can be so destructive, disruptive, and well, we just don't want them in our home, or trampling our garden, taking up our free time. They don't suit our lifestyle.

REALTOR . . . Understandable.

WIFE We didn't bring it up . . . well, sometimes people judge you. You say you don't want squirrels and people assume you're hateful, and we're not—

REALTOR Of course not.

WIFE —It's a *choice*, really.

REALTOR Absolutely.

[MAN *rushes in, breathless.*]

MAN Next door, neighbor . . . he says. . . . no squirrels in the house . . . not in his memory . . . Says there aren't that many squirrels on this block.

WIFE That's wonderful.

REALTOR Are you ready to make an offer?

MAN Could you give us a moment first?

REALTOR Of course. I'll be out front.

[REALTOR *exits.*]

MAN This is the one, isn't it?

WIFE This is it.

[*They stand together, arm in arm, looking out the window.*]

WIFE I love the garden.

MAN I know.

WIFE I hope I can keep it as beautiful as she did.

MAN I'm sure you will. We will. I can help in the garden.

WIFE We're going to love it here.

MAN We are.

[*Lights fade.*]

scene 2

[*Lights up. A bed and chair have appeared.* WIFE *sits in chair, reading. Something outside catches her eye. She gasps slightly, glances at the door, then looks harder. She is entranced.* MAN *enters, watches a moment.*]

MAN Honey?

WIFE Oh! Oh goodness, you startled me.

MAN What were you looking at?

WIFE Nothing.

MAN It wasn't nothing, you practically had your nose pressed against the glass.

WIFE I was just spying on a neighbor. [*Beat.* MAN *looks out window.*] She's gone now. Did you come to ask me something?

MAN A squirrel!

WIFE Just on the fence.

MAN You were looking at a squirrel.

WIFE Maybe it was a rabbit.

MAN It's not. I can see its poofy tail. Why were you looking at it?

WIFE Because it was there, because it caught my eye!

MAN Caught your eye. I bet you thought it was cute.

WIFE No!

MAN Maybe you'd like to ask it in for tea!

WIFE You're being ridiculous.

MAN Were you going to tell me? Were you even going to tell me it was in the yard?

WIFE It wasn't *in* the yard. It was on the fence. Perched on the fence, for half a moment—

MAN On the fence is a very dangerous place to be.

WIFE It's gone, now, see? You scared it away.

MAN Good!

WIFE Honey, it was barely even here. Barely even the idea of a squirrel. It was nothing.

MAN They said there were no squirrels. We were sold this house under false pretenses.

WIFE Honey, it's the suburbs, of course there are squirrels. You knew that.

MAN   You didn't lure it here, did you? You didn't will it here with a secret desire.

WIFE   No. There's no desire. Only for you.

MAN   Okay. [*Beat.*] Maybe I should get a BB gun.

WIFE   You can't hurt it.

MAN   Why do you care if I hurt it?

WIFE   Because you shouldn't hurt things. It's not Christian.

MAN   We're Buddhist.

WIFE   Even more so.

MAN   You're not changing your mind are you?

WIFE   No.

MAN   I mean the house, the yard, the garden gnomes. . . . It's not making you want squirrels, is it?

WIFE   No.

[*Lights fade.*]

scene 3

[MAN *is in bed, reading.* WOMAN *enters.*]

MAN   Sex?

WIFE   Not tonight.

MAN   All right.

[*Beat.*]

WIFE   There's a block party next week.

MAN   Is there?

WIFE   Good opportunity for you to meet the neighbors.

MAN   What about you?

WIFE   I've met the neighbors.

MAN All of them?

WIFE Well, no, not all of them. Some of them, at the neighborhood association meeting.

MAN Did you ask about squirrels? [*Beat.*] Dear?

WIFE I didn't want them to think I was weird.

MAN It's not weird!

WIFE Not at the first meeting.

MAN You should have asked. If there have been problems.

[*Beat.*]

WIFE I was talking with Alice—she lives behind us and two houses over—she was pointing out a hole beneath the eaves outside this window.

MAN What?

WIFE Next to the satellite dish. We were chatting, earlier, and she asked if we knew about it. You can see it clear as day from over there.

MAN There's a HOLE?

WIFE It's not big. Maybe the guys who installed the dish—

MAN [*Getting out of bed.*] There's a breach in our perimeter!

WIFE Honey, you won't be able to see it right now.

MAN [*Leaning out window.*] We've been living in an unprotected house! There could be a whole colony.

WIFE We would have heard them. You can patch it up tomorrow.

MAN Why didn't you tell me earlier?

WIFE I didn't want to ruin the evening.

MAN Did you put that hole there?

WIFE What are you talking about?

MAN Did you?

WIFE   No! It had to have been the guys installing the dish. It's right next to it.

MAN   We're going to have to get the exterminator back in here. Have the house reexamined.

WIFE   You can patch it in the morning. Everything will be fine. It's good that we know.

MAN   You're right. It's good that we know.

[*Pause. They read. Suddenly the pitter-patter of little feet from inside the wall.* WIFE *looks at ceiling, looks at* MAN. *No reaction.*]

WIFE   Did you hear something?

MAN   No.

[*They listen. more pitter-patter.* MAN *does not hear it.* WIFE *looks at ceiling, then at* MAN.]

WIFE   You don't hear that?

MAN   No. Are you all right?

WIFE   We should go to sleep.

MAN   Sleep or . . . ?

WIFE   Sleep.

[*Lights fade.*]

scene 4

[*The pounding of a hammer precedes the lights coming up on* WIFE *sitting in chair, holding her hands over her ears.* MAN *stands on ladder, hammering. hammering stops.*]

WIFE   Honey, don't damage our house.

MAN   You don't want a squirrel in here, do you?

WIFE   No.

MAN I'm doing this for you. For us. To protect us.

WIFE Just don't hurt the house.

[*More hammering. More ear-holding. He stops.*]

MAN Okay. I think we're secure, now.

[WIFE *is relieved. pitter-patter of little feet as* MAN *comes down ladder. Only* WIFE *hears it.*]

WIFE [*Quietly.*] Oh my God.

MAN Did you say something?

WIFE No.

[MAN *is now level with wife, though still on ladder.*]

MAN Look, we're like Romeo and Juliet. How does it go?

WIFE I have no idea.

MAN Something about the East and Juliet is glowing like the sun.

WIFE I don't think that's it.

MAN Regardless. You're glowing.

WIFE Don't say that.

MAN You should kiss me.

[*Beat. She leans out window and kisses him.*]

MAN [*Continued.*] I love you.

WIFE I love you, too.

MAN This is perfect, isn't it?

[*Beat.*]

WIFE Yes.

[*Pitter-patter. Lights fade.*]

scene 5

[WIFE *is in bed, reading. Pitter-patter of little feet. She puts her hand to the wall.*]

WIFE [*Whisper.*] Stop. You have to stop. [*It stops.*] I haven't forgotten you're in here. Trust me. I have *not* forgotten for even one moment. But I . . . I haven't decided what to do about you yet, OK?

[MAN *enters, stops when he sees* WIFE *with hand on the wall.*]

MAN Were you talking to someone?

WIFE No. [*Beat.*] Going over a brief for tomorrow's meeting. Didn't even realize I was speaking out loud.

MAN Are you feeling all right?

WIFE Of course.

MAN You didn't eat much at dinner.

WIFE I wasn't hungry.

MAN And you've seemed especially tired.

WIFE It's been busy at work.

[*Pitter-patter, scamper, scramble.*]

MAN Oh my God.

WIFE What?

[*Pitter-patter, scamper, scramble.*]

MAN Don't you hear that? [*Pitter-patter, scamper, scramble.*] There's a squirrel up there.

WIFE No.

[*They stare at the ceiling. More squirrel noise.*]

MAN I've shut it in there.

WIFE Maybe there's another hole?

MAN No, no, I checked. I checked every inch of the house. I nailed it in.

[*Scamper, scramble.*]

WIFE What . . . do we do?

MAN We're going to have to kill it.

WIFE Tom!

MAN Well, it can't stay up there. It'll nest in the insulation, it could chew the wiring, set the house on fire, burn it down, screw up the cable!

WIFE We have satellite.

MAN There are still wires!

WIFE Are there?

[*Pitter-patter. MAN is nearly hyperventilating.*]

MAN Is it dancing?

WIFE We'll get a trap. One of those humane traps and we'll release it.

MAN No, I can't go up there, I can't face it.

WIFE *I* can put the trap up there.

MAN How?

WIFE Through the trap door in the ceiling of our closet.

MAN No, you can't allow it into the house.

WIFE I won't.

MAN Right now it's contained, isolated. You can't engage with it or you'll get attached. You know how you are, Sarah.

WIFE So open the hole up and we'll wait for it to leave.

MAN More will come! Do you want multiples?

WIFE You're being hysterical.

MAN We have to let it die up there.

WIFE Tom!

MAN   It's the only solution.

WIFE   It'll smell. Our whole house will smell of death.

MAN   No, it's dry, it's sealed off. Promise me you won't go up there, Sarah, promise me you won't let it in.

WIFE   I promise. I won't let it in.

MAN   They're dangerous, they spread disease.

WIFE   We should go to sleep.

MAN   How can we sleep?

WIFE   It's not making noise anymore.

[MAN *stares at ceiling long moment.*]

MAN   I'm going to sleep downstairs.

[MAN *takes pillow and exits.* WIFE *looks at ceiling, hers hands pressed on her belly. She looks ill. Lights fade.*]

scene 6

[WIFE *enters with* EXTERMINATOR. EXTERMINATOR *carries a small Have-A-Heart trap and a pith helmet with a light on it.*]

WIFE   It's over here.

[*The* WIFE *goes to the raised platform and pulls down or sets up a ladder. They climb the ladder, push the trap door up slowly and peer around.*]

WIFE   [*Continued.*] Thank you for doing this with me.

EXTERMINATOR   It's not a problem.

WIFE   I'm nervous.

EXTERMINATOR   Lots of people are.

[*The whooshing sound of an ultrasound as the* EXTERMINATOR *scans with the light. A tiny fast heartbeat.*]

EXTERMINATOR   [*Continued.*] There we go—over there.

[WIFE *gasps.*]

WIFE It's so little.

EXTERMINATOR Common gray tree squirrel.

WIFE He looks scared.

EXTERMINATOR You shouldn't anthropomorphize. It's not a person. It'll only make you feel worse.

WIFE You don't think it's afraid?

EXTERMINATOR *You* don't think it belongs in your attic. That's all that matters. [*Setting up the trap.*] You figure out how it got in?

WIFE A hole. My husband sealed it up.

EXTERMINATOR Sometimes if you leave it open and put a bright light up here, play loud music, create an inhospitable environment, they leave all on their own. Too late for that, though.

Well, that should do it. You can check it in the morning.

WIFE I'll be right down.

EXTERMINATOR . . . Okay.

[EXTERMINATOR *descends and waits.*]

WIFE [*Quietly.*] Hello. Hi. Okay, stay over there. I'm sorry you got locked in here, but you're going to have to leave. I've brought this nice trap, it won't hurt you. All you have to do is get caught and we'll take you somewhere. Somewhere nice. Far away. It's nothing personal, I don't hate you. We just don't want. . . . I'd be a terrible—It's better this way. And Tom. . . . he really can't handle it. [*She sneezes. Beat.*] Where'd you go? Oh, okay. Sorry if I startled you. Allergies . . . Anyhow, I'll come and get you in the morning, OK? [WIFE *descends.*] What if it doesn't work?

EXTERMINATOR We try poison.

[*Lights out.*]

scene 7

[*In the darkness, the sound of the tiny fast heartbeat continues.*]

[*Lights up on* MAN *listening to the wall with a stethoscope.* WIFE *enters.*]

WIFE   What are you doing? I said dinner is ready.

[*She sneezes.*]

MAN   It's still in there.

WIFE   Of course it's still in there. It's only been a day.

MAN   I can hear its heart beating.

WIFE   What? No you can't.

MAN   I can. I can hear its heart. I think it's right on the other side of this wall, taunting me.

WIFE   You're being crazy.

MAN   Listen.

[*She listens. The heartbeat is loud.*]

WIFE   Oh my god.

MAN   See?

WIFE   I don't think I should have listened to that.

MAN   You can't deny it anymore, after you hear that.

[*She goes to listen again. He punches the wall.*]

BOTH   Ow.

WIFE   Don't do that!

MAN   It's going to figure out how to get in here and suck the life out of us if it has to chew its way through the plaster.

WIFE   I think it's drywall.

MAN   They're voracious eaters. What if it never dies?

WIFE Everything dies.

MAN But what if it takes a long time?

WIFE It won't. It's only been a day. Come down to dinner.

[*She sneezes again.*]

MAN Are you sick?

WIFE It's a little cold. Come and eat.

MAN I'm not sleeping up here until it's dead.

WIFE You're hurting my feelings.

MAN It has nothing to do with you.

[*Lights fade.*]

scene 8

[WIFE *climbs back up to attic crawlspace. The trap is empty. She looks around with flashlight until she sees the squirrel.*]

WIFE Shit. Where are you? Look, you have got to get your butt into this trap. My marriage cannot survive your existence. My God, look what you did to the insulation! That's appalling. How could you have done so much damage in such a short time? Made yourself so at home? [*She sneezes.*] He *will* leave me. He will. He can't handle this. He won't. It's in the prenup.

Are you shaking? Am I scaring you? Don't tiny animals shake? Normally? As a habit? Maybe this is normal. [*Pause.*] It doesn't feel normal. You must be hungry. Maybe starving you isn't the right tactic. You'll just eat the house. Don't hurt my house.

[*She pulls out a small package of nuts.*]

WIFE [*Continued.*]So here's the deal: I put these nuts in the trap and you go in there. That's the deal.

[*Lights fade.*]

scene 9

[*Lights up on* WIFE *opening the trap door.*]

WIFE   Come on! You are not cooperating! And you ate the nuts. How did you—Sneaky. Sneaky critter. Smart. You look better today. Not so shaky. I, on the other hand, look like the walking dead. You don't understand what this is doing to me, *physically* doing to me. I don't want to kill you, I really don't want to kill you. You're cute and I'm sure you've got a nice personality . . .

I wish Tom could come in here and see you. Not so he could be won over, or change his mind. But so he could know. So you could be more than a faceless monster behind the wall. [*Pause.*]

I pray every night that you'll die on your own, peacefully, so I won't have to do anything drastic. Can you hear me? Can you hear me praying?

[*Lights fade.*]

scene 10

[WIFE *in bed, reading.* MAN *comes in wearing pajamas. He glances nervously at ceiling.*]

MAN   I just came up to say good night.

WIFE   Okay.

MAN   Have you heard it?

WIFE   Not since I got into bed. Won't you sleep up—

MAN   No. Are you all right? You look tired.

WIFE   I am.

MAN   Can you sleep with . . . ?

WIFE   He keeps me up sometimes.

MAN   He?

WIFE   What—I don't know.

MAN   "He." You're getting attached.

WIFE   No.

MAN   You should sleep downstairs with me.

WIFE   The bed is too small.

MAN   How do you know it's a he?

WIFE   I don't.

MAN   Then why would you say—

WIFE   I just imagined. Decided.

MAN   You're imagining.

WIFE   No.

MAN   Don't lie to me.

WIFE   Look. I should tell you . . . [*He recoils.*] I put a trap up there.

MAN   You promised!

WIFE   To not let him into the house. Yes, I promised.

MAN   Is it gone? Did you catch it?

WIFE   He won't get in the trap. He takes the food—

MAN   You're feeding it! No wonder it's still alive. You're nurturing it.

WIFE   I was trying to catch it. It's not working and I need to try
something more drastic. I know that. Tomorrow I'll switch to poison.

MAN   Don't let it hurt you.

WIFE   It's not hurting me.

MAN   You don't look good.

WIFE   It's not related. He, it, trusts me now. It'll take the poison and this
will be over.

MAN You're so brave.

WIFE It's hard on me.

MAN I know.

WIFE No. I mean your absence.

MAN I'm right here.

WIFE Your not sleeping with me.

MAN I can't. Not with it . . . up there.

WIFE You're the one who wanted the dish.

MAN Are you blaming me?

WIFE No. I feel as if you're blaming me.

MAN Once it's gone, everything will be fine.

WIFE You mean once it's dead.

MAN Gone, dead.

WIFE It's not the same.

MAN I'm going downstairs.

[WIFE *nods.* MAN *exits.* WIFE *looks at ceiling. Lights fade.*]

scene 11

[WIFE *climbs ladder and peers into attic. She holds a bottle of poison.*]

WIFE Look, I'm sorry. I feel really terrible about this, but I can't take
care of you. I don't want to. I'm not good with—

[*She takes a pill.*]

WIFE [*Continued.*] Anyhow, it was good to know you. I mean, I know I
don't really *know* you, that we're not on the same plane of existence.
But you seem really sweet. Little critter.

[*Lights fade.*]

scene 12

[WIFE *lies in bed, ill, her ear pressed again the wall or her hand on it.* MAN *sits with her, holding her hand.*]

MAN Do you think it's still alive?

[*Pause as* WIFE *listens for it.*]

WIFE [*With sadness.*] No.

MAN Oh, thank god. [*Beat.* WIFE *glares at him*] Are you all right?

[*Beat.*]

WIFE I'll be okay. They said I'll feel sick for a few days, not just because of the poison. They said I was having a reaction to the squirrel.

MAN I knew it. I shouldn't have made you deal with it on your own.

WIFE You were afraid.

MAN Yes. I'm sorry.

[EXTERMINATOR *peeks their head in.*]

EXTERMINATOR Hi.

WIFE Hi.

EXTERMINATOR The poison should have had its effect by now.

WIFE It has. It's dead.

MAN I'm going to . . .

[*He bolts.*]

WIFE I don't hear the pitter-patter anymore.

EXTERMINATOR You grew attached.

WIFE Yes.

EXTERMINATOR It happens.

WIFE I don't believe in killing things.

EXTERMINATOR Sometimes it's necessary.

WIFE It's against my religion.

EXTERMINATOR It's against most religions.

WIFE But mine means it. Will God hate me?

EXTERMINATOR I'm just the exterminator.

WIFE Say something that will make me feel better.

EXTERMINATOR The disruption is over. Things will return to normal.

WIFE Disruption.

[EXTERMINATOR *climbs the stairs. Lights fade as he opens the trap door, then lights rise as he closes the trap door and descends carrying a plastic bag with something in it and the empty trap.*]

EXTERMINATOR All done. It looked pretty sick. Probably would have died on its own soon.

WIFE Really? I'm not sure if that makes me feel better or worse. Could you tell me. . . . the gender?

[*Beat.*]

EXTERMINATOR You want to know the gender of the squirrel?

[*WIFE nods. After a stare,* EXTERMINATOR *looks in the bag, jostles it to see.*]

EXTERMINATOR [*Continued.*] Male.

[*She nods, swallowing the tears. MAN enters.*]

MAN Are you done?

EXTERMINATOR Yep.

[MAN, *seeing the bag, moves away from it. He sits at* WIFE's *bedside.*]

MAN Thank you.

WIFE Will we ever have another . . . ?

EXTERMINATOR Not if you're careful.

MAN   We'll be careful.

EXTERMINATOR   Not that it's impossible. Anything's possible. Nature is persistent.

WIFE   Yes.

MAN   We're going to be very VERY careful.

EXTERMINATOR   You can always call me again if you need to.

WIFE   I don't really like you.

MAN   Dear! Sorry.

EXTERMINATOR   It's all right. I'll see myself out.

[EXTERMINATOR *exits.*]

WIFE   I killed it.

MAN   We had to.

WIFE   That doesn't make it right.

MAN   I think it does. It didn't belong here, in our life.

WIFE   So we should kill everything we don't want?

MAN   If it's going to eat your house from the inside out.

WIFE   You don't know how it feels. *You* didn't do it. You didn't say sweet things while you were serving it poison.

[*Three beats.*]

MAN   I paid for the exterminator. [*She turns away from him.*] Do you hate me now?

WIFE   No. [*Beat.*] It was a boy. I was right.

[*Pause.*]

MAN   Did you love it?

[*Beat.*]

WIFE   Yes. I didn't mean to, but yes.

MAN More than me?

WIFE No! Of course not. It was just a tiny . . . critter. I hardly even knew him.

MAN But you loved it, still.

WIFE I tried not to.

MAN I'm glad it's gone. I'm sorry if that hurts you, but I'm glad. I can come back to bed, now.

WIFE Yes.

MAN You missed me.

WIFE Of course.

[*He climbs next to her in bed, rests her head on him.*]

MAN I love this house.

WIFE Yes.

MAN We're going to be so happy here.

[WIFE *cries.*]

• • •

The Artist Electric

Judah Skoff

The Artist Electric by Judah Skoff. Copyright © 2019 by Judah Skoff. All rights reserved. Reprinted by permission of the author.

CAUTION/ADVICE: Professionals and amateurs are hereby warned that performance of *The Artist Electric* is subject to a royalty. It is fully protected under the copyright laws of the United States of America, and of all countries covered by the International Copyright Union (including the Dominion of Canada and the rest of the British Commonwealth), and of all countries covered by the Pan-American Copyright Convention and the Universal Copyright Convention, the Berne Convention, and of all countries with which the United States has reciprocal copyright relations. All rights, including professional and amateur stage performing rights, motion picture, recitation, lecturing, public reading, radio broadcasting, television, video or sound recording, all other forms of mechanical or electronic reproduction, such as CD-ROM, DVD-ROM, information storage and retrieval systems, and photocopying, and the rights of translation into foreign languages, are strictly reserved. Particular emphasis is placed upon the matter of readings, permission for which must be secured from Judah Skoff in writing in advance. Inquiries concerning rights should be addressed to Judah Skoff at: judahskoff@gmail.com.

Judah Skoff

JUDAH SKOFF graduated from Brown University. He was named by the Jewish Week as one of the top "36 under 36" rising stars in the American Jewish Community. His plays have been performed in New York, London, and elsewhere at a variety of theatres and festivals, including Theatre503, Symphony Space, the Nylon Fusion Theatre, the Great Plains Theatre Conference, the Last Frontier Theatre Conference, the Midwest Dramatists Conference, and the Writers Theatre of New Jersey. His awards include the National Playwriting Competition, the New Jersey Playwrights Contest, and two Governor's Awards in the Arts. He was a playwriting fellow with the Athena Theatre Company. In the spring of 2019, Judah directed a production of his experimental drama *The Sinless* at the Theater at the 14th Street Y in New York. He can be reached at judahskoff@gmail.com.

··· production history ···

The Artist Electric was produced by The Write Hour Podcast, Episode 3. It was released on May 6, 2019. It was hosted by Kayla Marie Dreysee and Farokh Soltani. The cast featured Hannah Lawrence and Caitlin Innes-Edwards.
https://soundcloud.com/thewritehour/episode-3
https://thewritehourpodcast.com.

characters [in order of speaking]

BRITTNEY, early twenties.

LIZA, late twenties, early thirties.

setting

A theater.

time

The present.

···

[*At rise: Two chairs facing the audience at slight angles. LIZA wears an upscale but casual summer dress, fancy sandals, and has red painted toenails. BRITTNEY wears a darker, black, upscale party dress.*]

BRITTNEY On Sunday mornings Daddy and I would sit at the kitchen table and read the theatre reviews from the week before. He would make me toast with butter and I would smell his coffee and I would sit in my nightgown and cross my legs and accent my chin as if I were I were being photographed for some important magazine. I imagined myself being written about, gossiped about. Scandals about my lovers. And I told him this and he laughed and smiled.

[*She observes herself, is aware of herself.*]

Sometimes there was a quote from him, what he thought about some new writer or director. Everyone loved him. Even those who hated him loved him, because they had to listen. Had to hear him. What he said mattered. [*Beat.*] After my mother died. After the accident with that drunk driver. The person who did it never got caught. Every time he walked outside, as we tumbled into the narrow cobblestone streets in the West Village near our apartment, behind every wheel of every car was a potential killer. Sometimes he would chase the cars, my father. Just run after them. Throw little crumpled pieces of newspaper at them, as if he were throwing stones. He would wave his arms, wander, delirious through the streets, yelling at cars, "is that the one?" . . . "is that the one who . . . ?" [*Beat.*] But I was with him. I was with him the whole time. And that made him happy.

LIZA Was he depressed? Of course he was. I mean . . . everyone knew it but her. They were going to fire him at the theatre. He was done, washed out. His last few seasons, his last few shows, they were disasters. [*Beat.*] The last show he directed, the one that sent us out to that borrowed house on the beach (because he had to get away) it was about a goldfish who learned to talk. This goldfish starts dating a depressed girl with some type of eating disorder living alone in a third-floor walk up in Union City, New Jersey. It was supposed to be some kind of quirky comedy—I hate that term, quirky comedy—but it was savaged, laughed at. He started taking pills, and the pills were slowing him down. Because. Because he. He couldn't . . . He couldn't anymore. Not like when I first met him. Not like when I rejuvenated him after the death of his first wife. No, he slowed down. And he settled into a grim kind of life. And I did too. It was a decline. [*Beat.*] I never imagined I'd be a widow so young.

BRITTNEY When I was a little girl, I used to look through the old family albums and see him and Mom on vacation, in Morocco and China and Australia. I used to be so jealous because I wanted to go, wished that I had been there. And sometimes I used to wonder . . . Mom, did she jump in front of that car on purpose, so Daddy and I could be alone together, without distraction? Sometimes I believe she made that sacrifice for us. [*Beat.*] Daddy met Liza shortly after Mom died. Liza was a hanger on at that point, just followed him around like a lost cat. I mean who was she? Some social worker who found cheap meds for heroin addicts. She'd never been to the theatre. I spent so many nights with him at dim bars listening to bad poetry and drinking cheap beer; getting a headache from the glow of neon lights burning in from the sleazy laundromat across the street. And she? She got all self-righteous at the smell of cigarette smoke and thought beer wasn't ladylike. I can just tell she was a whore in college.

LIZA   At the funeral all of his friends gathered, people who had known him for years, decades, maybe they knew him since before I was born. They told stories and . . . it was almost like. It's almost like I wasn't part of his life. He has no family other than her and so, I was, it was . . . they should have been comforting me. [*Beat.*] Nice enough. That's what I heard, that was the whisper, nice enough. Over and over. That's what they said about me. I was nice enough for a second wife, a younger woman, someone to fuck. They ignored me, and just tripped over her. Brittney, his princess. [*Beat.*] I was no gold digger. I'll say that a million times or only once. I didn't marry him for his money. He didn't have much money. The house that we stayed at, the house on the beach, the house where he died, it was loaned to him by some actor friend. Some actor friend he made famous. He walked around at night in a silk bathrobe and slippers. Certainly he acted like he was entitled to it. He acted like he was entitled to a lot of things. [*Beat.*] He was a theatre director—he had a certain cache. A certain profile. And that was sexy. [*Beat.*] When we met I was living with some other girls in a small railcar apartment and we were all trying to make it. And mostly being ignored and—I was a social worker, working with at risk youth and he—. I went to graduate school. I had a savings account. I was doing things right. He was somebody. He liked to dress me up. But he had a daughter.

BRITTNEY   Daddy, are you out there?

LIZA   Did you know that she slept in her dead father's theatre the night after he died? She slept in the theatre in brand new silk pajamas she bought just for that occasion.

BRITTNEY   He liked to dress her up. Short skirts, cute little one-piece cotton dresses in the summer which bounced up around her thighs. Tight black stockings and boots in the fall, skinny jeans or leggings in the winter . . .

LIZA   And I would wear what he bought and it was a little show for him. I mean this is what men do, isn't it? They dress us up. We dress up for them. We wear nighties and short skirts and low-cut shirts and lingerie and we sculpt our faces with makeup and do our hair just so . . . and we become a kind of imaginary object. We spend time at the gym. We lift weights and crunch our stomachs. And it's because the human body, on its own, laid bare . . . it. It's not all that impressive. [*Beat.*] And what I am to her?

BRITTNEY   What is she to me? Is she my stepmother?

LIZA   Am I her stepmother?

BRITTNEY   Step-mommy Liza! Maybe just mommy Liza . . . Maybe just mommy. Or Mom.

LIZA   Aren't we, in some way . . . aren't we still family?

BRITTNEY   When I was a girl I ran across his stage. He sat there watching me. Do this Britt, do that. Act for me. You're better, so much better than those other girls—those real actors who work for me. I could live without them but not without you.

LIZA   We spent the summer at that house in the beach.

BRITTNEY   I came out to the house at the beach one weekend during the summer. The hottest weekend.

LIZA   It was midsummer, one of the hottest nights of the year and there were parties and bonfires on the beach. Young people. Young, pretty people, boys and girls and . . . he liked to be around them, pretended he was still one of them. And she came to stay with us.

BRITTNEY   He was having a party with some actor friends. And some young actors and actresses were sitting in the big living room, drinking wine and gazing out at the ocean. And there was a kind of bluish glow out from the moon. [*Beat.*] And I wore a black and white bikini bathing suit and high heels. I walked around the house and drank champagne. People sat around reading this new play by some hot playwright, trying out these different voices and personas. And I sat on this older actor's lap. I didn't know who he was or why he was there or even remember his name but I think it was Tommy. And I nibbled at his ear and laughed into him and giggled and scraped the tips of my nails against his chest. And Liza watched me and so did my father; they both watched me. When the play reading was over I took my new actor friend by the wrist and pulled him into a bathroom down the hall, not far from the living room. Everyone saw us walk away.

LIZA That night in the house on the beach. She came but he hardly noticed her. It was as if he didn't want her to be there. She stayed for the reading and I guess she was talking to the people there but . . .

BRITTNEY They all noticed me leave.

LIZA And then she was gone. I don't even remember when she left or who she left with. It was weird . . .

BRITTNEY They were jealous. Daddy was jealous of the attention I was getting.

LIZA And her father, he, he was having a wonderful time just being around people he loved, people who adored him; it was like all his problems never happened. He needed to be adored. He was drinking and laughing and reading the stage directions for this new play.

BRITTNEY I know Daddy watched me leave. Saw me leave with that older actor. I can just imagine him crushing the ice against his teeth, so angry, so angry at me.

LIZA It was the first time I'd seen him truly happy and I honestly think, the only thing which put any damper on it, was that she was there.

BRITTNEY And we went into the bathroom, me and this older actor, Tommy I think his name was, and he was just, my god at this point, he wanted me so badly. And so I let him have me. I had to, it would have been wrong not to, the way he was begging and pleading and just losing himself. It was sad, kind of, a little pathetic. I let him fuck me right there on the bathroom sink, with me leaning over, looking at myself in the mirror, watching him through the mirror.

LIZA At some point the party was over and everybody left and a few people just passed out on the couch and Brittney was . . . no one knew where she was, and honestly, no one cared. And then we were in the bedroom and his step was lighter and as I was getting ready for bed, he grabbed me from behind and he pulled me into bed and he . . . he touched me. He touched my legs and my thighs and my . . . and he kissed me and I was . . . And it was the first time in a long time. I always loved the way he touched me.

BRITTNEY After sex, the actor he, Tommy I guess his name was, he just disappeared out of a back door to the house. Didn't want to stick around, I guess. [*Beat.*] I went back to my room and slept a little. Dozed, really. Not restful, not deep. I didn't dream. At some point I had to pee. I walked down the corridor past the bedroom where . . . I could hear them, I could hear my father and Liza fucking and moaning and it sounded like ecstasy.

LIZA When he was . . . he said he wanted me. He said he needed me.

BRITTNEY And I knew in that moment he had forgotten my mother and embraced a kind of death, a kind of death that's an excuse for living.

LIZA He said he needed to be with me because he only felt alive when he was with me.

BRITTNEY I sat by the door. It was closed but I could hear. And I heard.

LIZA It felt so good.

BRITTNEY And I saw it in my mind. And I lay down on the floor outside the bedroom and curled up like I was a baby. I rocked back and forth and I sucked my thumb and I wanted to pee right there on the floor. But I stopped myself. I wasn't going to be his baby. [*Beat.*] I stayed by the door and fell asleep and woke up when the earliest rays of the sun were creeping along the carpet. The door to the bedroom was open a crack and I pushed my way in. The bed was empty. I saw jumbled sheets and a deep indentation on the mattress. Liza wasn't in the room. My father was lying on the floor dead in front of the large mirror. His face and his body and his arms and mouth were covered with thick disinfectant, the kind you would use to clean a bathroom, or kitchen floor. There was a harsh, sterile smell around him.

LIZA I found them after I got back from a run on the beach. She was lying there with his dead body.

BRITTNEY Liza found us. When she got home, she found us lying next to each other. She screamed. She screamed like a little baby girl, a terrified baby girl, maybe thinking we were both dead.

LIZA And then she got to be—she got to be pitied—she got to be all of their daughters. I never believed it was a suicide like they said.

BRITTNEY Daddy, I found your body discarded in front of that mirror. I lay down on the floor near you. I arranged your arms so you hugged me with your hands. It was a kind of happy moment, in the way that moments can sometimes be happy if you accept them, moments full and complete, separated from anything else, anything called reality. I can still see you out there. When I stood on your stage and danced and acted all I could see was the dark. All I could see was the lights on my face and the dark. An endless dark which ate me. Which consumed me.

LIZA There's a man waiting for me now. I have a date. His name is Johnny and I hear he's an aspiring actor. I see him now. He's wearing a sports jacket and shirt open at the collar. Shiny black shoes and freshly pressed pants. He looks nice. He's only a few years older than me. He has a smooth face and short hair which is curled. I see him and I see so much of myself and the world. I see him and I see a future.

BRITTNEY I can see you now. You gave me that gift. It made me electric, like I was praying, like I was talking to God. [*Beat.*]

I love you.

I love you.

I love you.

I love you.

[BRITTNEY *lays down and writhes gently on the floor.*]

I love you.

I love you.

[BRITTNEY *becomes strangely content.*]

• • •

CouchFullaLuv

Kato McNickle

CouchFullaLuv by Kato McNickle. Copyright © 2018 by Kato McNickle. All rights reserved. Reprinted by permission of the author.

CAUTION/ADVICE: Professionals and amateurs are hereby warned that performance of *CouchFullaLuv* is subject to a royalty. It is fully protected under the copyright laws of the United States of America, and of all countries covered by the International Copyright Union (including the Dominion of Canada and the rest of the British Commonwealth), and of all countries covered by the Pan-American Copyright Convention and the Universal Copyright Convention, the Berne Convention, and of all countries with which the United States has reciprocal copyright relations. All rights, including professional and amateur stage performing rights, motion picture, recitation, lecturing, public reading, radio broadcasting, television, video or sound recording, all other forms of mechanical or electronic reproduction, such as CD-ROM, DVD-ROM, information storage and retrieval systems, and photocopying, and the rights of translation into foreign languages, are strictly reserved. Particular emphasis is placed upon the matter of readings, permission for which must be secured from Kato McNickle in writing in advance. Inquiries concerning rights should be addressed to Kato McNickle at: katoagogo@aol.com.

Kato McNickle

KATO MCNICKLE is a Connecticut-based playwright, director, and artist. A graduate of Brown University, they hold a degree in Ancient Studies specializing in Greco-Roman and Sanskrit performance and continue to study the connection between art, perception, neuroscience, and performance. Kato is host of *Welcome to the TheaterVerse*, a podcast dedicated to encouraging theater-makers to pursue their craft wherever they are in the world. They have taught playwriting at the University of Connecticut, and writing, acting, and comic-book making at Artreach, Inc. in Norwich, CT. They are a member of the O'Neill Theater Center Artistic Council, Vice-President of the Mystic Paper Beasts Mask & Puppetry Company, producer of the Mayfly 24-Hour Theater in New London, and a member Dramatist Guild and the Star Wars Fan Club.

··· production history ···

CouchFullaLuv was performed as part of Table and Chairs, an evening of one-acts for Valentine's Day by the Stonington Players at the La Grua Center in Stonington, Connecticut, directed by Kato McNickle with stage manager Regan Morse.

The cast was as follows:

THE CLERK, Michael Vernon Davis

HARRIET, Helen Cronin

SYLVI, Alyssa Christian

CHAZ, Evan Brown

'NESSA, Tricia Montes

JOS, Emily Donnel

characters

THE CLERK, his name is really Jerry, but hardly anyone ever remembers that. This is his store—twenty-five years in couches.

HARRIET, an older woman dumped after twenty years of marriage. Her last couch "fell apart."

SYLVI, a young woman shopping with Chaz. She likes the mocha sofa.

CHAZ, a young man shopping with Sylvi. He doesn't know what mocha is.

'NESSA, A young woman in a new relationship and a new apartment to furnish with Jos.

JOS, A young woman with an old foldaway, who wants a couch big enough for napping.

requirements

A single set, a couch, and some feathers (okay, lots of feathers), twenty-five minutes.

note

The feathers may fall, be placed, be preset and there the whole time, or any other creative way to deliver the feathers to the couch that you can think of; and the brawl can be elaborate as described or simple with just some thrown pillows and a little fluff . . . *just make it magical and fantastic—super fun music can buy you lots of real estate.*

setting

A furniture showroom—a portion of the couch section. One couch is present.

• • •

[*The music starts—the angels sing! A thin shaft of light pierces the couch. A single feather falls from heaven to the cushion of the couch or is already there, illuminated by the light. It is beautiful and of modest size.*]

[*The* HEAD SALES CLERK *enters, inspecting the wares. The* CLERK *bends to pick up the feather when . . .*]

[*ZING!!—THWUMP!! Whir whir whir . . . !*]

[*The* CLERK *unfolds, standing upright—the feather in hand. The* CLERK *looks at the feather, rubs the back of his neck, and with unthinking befuddlement, places the feather neatly in his breast pocket.* HARRIET *enters the showroom.*]

HARRIET Excuse me? Can you help me?

CLERK Can I help—oh yes. I can help you. My—my card?

[*He hands her the feather, sees it, takes it back and places a card in her hand. He returns the feather to his pocket.*]

HARRIET Thank you. [*Reading from card.*] Jerry . . . ?

CLERK Yes. Jerry. Couch?

HARRIET Harriet, actually.

CLERK Harriet. Yes. Excuse me. You're looking for a couch?

HARRIET I—I—I've found myself in need of a—I need a couch. That's why I'm here. A couch. Sofa. Chaise lounge. You name it, I need it.

CLERK We have a large selection, in many styles, including many top-quality—anything in particular?

HARRIET Particular? Sturdy. No. Wild. Maybe not. But it could. Bright. Maybe. Or. Blue. Maybe. Red! No. Brown? Brown's boring, isn't it. Not brown. How about . . . different.

CLERK Different?

HARRIET Just something—different. That's all. Change.

CLERK Do—any of these look—different . . . ?

HARRIET Not really.

CLERK Well, let me show you some other styles. We have a wide assortment throughout the store. A couch is an important investment and we pride ourselves on supplying the perfect selection, satisfaction or your money back.

HARRIET My money back. That's funny. Well, not really. Show me some couches [*Reads card.*] Jerry.

[*They exit, another feather falls from heaven to the coach as* SYLVI *and* CHAZ *enter and cross to the couch, or perhaps the other feather is already there...?*]

SYLVI Do you like this one?

CHAZ I like it fine.

SYLVI Do you love it? There was the other one.

CHAZ Which one? There are about a hundred.

SYLVI The mocha one.

CHAZ The—mocha—one.

SYLVI The brown one.

CHAZ Sylvi, there are a hundred couches, and about fifty of 'em brown—

SYLVI The brown that was mocha.

CHAZ Mocha—is . . . ?

SYLVI Coffee and chocolate. Like a coffee mixed with chocolate. Mocha.

CHAZ Ah—Mocha.

SYLVI You still don't know which—

CHAZ —But I'm sure it was nice too.

SYLVI Chaz!

CHAZ It was comfortable, right?

SYLVI Comfortable . . . ? Maybe . . . ? Maybe not as comfortable . . .

CHAZ All I care about is comfortable . . .

SYLVI Then you have to remember whether or not you liked the mocha one!

CHAZ Sylvi . . . I . . . I . . . don't remember which brown the mocha was!

[CHAZ *notices the feather.*]

SYLVI The one that was more elegant! The one that we were just looking at! The one that would go so well next to the window with all the afternoon light! [CHAZ, *distracted by the feather, picks it up.*] Chaz!

CHAZ A feather. Look Sylvi, a feather.

SYLVI This is important, Chaz.

CHAZ You're right. It's important. It is important. Mocha.

[*The* CLERK *enters and moves quickly to the couple.* CHAZ *tries to avoid eye contact with the* CLERK. *The* CLERK *speaks anyway.*]

CLERK Can I help you find anything?

CHAZ Nah—naw—just lookin' Just lookin' around. That's all.

SYLVI We're looking at couches. Are you listening to me, Chaz?

CLERK Something in particular . . . ?

CHAZ We're looking.

CLERK We have a wide selection—

SYLVI We're looking for something nice. One that will last. Last a long time. Right, Chaz?

CHAZ Quality.

CLERK We have many top quality items throughout the showroom—

CHAZ Just gonna keep looking—c'mon Syl—you liked the mocha?

CLERK We offer many shades of brown—

CHAZ No kidding.

CLERK —including a number of taupes and beige, and cinnamon—

CHAZ We're checking up on mocha right now—

SYLVI Ooo—cinnamon—

CHAZ Mocha, honey.

CLERK We also have covers in honey tones—

CHAZ We're gonna look around.

[CHAZ *starts off, waits for* SYLVI *who approaches the* CLERK.]

SYLVI Card?

CLERK Oh! My card—!

[*The* CLERK *reaches into his breast pocket and pulls out the feather and hands it to* SYLVI.]

You need anything, you let me know. Twenty-five years, one thing I know, it's couches.

[*The* CLERK *sees the feather in* SYLVI's *hand.*]

Feather—!

[*He plunges his hand back into his breast pocket, produces a card, takes back the feather with one hand, switching it for the card with the other.*]

Card.

SYLVI Thanks.

CHAZ Syl, mocha . . . ?

SYLVI This couch is going to last, isn't it, Chaz? It better be one that lasts.

CHAZ Mocha lasts forever, right?

[SYLVI *exits with* CHAZ. HARRIET *enters.*]

HARRIET [*Reading from card.*] Jerry . . . yes. I have a question about the Moroccan Camel-back Lounger. I'd like an opinion. I'm not really sure if it's me.

CLERK It also comes in stripes or in paisley—

HARRIET Paisley. Really.

[*The* CLERK *exits with* HARRIET. *A third feather falls from heaven onto the couch accompanied by the music and pointed light, or has been there all along. The second couple,* JOS *and* 'NESSA *enter.*]

'NESSA Which one you like, baby?

JOS We want a big one, right?

'NESSA Not too big. We got a small place.

JOS Maybe we should getta bigger place? Then we can get a big couch—

'NESSA Or we get a smaller couch now, and when we get a bigger place, we get a bigger couch to go with it.

JOS Which one you want?

'NESSA Which one you want, baby?

JOS Aww, 'Nessa, I gotta old foldaway it's been just fine, and it's big—

'NESSA We are not bringing any kinda foldaway into our place, Josie-girl. We got a place and I'm planning to make it just cozy. I'm planning to make it just right—

JOS I want one big enough for me to lay down.

'NESSA Not too big. Just cozy—

JOS I want one for me to lay down and stretch out and just fall asleep—

'NESSA Not too big—

JOS That's what I want.

'NESSA I'm so happy. I'm so happy right now. We're gonna buy a couch. A nice cozy little couch—

JOS Maybe medium—?

'NESSA —and we're just gonna be so happy together. I know it. I can tell.

JOS Yeah.

['NESSA *gets close to* JOS]

'NESSA This couch is just gonna be ours. Our first real thing that's us, and I want it to be perfect. It's our anniversary, after all.

JOS Yeah, two weeks—

'NESSA And one whole day living together in our apartment.

JOS Our small, empty apartment.

[*The* CLERK *enters.* JOS *sees him first and immediately moves far away from* 'NESSA]

'NESSA Jos?

CLERK Can I help you ladies find anything?

'NESSA We're looking at couches—

JOS I'm—me—she's—she's looking for couches. Me—I'm helping.

'NESSA Right now we're looking—

JOS I'm just here to help, really—

CLERK Is there a particular style?

JOS Not too fancy. Unless—you want fancy . . . ?

'NESSA Okay then, baby. Not too fancy.

JOS She means—I'm just helping—helping out—I'm a helper. It can be fancy. Um. How 'bout one 'bout my height?

'NESSA Not too big. Cozy.

JOS She wants cozy. She's got a cozy little place—

[JOS *notices the feather on the couch and picks it up.*]

'NESSA We. We've got a place—

JOS —LOOK 'NESSA! A feather! I found—right here! Let's look at more couches! Over there! I'm sure there's some—

CLERK My card?

[*He pulls the feather from his pocket as* JOS *pulls* 'NESSA *away. The* CLERK *grumbles, finding a card and putting back the feather. As he does, another feather falls from heaven onto the couch. A moment later* HARRIET *enters.*]

Find anything that suits your fancy?

HARRIET Found a feather—

[HARRIET *picks up the feather as the* CLERK *takes the feather out of his pocket.*]

CLERK Yes. Here. Oh. There.

HARRIET But haven't found anything—fulfilling. Nothing that makes me happy. Nothing that says "You need me in your life and I need you always!" Know what I mean, [*reading from card*] Jerry.

[HARRIET *sits on the couch as she sighs.*]

[*ZING!! THWUMP!! "AHHHHHHHHH!" the angels play their celestial harps up the scale . . .*]

HARRIET Ooo! That's a surprise.

CLERK Everything all right—!?

HARRIET I like this couch. This. This is a—very—nice couch. It definitely speaks to me.

[*She bounces a bit.*] Oh, yes. Very nice.

CLERK This is a fairly midrange couch—or sofa—it comes in several color options—but no paisley I'm afraid—

[HARRIET *begins rubbing her hands all over the covering.*]

HARRIET I like this one. Just like it is. Have you tried this one? You should—come here—try this one—[*reading from card*] Jerry. Com'ere, Jerry.

CLERK Well—um—

HARRIET Something better to do?

CLERK Oh—um—no, not really.

[*The* CLERK *sits. ZING!! DOUBLE THWUMP!! "AHHHH-AHHHHHHH-HH!!" the angel harp plays* . . .]

CLERK I—see what you mean.

HARRIET Harriet. Call me Harriet. I love it when you call me Harriet.

CLERK Hel / lo—

HARRIET Married?

CLERK —Harriet. No. No. Never seemed to find—

HARRIET Me neither. Not married. Not now anyhow. That's why I need a couch. That's why I need a couch very—very badly—Jerry.

CLERK I see. Um-hm. This is a very, very nice—hmm-mmmmm.

[*He moves passionately toward her, but is stopped by her words. Crazy jungle drums sound, like a heartbeat—thump-thump-thumpthump! Starts up and builds through the following* . . .]

HARRIET My husband—

CLERK Husband?

HARRIET Ex-husband. I sawed the last one in half.

CLERK Husband?

HARRIET Couch. Chainsaws are surprisingly easy to wield. Now I need a new one.

CLERK Husband?

HARRIET Couch.

CLERK How wonderful.

HARRIET I found a feather, Jerry. A feather just like yours—on this couch.

CLERK Yes. That's odd—

HARRIET I NEED this couch, Jerry. RIGHT NOW!!

[*The jungle heartbeat is loud and furious*—HARRIET *grabs the* CLERK *and kisses him in a mad frenzy!*]

CLERK [*Breathlessly.*] We can—we can—I have the paper work in my office—

HARRIET This is a great couch, Jerry! This is a wonderful couch! WHERE HAS THIS COUCH BEEN ALL MY LIFE, JERRY!!

CLERK The paper work, and it's yours!

HARRIET Let's do it.

[*The two rush off to the office. The drum beat subsides as* 'NESSA *enters followed by* JOS.]

JOS Aww, 'Nessa. Don't be all like that. You know how much I love you.

'NESSA I cannot believe how you were being. I did not even know who you were. You who?

JOS It's just we're in a store.

'NESSA We're looking for a couch.

JOS We're in a couch store.

'NESSA Furniture showroom.

JOS Yeah, that. And I can't be all like I'm with you is all.

'NESSA We are buying a couch. Together. Us. And you are with me. And I'm with you. That's together.

JOS Yeah, yeah. But I don't want to look together is all. I don't want that snooty old clerk looking all at us and giving us some kinda attitude—

'NESSA So he's looking at us like you're some crazy person all excited and in my face 'cuz you found some feather—

JOS You can have it. I'll give it to you.

'NESSA I do not want some kinda feather you found on the floor of the furniture showroom!

JOS 'Nessa . . . ?

'NESSA What, Jos.

JOS 'Nessa . . . this is our first fight, isn't it. This is our first ever fight.

'NESSA No. No. We are not fighting. We are not going to fight.

JOS F'you say so.

'NESSA We are not going to be like that. I've been all that. Not that no more. Not since you.

JOS Yeah but, you don't know, maybe it'll be all like that, maybe.

'NESSA I'm all—I love you, Josie-girl. Real time. You're all I need now. You and me. And a couch.

JOS Yeah, that.

'NESSA I found you and I looked at you, and I forgot about everybody else. Adios I said everybody else. Didn't I? Didn't I say that?

JOS Yeah.

'NESSA And you said all kindsa sweet to me.

JOS But you ain't been like this too long, 'Nes. Just two weeks and one day, and it's all new and all glowy still for you. But I been like this a long time now, and it's just I don't like getting all kindsa attitude from clerks is all. I mean, lookit me.

'NESSA Don't you want us to be perfect?

JOS Yeah.

'NESSA Then we need the perfect couch.

JOS I got a all paid for foldaway—

'NESSA I already told you—no old foldaway in our perfect, cozy place!

JOS I know.

'NESSA We—us—we—are buying—a couch.

JOS Uh huh.

'NESSA I'm gonna go find that clerk, and we—us—we—are going to talk to him about—our purchase—of a couch.

JOS 'M gonna wait here.

'NESSA Okay. You be ready when I get back.

JOS I'll be.

[*'NESSA exits in search of the* CLERK. JOS *wanders around the front side of the couch and takes a seat. ZING!! THWUMP!! The celestial harpist plays a clever little tune . . .*]

JOS This is a really nice couch. [*She bounces a bit.*] I really like this couch. [*She lies down. It is exactly long enough for her to lie down upon.*] Perfect. [*She sits up and looks around.*] 'Nessa! [*She looks behind.*] 'Ness! [*She scoots up on her knees peering over the back.*]

'NESSA! 'NES-SAA-A-A-A! [*She runs her hands all over the fabric.*] This is the most perfect cozy couch ever invented. I shoulda got a new couch a long time ago. Who wants a old foldaway anyhow? 'NESSA! You gotta com'ere and—TRY THIS COUCH! [*She looks around, with growing anxiety, unable to lose contact with the couch. Heavy drumbeats with cymbals crashing start to sound . . .*] 'Ness? You comin' back? You comin' back to me, right? I found a couch. Found the perfect couch. You gotta try this. 'Ness? [*She gets up. She keeps both hands on the couch.*] Over here . . . 'Nes-saaaa . . . [*She pulls one hand away.*] 'Ness baby . . . ?

[*She pulls that hand away, but keeps her foot against the couch, pushing her body in the direction that 'NESSA exited. She extends her body as far away as physically possible without disconnecting from the couch.*] Found the perfect— [*She falls, breaking contact with the couch. In a spastic panic, she reattaches herself across the couch's back.*] I love this couch. 'Nessa! I love this couch! I want you to see— [*She begins to pull at the couch. But it won't budge! Remaining connected, she moves to the opposite side of the couch and tries to push. Nuthin.*] Come on! [*She collapses, breathing hard, her face pushed into the cushion.*] . . . OK. [*She gets back up. And tries one last tug.*] ARRRRGGGHHHH!!! OK. I'll find you. I'll find you, 'Nessa! You gotta see this couch. [*With Herculean effort, she pulls her hand off the couch—she almost puts it back—stops.*] Get 'Nessa. 'Ness will love this couch. 'Nessa's gotta love—'Nessa! 'Nessa! [*She runs off—searching—the crashing drum solo ends.*] 'Nessssssaaaa-aaaaa!

[CHAZ *enters. He calls offstage.*]

CHAZ Syl, I'm remembering what mocha felt like. See? I'm remembering. Now I'm gonna try the other one we liked and I let you know which is better.

[CHAZ *goes to the couch and sits down hard. ZING!! THWUMP!! OooooooOOoOOoOoooh those celestial harps play . . . !*]

This is a really nice couch.

[*He bounces a bit.*]

I really like this couch. This is the one. Comfort. Style. It'll go so nice next to the window with all the afternoon light.

['NESSA *enters, still searching for the* CLERK, *expecting to find* JOS. *She sees* CHAZ *running his hands all over the couch.*]

'NESSA Chaz . . . ?

CHAZ Syl, look. I LOVE—

[*He sees* 'NESSA *and jumps to his feet—and quickly puts a hand on the couch, occasionally stroking the fabric.*]

Vanessa. You're—you . . . Uh. Funny. How you been?

'NESSA You finally buying a decent piece-a furniture?

CHAZ Looking. This one's nice.

'NESSA Finally get ridda that old foldaway?

CHAZ Come on. You liked that old thing. Made that cover for it.

'NESSA Suppose you're with somebody now.

CHAZ —a little—kinda—you could say—yeah. 'n you?

'NESSA Oh, I'm with somebody.

CHAZ Oh. Yeah. 'Course.

'NESSA I'm a whole lot different now, Chuck.

CHAZ You know I hate that.

'NESSA You wouldn't even recognize me nowadays.

CHAZ I recognized you fine. Hey, uh, you wanna check out this couch with me—old times sake?

'NESSA I got my own couch to buy. So. Bye.

['NESSA *exits.* CHAZ *fondles the couch a moment more.*]

CHAZ Yeah. This—is one great couch.

[JOS *enters and sees* CHAZ *with his hands on the couch. A banjo plunks an Old West hoedown tune.* JOS *and* CHAZ *lock eyes. On the same beat they both dive onto their beloved couch. Each tries to lay claim to the couch by occupying as much space as possible. They attempt to push the other off with their backs, while their hands are busy clinging to the couch.*]

CHAZ I was—here—FIRST!!

JOS Me!! This is my—couch!!

CHAZ There are—plenty—of other—COUCHES!

JOS Go—find—one a THOSE then!

[*They turn to face each other, poised to come to blows. Stop. Then. The two embrace and engage in a mad, thoughtless, energetic kiss as* 'NESSA *and* SYLVI *enter, agog at the spectacle they are trying to process. The hoedown music halts as* SYLVI *and* 'NESSA *shout their names . . .*]

SYLVI Chaz!!

'NESSA Josie??!!

[CHAZ *and* JOS *push apart, see each other and scream "AHHHHHHHHHH!" as they retreat to opposite arms of the couch.* JOS *wipes at her mouth,* CHAZ *signals for* SYLVI *to approach. Instead,* SYLVI *purses her lips and folds her arms shaking her head.* 'NESSA *moves to* CHAZ *and socks him in the mouth.*]

SYLVI Hey!

[SYLVI *cups* CHAZ's *face as* 'NESSA *moves back to* JOS.]

CHAZ This—is a great couch.

JOS This is my couch—

CHAZ My couch—

JOS Mine—

'NESSA This couch is too big, baby, and why were you kissing on Chaz?

JOS 'Nessa, you gotta try this couch—

CHAZ Sylvi, this is the couch. This is the late in the afternoon by the window couch. Help me out here.

SYLVI First, you explain who this woman is.

CHAZ I—I—I don't know who this woman is—

'NESSA This is Josie, Chaz. This is here is Josie, and I cannot believe you were here kissing on her.

JOS You know him?

'NESSA That's Chaz. I told you about Chaz. Before you?

JOS That's Chaz? He's not so bad.

CHAZ Try this couch, Sylvi.

SYLVI Wait a minute. Wait a minute. Something's not right. Who is this, Chaz?

CHAZ That's Vanessa. I was living with Vanessa when we—when we—you know—met.

SYLVI Oh. Yeah.

JOS Van-nessa?

'NESSA Oh. So this is. You met. Yeah. You two "met" before we broke up. I knew it. I knew that one.

SYLVI And the other one?

CHAZ What other one?

SYLVI The one you were kissing?!

CHAZ Her? I don't know her.

SYLVI   Then why were you kissing her?

CHAZ   I—I—I missed you sooooo much, Sylvi-doll—

SYLVI   Is that how it is?! Is that how it always is with you?!

'NESSA   That's how he always is. But Jos—what's wrong with you?!

SYLVI   We are buying a couch!! A couch that's supposed to last—!

'NESSA   Why were you kissing him?

JOS   I want this couch, 'Nessa. This one is all that.

CHAZ   My couch!!

SYLVI   I don't know if I want to buy a couch with you anymore, Chaz. I thought we were good and you were ready to settle down and that I could trust—

CHAZ   TRUST ME!!!

[CHAZ *grabs* SYLVI *and bodily hauls her onto the couch. THWUMP!! The gong of enlightenment rings.*]

SYLVI   I see what you mean about the couch.

CHAZ   I told you.

[JOS *grabs* 'NESSA's *hand, and in a fabulous spin, winds* 'NESSA *across her lap and onto the couch. PING! PING! PING!!*]

'NESSA   This is a wonderful couch.

[*The music is wild and both couples engage in robust necking. The* CLERK *and* HARRIET *enter, disheveled, deliriously happy, until they realize there are people on the couch.*]

HARRIET   Get off my couch! Jerry! There are people all over my couch!

[*The couples come out of their trance.*]

CHAZ / SYLVI / JOS   This is my couch!

'NESSA   Our couch, baby.

['NESSA *holds* JOS *tight.*]

CHAZ   Our couch!

   [*Holds* SYLVI *tight—then looks at* 'NESSA.]

   Are you with a woman?

JOS   Suck it up, Chuck!

[JOS *kisses* 'NESSA *like a movie star.*]

HARRIET   Jerry! There are lesbians and hipsters engaged in an orgy on my couch!

CLERK   I gotta keep more of these in stock.

CHAZ / SYLVI / 'NESSA / JOS   This is the best couch ever!

HARRIET   Get them off my couch, Jerry!

CLERK   She's a very nice customer! Much nicer than any of you, I might add.

HARRIET   It's mine! Bought and paid for! I have a receipt!

[HARRIET *moves in with force from the backside of the couch, screaming like a banshee and waving her receipt like a flag—TIME SLOWS DOWN as* CHAZ *strips away her receipt. A melodious cheesy love song with a whole lotta strings plays as the mob brawls in slow motion. A storm of white goose down blows in, like a kooky indoor blizzard.*

The fight is a mix of attack and passion. People are trying to carry others away, all the while grappling for a piece of the couch. The cover on the couch begins to tear, and the inner cushions are exposed. These are shredded by the desperate lovers. The couch is torn asunder as the members of the melee fall to the floor.

For just a moment it seems like a swarm of tiny cherubs fly out of the battered couch—they look like little bits of light flying back to heaven, or maybe they look like something else. It's hard to tell. The group watches, dumbfounded. The CLERK is the first to rise, picking up clumps of pillows and foam, attempting to repair the couch. The others get up and survey the damage.]

CHAZ   Here's your receipt.

HARRIET   I don't think I'll be accepting delivery.

CLERK   I understand.

CHAZ We were—looking at mocha. Right Syl? Mocha that will last?

SYLVI Mocha.

JOS And we—us—we're looking for something.

'NESSA Cozy.

HARRIET And I still need a couch, very, very badly, Jerry.

[HARRIET *kisses* JERRY—*breathing life back into him!*]

CLERK Store's closed! Everybody out. Come back tomorrow. Open bright and early at nine—[*He looks at HARRIET.*] N-n-n-noon. Do come back TOMORROW!

[*Beautiful music plays. All three couples dance away in a romantic haze. The lights fade to silhouette and then nothing except little dots of stars and cherubs.*]

• • •

Chocolate

Judd Lear Silverman

Chocolate by Judd Lear Silverman. Copyright © 2018 by Judd Lear Silverman All rights reserved. Reprinted by permission of the author.

CAUTION/ADVICE: Professionals and amateurs are hereby warned that performance of *Chocolate* is subject to a royalty. It is fully protected under the copyright laws of the United States of America, and of all countries covered by the International Copyright Union (including the Dominion of Canada and the rest of the British Commonwealth), and of all countries covered by the Pan-American Copyright Convention and the Universal Copyright Convention, the Berne Convention, and of all countries with which the United States has reciprocal copyright relations. All rights, including professional and amateur stage performing rights, motion picture, recitation, lecturing, public reading, radio broadcasting, television, video or sound recording, all other forms of mechanical or electronic reproduction, such as CD-ROM, DVD-ROM, information storage and retrieval systems, and photocopying, and the rights of translation into foreign languages, are strictly reserved. Particular emphasis is placed upon the matter of readings, permission for which must be secured from Judd Lear Silverman in writing in advance. Inquiries concerning rights should be addressed to Judd Lear Silverman: juddls@sprynet.com.

Judd Lear Silverman

JUDD LEAR SILVERMAN is a Brooklyn-based playwright and a grant recipient from the Berrilla Kerr Foundation. Published by ArtAge, Samuel French, Focus Publications, Stage It! and Applause Theatre Books (*Best American Short Plays*), his work has been seen across the country and in numerous global fringe festivals. Recent presentations include *Consequences* (Articulate Theatre Company, NYC), *Handiwork* (Take Ten Festival, Between Us Productions, NYC), *Satisfaction Guaranteed* (Mid-America Theatre Conference, Cleveland, OH; StageIt Festival, Bonita Springs, FL; Plays and Pizza, NYC), *A View to the Future* (reading, Durango Arts Center, Durango, CO), *Change of Venue* (Lion's Paw Theatre, MO), *A Shot at the Big Time* (reading, Actors Studio, Newburyport, MA), *THE HORROR* (reading, Village Players, NYC), and productions of *Chocolate* (Owensboro Workshop Theatre, KY), *In the Wondrous Woods* (Bonita Springs Arts Center, FL), and *Your Turn* (Know Theatre, Binghamton, NY). He teaches Playwriting and English at Pace University in NYC.

··· **production history** ···

The premiere production of *Chocolate* occurred at the Theatre Workshop of Owensboro in their Summer Shorts Festival in July 2019 under the direction of Kelley Elder. Rose was played by Beth McCormick-Worth and Beau was played by Joseph Acquisto.

characters

> **ROSE**, a young woman with a shotgun.
>
> **BEAU**, a young man passing through.

setting

A coastline, possibly along a beach or hill, with a large boulder or lookout point.

···

[*Atop a high rock or boulder that looks out on the ocean,* ROSE, *a young girl, stands guard like a sentry, hair pulled back, rifle drawn.* BEAU, *a young man not much older than* ROSE, *saunters in and sees her looking out to scan the horizon, rifle ready. He watches for a moment.*]

BEAU That's no way to catch fish.

ROSE [*Surprised.*] What?

BEAU Unless you're shooting them in a barrel. A rod would be much more effective.

ROSE I'm not—mind your own business!

BEAU Sorry, ma'am. Just passin' through.

[*He takes a few steps closer, although he pretends to be passing by. He has almost left. But he pauses. He turns to speak, but she intercepts him.*]

ROSE Keep walkin'.

BEAU A man can do what he wants to do.

ROSE You're no man.

BEAU   Try me.

ROSE   I'm warning you!

BEAU   I am so warned.

[*Pause.*]

What are you doing with that thing? A body could get hurt.

ROSE   That's just the point.

BEAU   To hurt?

ROSE   To avoid hurt. Keep movin'.

BEAU   I have no plans to hurt anyone.

ROSE   That's just how it happens. Carelessly. Without any plan. Use and discard.

BEAU   Whoa! Did someone get burned?

ROSE   Close enough not to fall for that stupid mistake again. You just keep your hands to yourself and mosey on.

BEAU   My hands are attached to my arms, my arms to my shoulders, my shoulders to my torso, and so on. They go where I go.

ROSE   Then get them all gone.

[*Pause.*]

BEAU   Strange.

ROSE   What?

BEAU   You're using a hunting rifle. That means you're actually hunting for something. Looking.

ROSE   [*Shaking her head.*] Warding off predators.

BEAU   From up there?

ROSE   By land or sea.

BEAU   Oh. Are you a good shot?

ROSE   Crack shot.

BEAU I see.

ROSE Don't underestimate me.

BEAU I won't.

[*Pause.*]

What kind of predators?

ROSE Thieves. They take, they plunder.

BEAU Do you have anything worth stealing?

ROSE I have enough.

BEAU Possessions are just things.

ROSE My personage. Myself. I am of value.

BEAU Clearly. So you fear—

ROSE Someone will take what they may. I won't let them.

BEAU No. Of course not.

ROSE I am ever vigilant. Intact.

BEAU More than I needed to know. And anyone who comes within range—

ROSE Will be blown to bits.

BEAU Right. No one gets near.

ROSE Right.

BEAU Or they'll be blown to bits.

ROSE Right.

[*Pause.*]

BEAU And how do I know you'll do this? That you'll carry through?

ROSE You don't have to know. I don't have to prove it. That's on you.

BEAU Hmm. Well, I don't see the bones or remains of anyone else who's tried, do you?

ROSE How do you know they didn't try from the waterfront approach?

BEAU Good point. You got me there.

[*Pause.*]

Still, you must get tired up there. Every sentry has his—excuse me, *their* relief replacement.

ROSE I'm fine.

BEAU Can't be on guard 24/7.

ROSE Watch me.

BEAU I'm watchin'.

[*Pause.*]

Don't you get lonely up there?

ROSE No. It's me, the gulls, and the world. That's enough.

BEAU You speak gull?

ROSE Enough so that we understand each other. They pretty much leave me alone. That's why I like them.

BEAU Oh. No thirst, then?

ROSE I've drunk my fill of insensitive bastards who would take my—

BEAU Cherry?

ROSE Maidenhood! See, that's just how crude all boys are!

BEAU That's just how self-contained most girls are, holding themselves up as a teasing prize!

ROSE Teasing? Do I appear to be teasing?

BEAU Dressed in that top and those slacks, your hair tied back like a pirate, and your rifle drawn?

ROSE It should make your blood run cold.

BEAU You're up on a rock, with a rifle, dressed like that! You've meant to draw attention!

ROSE Not so. I don't want anyone's attention. Especially someone like you.

BEAU A man.

ROSE A boy. Move on.

BEAU I've no intention of sticking around where I'm not welcome.

ROSE Well, you're not.

BEAU Thank you.

ROSE You're welcome.

BEAU See? Make up your mind!

[*Pause.*]

How long have you been up there?

ROSE Not long.

BEAU Long enough.

ROSE Not long enough. You're still here.

[*Pause.*]

BEAU Are you hungry?

[*Pause.*]

I say, are you hungry?

ROSE I'll live.

BEAU That wasn't the question. When did you last eat?

ROSE I've eaten.

BEAU Something salty?

ROSE Everything is salty.

BEAU But not everything is sweet.

[*Pause.*]

I have some chocolate on me. Do you want some?

ROSE Why would you share your chocolate with me?

BEAU I like to share. It makes me happy. It lightens my load.

ROSE It does not!

BEAU At least by the weight of a chocolate bar. Would you like some?

ROSE No.

[*Pause.*]

Thank you.

BEAU You're welcome.

ROSE Don't fake politeness. It's . . . Impolite.

BEAU Who's faking? Besides, it wasn't "you're welcome" to your thank you. It was "you're welcome to join me." Beats serving sentry up on a rock all day.

[*Pause.*]

No strings attached to the candy bar.

ROSE Why would a candy bar have strings attached?

BEAU Is this a riddle?

ROSE Is what a riddle?

BEAU Are you a riddle? A puzzle to be solved.

ROSE [*Proudly.*] I'm a puzzle that no one can solve!

BEAU And that would be good because—

ROSE If I were solved, I would be finished. Done.

BEAU Completed.

ROSE Yes. Wait . . .

BEAU What's worse? To feel empty gaps or to feel complete?

ROSE To be complete means you have nowhere else to go, nothing else to pursue.

BEAU And you like pursuit?

ROSE Yes!

BEAU Then why ward off all invaders with a rifle? Why not pursue? All you're doing is maintaining the status quo!

ROSE What?

BEAU You're keeping everything just the same. Nothing will happen.

ROSE Exactly.

BEAU And you want nothing to happen? Ever? What's the point of that?

ROSE I won't get hurt.

BEAU You won't get anything.

ROSE And what would I get if I stepped off this rock?

BEAU I don't know. No one does. You might get hurt. You might not. You might get joy. I do know one thing you could get.

ROSE What?

BEAU A piece of chocolate. That sounds like a win-win situation to me. [*Pause.*]

ROSE You won't try to disarm me?

BEAU Quite the contrary. You've disarmed me. You're quite, quite safe. And it is quite good chocolate.

[ROSE *considers a moment. Then slowly, warily, she begins to come down off the rock, rifle in hand.* BEAU *moves in to help her down, but she points the rifle at him.*]

ROSE No funny business!

BEAU Clearly.

[*The rifle impeding her descent, she eventually figures a way down. She puts the rifle on the rock, lowers herself to the ground, then regains the rifle, and immediately points it at* BEAU.]

BEAU Welcome to solid land!

ROSE I said no funny business!

BEAU It's all funny business.

[*He goes to reach into his pocket.* ROSE *aims the rifle at him with some seriousness.*]

ROSE Hey!

BEAU I have to get the chocolate out, don't I?

[*He reaches into a jacket pocket and fishes out his candy bar.*]

ROSE You wear a jacket on a hot day?

BEAU It has pockets for things.

ROSE Like what?

BEAU Chocolate bars.

ROSE You wear a jacket just for a chocolate bar?

BEAU Well, it would melt if it rested against my body.

ROSE Is that so?

BEAU Or yours.

ROSE [*Pointing rifle.*] Hey!

BEAU Or anybody's.

[*He takes the bar out of his pocket, then offers it to her.*]

ROSE I don't want the whole thing.

BEAU No?

ROSE Only a taste.

BEAU I'll split it with you.

ROSE Break me off just a piece.

BEAU I'll break it in half.

  [*He does so.*]

  There. It's more or less in half.

ROSE You take the bigger half.

BEAU   There is no bigger half. A half is a half. Each the same. I suppose I could weigh them to see which is more—but I don't have a scale. One half could weigh more if it has nuts. Whoops! I forgot to ask! Do you like nuts?

ROSE   Depends.

BEAU   On?

ROSE   What kind.

BEAU   Oh. Well, I think these are almonds. No peanuts—in case you have an allergy and are worried.

ROSE   [*Distrusting.*] I can have almonds.

BEAU   Okay. Then. Come claim your half.

ROSE   You can lay it on the rock.

BEAU   No. You must choose. *You* must choose. Meet me halfway.

[*They move closer. Closer—although the rifle is drawn. He looks at her, daring her to move in.*]

ROSE   I'm not coming any closer.

BEAU   Even a piece of chocolate has its risks.

ROSE   You stay where you are!

BEAU   If I do, then you'll have to come closer to get your half.

ROSE   I don't really even want it now.

BEAU   Scared?

ROSE   No.

BEAU   What's the point? If you're just gonna spend life scared—

ROSE   I said I'm not scared!

BEAU   Then come take it!

[*She moves in slowly, but clearly, she cannot keep the rifle pointed at him and still reach the chocolate in his hand. Slowly, she lowers the rifle. Gingerly she moves closer. He holds out his hand.*]

ROSE   You eat it first.

BEAU   To prove it's safe? Okay. You choose which piece I get.

ROSE   [*Pointing.*] That one.

BEAU   Okay. And you get this one.

[*He hands her one half. He takes his half and unwraps it, if there's any wrapping left, and takes a bite.*]

BEAU   Hmmm. I love a good piece of chocolate. And there are raisins, too. I forgot about the raisins. Chocolate and nuts and raisins. The best plans of God and man.

ROSE   Of God and woman.

BEAU   Same thing.

   [*Pause.*]

   Eat it before it melts.

[*ROSE reticently unwraps her portion. BEAU watches. She gets her first taste—and cannot hide her enjoyment. He smiles. She tries not to but smiles anyhow.*]

ROSE   You remind me of someone?

BEAU   Yes.

ROSE   The snake. In the garden of Eden.

BEAU   Well, she didn't come away empty-handed, after all.

ROSE   She was banned from Eden!

BEAU   She came away with knowledge. And a juicy apple. And Adam.

ROSE   I suppose two out of three ain't bad.

[*Lights fade to black.*]

• • •

Unabridged

Sean Abley

Unabridged by Sean Abley. Copyright © 2018 by Sean Abley. All rights reserved. Reprinted by permission of the author.

CAUTION/ADVICE: Professionals and amateurs are hereby warned that performance of *Unabridged* is subject to a royalty. It is fully protected under the copyright laws of the United States of America, and of all countries covered by the International Copyright Union (including the Dominion of Canada and the rest of the British Commonwealth), and of all countries covered by the Pan-American Copyright Convention and the Universal Copyright Convention, the Berne Convention, and of all countries with which the United States has reciprocal copyright relations. All rights, including professional and amateur stage performing rights, motion picture, recitation, lecturing, public reading, radio broadcasting, television, video or sound recording, all other forms of mechanical or electronic reproduction, such as CD-ROM, DVD-ROM, information storage and retrieval systems, and photocopying, and the rights of translation into foreign languages, are strictly reserved. Particular emphasis is placed upon the matter of readings, permission for which must be secured from Sean Abley in writing in advance. Inquiries concerning rights should be addressed to Sean Abley at SeanAbleyPlaywright@yahoo.com.

Sean Abley

SEAN ABLEY has over thirty plays published by Playscripts, Brooklyn Publishers, Heuer Publishing, Next Stage Press, Stage Partners, Plays to Order, Eldridge Plays and Musicals, and Applause with titles like *End of the World (With Prom to Follow)*, *The Adventures of Rose Red (Snow White's Less-Famous Sister)*, *Horror High: The Musical*, and *Two-Faced: A Traged . . . Sort Of*. His plays have been developed and performed at the Kennedy Center, Antaeus Theatre Company, Goodman Theatre, Celebration Theatre, Write/Act Repertory, Factory Theater, Merry-Go-Round Youth Theatre, SkyPilot Theatre Company, Virginia City Players, and academically at the Playwrights Lab at Hollins University and California State University-Stanislaus. His plays for young audiences have been performed in over 300 professional and educational productions in the United States, Canada, Australia, Mexico, New Zealand, Saudi Arabia, South Africa, Argentina, Belgium, Singapore, and United Arab Emirates. Sean is a member of the Dramatists Guild and the Writers Guild of America, and holds an MFA in Playwriting from The Playwrights' Lab at Hollins University.

··· production history ···

Unabridged was first performed in a full production on July 20, 2018, at the Gaslight Theatre in St. Louis, MO, as part of the LaBute New Theater Festival presented by St. Louis Actors' Studio (William Roth, Founder and Artistic Director; John Pierson, Associate Artistic Director) under the direction of Ryan Scott Foizey, with stage management by Amy J. Paige; set design by Patrick Huber; lighting design by Patrick Huber and Dalton Robison; sound design by John Pierson, Wendy Greenwood, and Ryan Scott Foizey; costume design by Megan Harshaw; prop design by Jess Stamper; and technical direction by Joseph Novak. The cast was as follows:

BARKER, Zak Farmer

CESAR, Spencer Sickmann

MAN, Eric Dean White

Unabridged was originally developed as part of the Playwrights' Lab at Hollins University (Todd William Ristau, Program Director). This final version of the script was subsequently presented as part of the 2018 Playwrights Festival under the direction of Michael Mansfield, with the following cast:

BARKER, Kate Burke-Benedict

CESAR, Stephen Baltz

MAN, Walter Dodd

Stage directions read by Shelby Taylor Love.

characters

CESAR, a criminal junkie type.

BARKER, a dealer of sorts.

MAN (OR ANY PERSON), a suburban person.

note on casting

All roles are gender irrelevant. Change pronouns, gender-specific dialogue, and intentions when/if necessary. A cast of diverse human beings would be the playwright's preference.

setting

What appears to be an old library, empty of books, with the exception of a large dictionary at the desk.

production notes on characters speaking

If parenthetical word references ("angry") are followed in the spoken dialogue with a word that appears to be a simpler version of the parenthetical, the intention is to indicate what the character is trying to say with that alternate, simpler word. If there is no alternate word after the parenthetical reference, the character should use gestures and expressions to convey what they're trying to say. This shouldn't slow down the actors' pace as this situation is not new for the characters—they have been living this way for ages, and have learned to speak fluently yet simply.

• • •

[*Winter. The future. Or not. Possibly an alternate universe where everything looks like our current timeline. Regardless of time period, the room in which we find ourselves appears to be the front desk area of a rundown library. The door to the outside is at one end of the space, the front desk at the other. There is at least one entrance leading offstage from the front desk area to the nonpublic areas of the building. The shelves we can see are empty, implying the entire library is empty as well. The front desk is bare with the exception of a low bookstand upon which rests a large dictionary. The world outside is chilled by wind and snow, the space inside warmed by a space heater.*

CESAR *enters from the front door. He is wiry, squirrelly, but wears a heavy, shapeless winter coat, making him look like a kid in his father's clothes. He cautiously moves into the space. As he makes his way toward the front desk his confidence grows. He steps up to the desk as if to be served.*]

CESAR It is cold out there! You should knock some of that stuff off that part over the door! [*A moment.*] Hey! I need one! [*A moment.*] Hey! I'm back! You open or what?

[CESAR *looks around, checks between the shelves, takes tentative steps toward the front desk. Nothing.*]

CESAR Hey! I'm leaving! Guess you don't want my cash.

[*He waits, planted in place. After a moment he reaches up and opens the dictionary.*]

BARKER [*Offstage.*] Read one word and I'll blow your fucking head off.

[BARKER *enters holding a really big gun pointed right at* CESAR's *head.* CESAR's *hands immediately go up.*]

CESAR Whoa! Hold up! I'm cool!

BARKER Uh huh.

CESAR I wasn't gonna read your thing. I was just looking at it.

BARKER You don't look with your fucking fingers.

CESAR "Fingers!" I know that one! Got that one last month.

[BARKER *cocks the gun.*]

CESAR Okay, okay! My fucking bad. Noted. Can you put that ["*gun*"] down? You act like wanting to see something is a ["*crime*"] bad thing. I just wanna . . . you know . . . [*Gestures to dictionary.*] What do you call that thing again?

BARKER Stop fishing. No freebies. [*He lowers the gun.*]

CESAR "Freebies." Of course! I know that one. You never let me forget that one. You can't be giving that shit away. That's a bad way to do your stuff you do. Anyway, I got money.

[CESAR *retrieves a bill from his pocket and holds it out toward BARKER. BARKER snatches it away from him, moves behind the front desk, and drops it into a drawer. He pulls out a ledger, consults a page, then gestures to the dictionary as he pulls out a small pad and a pen and starts writing.*]

BARKER You want to know what this is? That's what you're paying for?

CESAR Yeah. No! Wait, no, no, no! Stop! No, that's not it! I didn't say that! You did. That's not what I want. That's not what I came here for.

BARKER Then what do you want? Jesus, Cesar, do we have to go through this every time?

CESAR No, no, you're right. Sorry. My bad. Sorry. What I want is . . . My wife sent me. She wants to know the word for that stuff you use to make kosher dill pickles. You gave me "kosher" and "dill" last time, remember? And "pickles" two times before that. Those were so great. She loved "pickles," and when I got her "kosher dill," I swear it was like our night we got ["*married*"]. And bee-tee-double-u, it was like our night we got ["*married*"], if you know what I mean. The best. And now she wants to know what that taste word is. So . . .

BARKER Cesar, you're in here what? Four, five days a week? Don't you have kids?

CESAR Yeah, I got kids. My wife's looking out for them. What about it?

BARKER Your wife's looking out for them.

CESAR Sure. Or at least she's got 'em sorta set up so they can't do anything bad while she's gone. Hey, this stuff doesn't pay for itself. Somebody's got to make the cash, and while I'm doing what I'm doing she's out doing that. And?

BARKER I've seen a lot of guys come through here, and it never ends well for the ones with kids.

CESAR What, now I gotta get a talking to before I get my buy?

BARKER You're hooked, Cesar. You and your wife are hooked. And if you're not careful, your kids will be hooked—

CESAR How the fuck is that gonna happen? We never let the kids into our stash.

BARKER You get drunk, you say a few words, say a few more, don't realize the kids are listening from the other room...

CESAR Naw, it's not like that. We're careful. Real careful. One time it happened, one time, and we felt like shit about it, and it never happened again. We watch what we say whenever they're awake. We don't leave our stash lying around.

BARKER Just once, huh?

CESAR Like one time. Maybe there was another time, with the girl, but I can't think if that is true or not, but it's not like a thing that happens.

I mean, kids are kids, right? They get into shit. I did this thing when I was a kid and I ate a [*"insect"*] thing that . . .

BARKER Bug.

CESAR A bug! Right. You sold me that one, I remember. [*Tapping his head.*] I wish they lasted longer, right? But I guess that would kinda kill what you're doing here. Anyway, I ate a bug and nothing. I was fine. Kids are fine. They got this thing where they're [*"tough"*] and they're okay. They're good. I swear. Now can I get my "kosher dill pickle" word?

[BARKER *starts writing on the pad.*]

BARKER Easy one. Don't even have to crack open the stash. It's a two-fer, but I won't charge you because you buy from me a lot.

[BARKER *rips off the page from the pad and hands it to* CESAR, *then logs the buy in the ledger.*]

CESAR [*Reads.*] "White vinegar." Holy shit! "White vinegar!" I fucking love that. She's gonna go nuts for this, Barker, I swear. "White vinegar." Damn, buddy, you are the best. Seriously. You got the best product out there. Ain't nobody can sling words like you can. Burger? Charlie Burger? From like two stops down? His shit is shit. Like, unsayable. And he's a he steals stuff. Tried to from me. I paid him for something that goes on a sandwich—a word which I bought from you, thank you very much, I should have known better than to stray—and before I can tell him the whole thing he hands me "meat." And I'm like, "meat"? Are you fucking kidding me? "Meat." Nice. I know "meat," asshole! I know "meat" because it's "meat" and I already got that one, and you didn't let me say what I want and so let me say what I want and give me another one. And I had to fucking pry "mayonnaise" outta that asshole because he wanted to say it wasn't his fault I wasn't [*"clear"*] I didn't tell him right.

BARKER We all do our business the way we see fit.

CESAR "Business." I like that one. I forgot that earlier. Really wish they stuck up here [*points to his head*] long. Got that one a long time ago, from you eff-why-eye. Also and another thing, Charlie Burger does his business like a fucking boat. ["*Yesterday*"] The before day he was holdin' up—

BARKER   Like a what?

CESAR   A boat. You know, like a guy who looks down on you because you don't have as many words, but he has so many because he has money and fuck him.

BARKER   Did Charles sell you "boat"?

CESAR   Yeah.

[BARKER *chuckles as* CESAR *continues.*]

CESAR   Anyway, he was holding up his ["*dictionary*"] that and saying how it has all the words in it and how you, Mr. Barker, are nothing and he's going to fuck up your business and stuff.

BARKER   He said his ["*dictionary*"] has all the words in it?

CESAR   Yup.

BARKER   Did he use a word that meant "all the words"?

CESAR   Yeah, as a matter of fact he did. It was a long one. It was something like, sounded like—Whoa, wait a minute! Ha! You almost fooled me! Look at that! Ol' Cesar was gonna give up a word to Mr. Barker for free and all. Now how does that work, Mr. Business Guy? You pull a ["*gun*"] on me for trying to touch your ["*dictionary*"], and now you want a free one from me. Man, some people might say you're being a real boat, Mr. Barker.

BARKER   Okay, you got me. How about this—I give you one for free, and you try and pull the one Charles told you out of your [*taps* CESAR *on the forehead*] as a one-for-you one-for-me.

[CESAR *sticks out his hand to shake.*]

CESAR   Deal!

[*They shake on it.*]

BARKER   How about I just pick one out of here? Make it a surprise?

CESAR   "Surprise?"

BARKER   I didn't give you that one before?

CESAR   Nope! And that's not part of the one-for-you one-for-me! You were gonna pick one out of your that for that!

BARKER   You got me there.

CESAR   Ha! I got you! I fucking got you!

BARKER   You're a lot more knowing than people say you are.

CESAR   I am! I am a lot more knowing. Now you have to tell me what it means. Tell me "surprise."

BARKER   "Surprise" means a thing when you don't think a thing is going to be and then it is.

CESAR   "Surprise." Nice. [*Indicates the area behind the desk.*] Like when you came out of there with your [*"gun"*]. "Surprise!" Nice one. Okay, now the real one.

[BARKER *flips open the dictionary and picks a word at random. He writes it down on the pad and hands it to* CESAR, *then logs this in the ledger.*]

BARKER   "Scrambled." How does that sound?

CESAR   Big! What's it mean?

BARKER   It's what you do to eggs when you [*"beat"*] 'em and [*"cook"*] make them.

CESAR   Oh, yeah! Nice! We had that this morning. "Scrambled." My wife's gonna shit. Fucking "scrambled." Here you go, honey. "Scrambled." Isn't that a nice "surprise?"[*Wife's voice.*] Oh, my god, that's so good! You're so good, Cesar, I'm gonna do sex with you right now—

BARKER   Okay, okay. And you're going to give me . . . ?

CESAR   Okay, yes, I can now do "business." [*Points to dictionary.*] He said his was a . . . "unabridged"?

BARKER   Charles Burger has an unabridged?

CESAR I guess?

[*Grabs* CESAR *by the shirt and points the gun at his head.*]

BARKER Say it again—Charles Burger has an unabridged?! He said that word to you?

CESAR Yeah! [*Wrestles free.*] Yeah, he said he has an unabridged.

BARKER Get out.

CESAR What'd I do?

BARKER Just get out.

CESAR Jesus, are you outta your ["*mind*"]? That's two times you pointed that at me today. You don't point that at me!

BARKER Get the fuck out you sack of nothing before I change my mind and decide to use it!

CESAR Ahhh, I get it. He's got a big, fat, unabridged, and you don't got one and you're mad.

BARKER Cesar . . .

CESAR And I'm guessing you'd do just about anything to get your hands on an unabridged. Including acting like a fucking boat and sticking one of those things in Cesar's ["*face*"] cuz you're so fucking mad at Charlie Burger that blowing Cesar's ["*head*"] off would make you feel all better.

BARKER Cesar, I'm begging you, get the fuck out.

CESAR You know, Burger is a shitheel, but he's got one of them things, and he never once pointed it at my ["*face*"]. But I feel ya. I got it. I know what makes you ["*tick*"] be like you are. But what if ol' Cesar did Mr. Barker a piano? A nice, freebie piano. How would that sit with Mr. Barker. Cesar could go get that unabridged, and maybe then, just saying out loud, maybe then we could be business guys together.

[BARKER *laughs.*]

CESAR Now don't ha ha ha at me, Mr. Barker. Don't ha ha ha at me. If I do a piano for you, you should do a piano for me.

BARKER I don't need any pianos from you, Cesar. And even if you did a piano for me, we certainly wouldn't be in business together.

CESAR Why not?

BARKER [*Indicates the dictionary.*] Because you can't handle this like I can. I got a high ["*tolerance*"] because I never stopped using. People like you wanted their ["*head*"] all soft and empty and then when they took it all away you didn't do anything. And then it was all, "Oh, no, we want that back!" But it was too late. Guys like me weren't sitting around letting our ["*mind*"] get all stupid because we knew there was something we could do after it all went down. And now you want in on it after I did all the hard work. No thanks.

CESAR But I could—

BARKER We're different people, right down to our bones. And bones don't change. You have your words, now go.

CESAR But I know stuff.

BARKER Go. An unabridged isn't as ["*important*"] as you may think. I was just surprised. It's been a long day and I was acting like a boat. I'm sorry.

CESAR You don't got to say sorry to me. I feel you. And I'm gonna get you that unabridged!

BARKER Go home to your wife and kids. She's waiting for her "white vinegar." And her "scrambled." You'll be the big man today.

CESAR Yeah, okay. Thanks, Mr. Barker. And don't forget, if you ever need a piano—

BARKER I know who to call. I don't want to see you around here for a couple days. Give it a rest. Be with your family for awhile.

CESAR Okay. Later.

[CESAR *exits.* BARKER *whips out his phone and dials.*]

BARKER [*Into phone.*] We have a situation, and it's name is Charles Burger . . . An unabridged situation . . . Yes, I'm sure. The junky who comes in here thrice a week . . . Thrice . . . It means three, you mongrel. Put down the thesaurus and listen to me . . . Because I'm on speaker phone and the only time I'm on speaker phone is when you're reading and can't hold the fucking phone . . . Where the hell did you get an encyclopedia? . . . We're going to have a further discussion about that, but right now I need you to investigate this junky's intel . . . He's been cross pollinating at Burger's for his fixes. He said Burger has the unabridged, the one we've been waiting for . . . Yes, well, Burger's been cutting his supply with slang to stretch it, unless "boat" means something different now . . . I want you to recruit some of those domesticated animals you call associates, get over to Burger's hovel and relieve him of my unabridged . . .

[*A* MAN *tentatively enters, overhearing the last of* BARKER*'s conversation.*]

BARKER   Don't argue with me, you cretin. It was your gross negligence that allowed the unabridged to find its way into Burger's sour little hands in the first place. Get your ass over to that hovel, retrieve the tome, and bring it back to me before the sun sets or regret the decision not to.

[BARKER *hangs up the phone, then notices the* MAN *standing in the doorway.*]

BARKER   Can I help you?

MAN   I'm . . . no. Thanks.

[MAN *exits.* BARKER *is unfazed. He opens a drawer and counts money. The* MAN *enters again, shaking off the cold from outside. He stands for a moment, looking around.*]

BARKER   Back again.

MAN   Yeah, I think so. You sounded really mad when I was in here ["*earlier*"].

BARKER   How much of that did you hear?

MAN   Not much. Nothing really. Just you being mad.

BARKER   Uh huh. So, what do you want?

MAN Well, my wife and I, it's our the day that we got [*"married"*] a couple years ago. And I wanted to get her a [*"gift"*] thing for that.

BARKER Uh huh.

MAN Something [*"fancy"*] big. I have money. How do we do this? Do I just give you money and you give me words?

[MAN *pulls out a wad of cash.*]

BARKER Well, for that much, I can give you some very nice words.

MAN Great. I guess. I'm not sure how much this all costs. We've never done it before.

BARKER Never?

MAN No. We're sort of, you know [*"naive"*] regular. We don't do a lot of stuff like this. We hear about it, though. You know, people getting together, big groups, doing stuff like learning word after word all night long. Study groups? Learning words with other people's wives or husbands and stuff. Guys learning words together.

BARKER Is that something that you want to do?

MAN Oh, no. No, no. Nothing that big or out there. Just small stuff. You know, sometimes after work to [*"relax"*].

BARKER Well, I have some good news for you. I have something that will make your wife happy, and be something you can learn together.

MAN "Happy"?

BARKER [*Does "happy."*]

MAN Oh, right! Yeah! That sounds good! What is it?

BARKER Hang on. I need a name.

[BARKER *opens the ledger to a new page.*]

MAN For?

BARKER To keep track of what you buy in case you come back. And I'm more than a little sure you're coming back.

MAN Oh, is that . . . okay? Does anybody see that thing besides you?

BARKER If they do, that means I'm dead.

MAN Oh, okay.

BARKER Name.

MAN Bill . . . Smith.

BARKER Okay, Mister Smith, I'll put you right here by all the rest of the Smiths.

MAN Great.

BARKER Now give me a minute.

[BARKER *starts writing down a list of words. The* MAN *wanders around the space, walking back into the empty shelves, etc.*]

MAN This place is really [*"interesting."*] a lot. I heard you used to be able to just come in here and take stuff.

BARKER Did you now.

MAN I did. What you did was it used to be you didn't have to pay. People were just [*"responsible."*] okay and it all worked out.

BARKER Uh huh.

MAN This place was filled with stuff on all these things.

BARKER That is true. But if you don't use it, you lose it.

MAN Ah, okay. Sounds about right.

[*The* MAN *disappears far back into the shelves.*]

MAN [*Offstage.*] It's dirty back here . . .

[*There is quiet for a moment, then—*]

MAN [*Offstage.*] Uh, hey . . . I found something.

[BARKER *isn't listening, concentrating on his work. The* MAN *emerges from the stacks carrying a dusty children's book, Dr. Seuss or something similar, as if it were a snake.*]

MAN I found this. Is this something of yours?

[BARKER *finally looks up and for one second appears startled, but quickly regains his composure.*]

BARKER Oh, yeah. That's mine.

MAN I didn't look at it.

BARKER You shouldn't.

MAN I didn't. I didn't see any of the words. I just saw the part here [*indicates the corner he's holding*] under one of those things, and I grabbed it. But I didn't look.

BARKER You shouldn't. It's really too much for you. I'll take it.

[BARKER *takes the book from the MAN and flips open the cover to the first page.*]

MAN I mean, I opened it. But I just saw that part that was [*"handwritten"*] on the first part. Not the real part.

[BARKER *places the book out of sight behind the front desk then goes back to writing out the list for the MAN.*]

BARKER There are some big words in there, and you're just starting out.

MAN Are you Jessica? [*Off* BARKER's *reaction.*] "For my Jessica. Love, Mom."

BARKER No.

MAN Someone you know?

BARKER That's none of your for you to know.

MAN Sorry, right. None of my stuff that I need to know. [*A moment.*] Do you ever have those study groups here?

BARKER You a guy who does the law? Because you're starting to sound like a guy who does the law.

MAN Oh, no! No! Not at all. Do I look like a guy who does the law? Just curious.

[BARKER *finally tears the page off the pad he's been working on and holds it up.*]

BARKER This is for you.

MAN Wow, what is that?

BARKER It's called a "grocery list."

[BARKER *hands the grocery list to the* MAN, *who looks at it in awe.*]

MAN A "grocery list." What's it do?

BARKER "Grocery" is what you buy at the store. I'm adding that word for free, by the way. First time buyer gets a freebie. That's one you don't have to pay for.

MAN Wow, thanks! "Freebie." Stuff you don't pay for. "Grocery." Stuff you buy at the store. I like those.

BARKER This is a list of words for food and things that you need to buy at the store, also known as "groceries." So the next time one of you goes to the store, if you're out of one of these things, you can just put it on the list, then check it off when you buy it.

MAN Can I read it once in here? Is that okay?

BARKER Of course.

MAN [*Reads.*] "Salad, bread, rice." Wow, I don't know what any of these mean!

BARKER Keep going.

MAN [*Reads.*] "Tuna, vinaigrette dressing." Whoa, that one's a little crazy.

BARKER That one's for . . . you know, just between you and your wife.

MAN Right, right. Of course. [*Reads.*] "Chicken." Ha, that one cracks me up. "Fish sticks, crackers." Ha! [*Kooky voice.*] "Fish sticks! Crackers!" That's so funny. She'll love this! Man, I can see why people do this for fun. I could read more right now. I'm not even tired.

BARKER Well, take this one home and have fun with your wife. When you need another list, or even just a word, I have a lot for people just starting out like you.

MAN How do I know what they mean?

BARKER On the back, I've written some words I bet you know for a few of them.

MAN [*Reads the back of the list.*] "Chicken—the bird you eat. Tuna—fish you eat."

BARKER The rest you'll just have to enjoy as is.

MAN Wow, this is great. Thank you! Thanks!

BARKER Have a good one.

[*The* MAN *heads out, but stops short.*]

MAN I had an idea. I have more money still.

[*The* MAN *takes out the rest of a big wad of bills.*]

MAN Can I get a list like that for my kids?

BARKER Your what?

MAN My kids. Like, just some easy stuff.

BARKER You have kids.

MAN Yeah. Two.

BARKER And you want to buy words for them?

MAN Well, yeah. I mean, they're not ["*young*"]. They're almost ["*teenagers*"]. And we're ["*naive*"] regular but we're not ["*prudes*"]. We want to be the cool mom and dad. So nothing too big, but . . . Christmas is coming, and it would be nice to have something they would think was fun.

BARKER Look, I'm not their mom or dad. You can do what you want. But you can't tell me you're going to give this stuff to your kids. I don't deal with kids. I give you this stuff and you give it to them and then you come back here later and tell me "oh no my kids have been up learning all night what am I gonna do" and then I'm dealing with kids.

MAN They're good kids. They are. And we won't let them learn unless we're in the room. You can take all this money. We have more.

[*A moment.* BARKER *reluctantly takes the money, then pulls out his pad and begins writing again.*]

MAN We figure if they get it at where we live, with us there, they won't get it out of where we live. You know, give them a ["*taste*"] so they'll know what it is and it won't be ["*tantalizing*"].

BARKER I'm going to tell you these as I put them on the list.

MAN Great!

BARKER Don't give it to them all at once.

MAN Of course.

BARKER Uh . . . we'll start with some that aren't words, they're just letters.

MAN "Letters?"

BARKER It's the parts that make a word.

[BARKER *points to individual letters on the* MAN's *list.*]

MAN Ooooh . . . Yeah, got it. Damn, this feels great!

BARKER Just . . . slow down. Okay . . . [*Writing.*] "PBJ, BLT . . . " Um . . . "Boogers." Kids like that . . .

MAN Make sure you write something so we know what it is. Man, this is great. It's so great! Say another one! I'll pay you!

[*The* MAN *tosses another bill at* BARKER.]

BARKER "Balloon."

MAN "Balloon!"

BARKER It's a [*mimes blowing up a balloon*]. It goes in the air.

MAN Fuck yes! That's so great! We have those on the day we were born day. I can't wait to tell Bridget about this. She's going to be so "happy"! And the kids are going to ["*go crazy*"].

[BARKER *crumples up the kids' list.*]

BARKER No.

MAN Whoa, what are you doing?

[BARKER *gathers up the MAN's money, all of it, even from the drawer, and shoves it back into his hands.*]

BARKER Take your fucking money.

MAN What? What are you doing?

BARKER Take your fucking money and get the fuck out of here!

MAN Wait, I paid you! I paid you that money! I want these words!

BARKER Take your fucking words, and your money, and get the fuck out of here.

MAN I don't get it—

[BARKER *pulls the gun out and points it at the* MAN.]

BARKER I'm not going to say it again. Get. Out.

MAN Okay. Okay. Don't do anything.

[*The* MAN *backs toward the door, clutching his list and trying to wrangle the wadded up bills. When he reaches the door he bolts out.*]

BARKER And don't come back!

[*A beat, then* BARKER *yanks open the front door and shouts out into the street.*]

BARKER And don't go to Burger's place, either! [*Realizes.*] Fuck! Burger!

[BARKER *pulls out his cell phone and dials.*]

BARKER [*Into phone.*] No, I don't want to leave a message, you knowledge-inhaling gargoyle. Where the fuck is the unabridged?!

[CESAR *bursts in the door. The blood streaming from various deep cuts all the way down onto his shirt, and the deep bruises and abrasions on his face suggest a violent confrontation in his recent past. He staggers, both from his injuries and the effort required to carry the unabridged dictionary he clutches to his chest. Despite this, he is amped up beyond belief.*]

CESAR   I got your unabridged! I got your fucking unabridged! AND I BEEN FUCKING READING IT!!

[CESAR *slams the unabridged dictionary onto the floor, then drops down and flips the book open.*]

BARKER   Cesar, where did you get that?

CESAR   [*Reading.*] "Ocean! A body of water!"

BARKER   Cesar, answer me!

CESAR   [*Reading.*] "Omelette! A dish made of eggs!"

BARKER   Cesar—

CESAR   [*Reading.*] "Octuplets!" Oc-fucking-tuplets! "Eight identical or fraternal children!" I got your unabridged and we are business guys now!!

BARKER   Okay, Cesar, let's keep calm.

CESAR   Don't use small words to me! Use big words! I don't give a shit about small words. I know what you have and you're going to use it on me!

BARKER   Cesar, tell me what happened.

[CESAR *collapses, spent.*]

CESAR   I got home, and gave Cindy the words, and she wanted to learn more words. And she wasn't gonna go out again and learn those words because we have kids, and she'd been out all day and no takers. And she's really ["*hurting*"], and I thought, "How can I get more words?" And then I thought, "Mr. Barker has words, but he's a good guy even though he pointed a snow in my face."

BARKER   A "snow?"

[CESAR *pulls out a gun from his jacket and points it at* BARKER.]

CESAR   A snow. A fucking snow. And my next thought was, "Charlie Burger two stops down from Mr. Barker has words. He's got a big unabridged full of words." So I go down to Charlie Burger's place, and I see two guys, big guys, and they're about to go into this place so I hang back. You don't want to crowd nobody when they're getting their learn on. And as soon as they open the door—["*Bang! Bang!*"] Surprise! Surprise! They take one to the ["*chest*"], each of 'em, and then fall back onto the . . . [*Smacks his hand onto the floor, then does so again, as if insisting* BARKER *tell him the word.*]

BARKER   Ground.

CESAR   The ground. That'll be free of charge, business guy. So they fall back, and I see they got the same things in their hands that you pointed at my—[*Angrily points at his face, asking for the word.*]

BARKER   That's your face, Cesar.

CESAR   My face. So I go over to them, and by now that stuff is falling from the sky. You know the ["*snow*"]. Anyway, so I took this [*shakes the gun*] and held it up above his face so he could see it, and said, "What. The fuck. Is this?" And he's looking real bad, and he goes like this [*points up*] and he says, "Snow." And then he's gone.

BARKER   Cesar . . .

CESAR   So I took this snow into Charlie Burger's place, and pointed it at him. I wasn't really ready, so he got a hold of me before I could use it on him and we gave each other a real fight. And when I finally got him on the ground, I took that unabridged and I held it way up—

[CESAR *raises the unabridged dictionary above his head, and we can now see the blood on the back cover.*]

CESAR   —and said, "What is the word for what I'm about to do to you?" And he said, "Please." And I brought that unabridged down onto his face and pleased him right there.

[CESAR *slams the book down, then collapses again.*]

BARKER   Cesar . . .

CESAR   So we're business guys together, right? Because that's my unabridged. But I'm going to use it with you if you want.

[BARKER *has moved out of* CESAR's *direct sight line. He silently aims the gun at* CESAR's *head.*]

CESAR   Cindy will be happy. And the kids.

[BARKER *lowers the gun.*]

CESAR   Happy. I learned happy.

[CESAR *slides into unconsciousness as the lights fade to black.*]

• • •

Lacrimosa

A Humorous Tragedy

Christopher R. Marshall

Lacrimosa by Christopher R. Marshall. Copyright © 2018 by Christopher R. Marshall. All rights reserved. Reprinted by permission of the author.

CAUTION/ADVICE: Professionals and amateurs are hereby warned that performance of *Lacrimosa* is subject to a royalty. It is fully protected under the copyright laws of the United States of America, and of all countries covered by the International Copyright Union (including the Dominion of Canada and the rest of the British Commonwealth), and of all countries covered by the Pan-American Copyright Convention and the Universal Copyright Convention, the Berne Convention, and of all countries with which the United States has reciprocal copyright relations. All rights, including professional and amateur stage performing rights, motion picture, recitation, lecturing, public reading, radio broadcasting, television, video or sound recording, all other forms of mechanical or electronic reproduction, such as CD-ROM, DVD-ROM, information storage and retrieval systems, and photocopying, and the rights of translation into foreign languages, are strictly reserved. Particular emphasis is placed upon the matter of readings, permission for which must be secured from Christopher R. Marshall in writing in advance. Inquiries concerning rights should be addressed to Christopher R. Marshall at kalifilmactor@gmail.com.

Christopher R. Marshall

CHRISTOPHER R. MARSHALL is an actor, writer, and director who has directed more than forty plays and films since the start of his career in 2011. As an actor, he has studied Lecoq, Linklater, and British Classical Acting. He's written ten full-length plays and over twenty short plays and films. In college, his first directorial experience was as an assistant director for *The Colored Museum*. His directorial debut was for his own National award-winning play *Vodou and the Priestess* in 2012. Since then, he directed one touring show, numerous stage plays and staged readings, and six short films. In February 2018, he wrote and directed his award-winning play *Turnabout* at The Player's Theater. In August 2018, *Lacrimosa* was selected in the top thirty out of 850 plays for the Samuel French OOB festival. He also directed it Off-Broadway at The Vineyard.

···production history···

Lacrimosa was first debuted in Manhattan, NY on August 21, 2018. It was selected in the top 30 out of 850 submitted plays to be performed in the Samuel French OOB festival.

Original Cast

CHARLES, Deangelo Kearns

JOANNE, Kristin Dodson

Original Crew

Writer, Christopher Marshall

Director, Christopher Marshall

Stage Manager, Carleton King

characters

CHARLES, early to mid thirties. Very apathetic. Finds pleasure in his wife's distress.

JOANNE, late twenties, early thirties. Glum, dissatisfied wife. Becomes more frustrated as the play progresses.

setting

In the living/dining room area of Charles and Joanne's home.

note

Charles never takes his eyes off of his newspaper except for stage directional indications. Also this piece is written specifically without a time period so that it can adopt any time period based on the director's discretion.

• • •

Day 1

[*At rise, the song* Lacrimosa *by Wolfgang Amadeus Mozart plays.* CHARLES *is sitting at the dining room table drinking tea and reading a newspaper. His movements are very routine and expressionless. The music continues.* JOANNE *comes in wearing a black dress and a black veil with a teapot. She enters very sullen. He sits the tea mug down, and she pours him more tea. He doesn't look at her; she doesn't look at him. Music fades down but does not cut out. In a voice lacking emotion, he speaks.*]

[*Music pauses when she puts teapot down.*]

CHARLES   Good morning, dear.

JOANNE   What's so good about it?

CHARLES   Would you prefer I wish you a bad morning?

JOANNE   I'd prefer you wish me a quick death.

CHARLES   Beg your pardon?

JOANNE   Not too quick though. One would think that I would love to savor such a thrill as dying.

CHARLES   Are you alright, dear?

JOANNE   Yes, dear. I'm just in mourning.

CHARLES   Really? Who passed away?

JOANNE   My hopes and dreams! It was a touching service. Open casket and all.

CHARLES   Sounds a bit melancholy.

JOANNE   Yes . . . And now, I'm in mourning.

CHARLES   Well do enjoy yourself dear.

JOANNE   Indeed.

CHARLES   Yes . . . of course.

[*Music picks up again from where it was paused.*]

[Lacrimosa *starts playing again. She stares at him for a while. He continues to look through his newspaper. She sits the teapot down and picks up the candelabra and starts dusting it with a rag. She walks behind him. She gets an idea and looks between him and the candelabra. He continues to read his paper. She raises it to hit him on the head but notices a spot on his shoulder. Frustrated, she uses her free hand to dust off his shoulder and pats his head. She places the candelabra down on the table, and then she walks back to the kitchen. He's left onstage, looking through his newspaper, and drinking his tea.*]

[*When she exits offstage, blackout. Music fades out.*]

Day 2

[Lacrimosa *starts to play on the fourth beat. Lights come up after two beats.*]

[CHARLES *sits at the dining room table in the same spot. He's flipping through a newspaper and drinking his tea.* JOANNE *enters with the teapot and pours him a cup.*]

[*Music pauses when she puts teapot down.*]

CHARLES   Good morning, dear!

JOANNE   What's so good about it?

CHARLES   I do love a good riddle. I give up, what?

JOANNE   Well clearly I don't know, or I wouldn't have asked.

CHARLES   And why would you presume that I would know?

JOANNE   Maybe because you asserted how good the morning was.

CHARLES   Well if you don't know and I don't know, how will we ever come to an agreement.

JOANNE   By agreeing to agree.

CHARLES   Agreed!

JOANNE   [*Annoyed.*] Or by agreeing that we do not agree . . .

CHARLES   Splendid!

JOANNE   [*Petulant.*] Or we can agree on having breakfast, I'm famished.

CHARLES   Marvelous idea!

JOANNE   Great! . . . I made you some already. Be right back.

[*Music plays as she exits, and cuts when she reenters.*]

[*She exits and comes back with a tray of biscuits.*]

CHARLES Something smells delicious. What is it?

JOANNE I made you some biscuits for breakfast.

CHARLES That's lovely, darling, but sadly it's not the time of year for biscuits.

JOANNE The time of year?

CHARLES Hardly.

JOANNE When pray tell is the time of year?

CHARLES I'd assume during spring when wheat and flour are harvested.

JOANNE Well that's rather unfortunate. Are you sure you don't want to try the biscuits?

CHARLES Positive. I am rather in the mood for a croissant or a crepe.

JOANNE Well one would assume that the same wheat and flour that make biscuits are the same wheat and flour that make your crepe or croissant.

CHARLES Yes. One would assume.

JOANNE I do wish you would try just one. I spent all morning making these for you.

CHARLES Oh no, darling, it's quite alright. Watching my figure and all.

JOANNE But I used a few special ingredients. For extra flavor.

CHARLES Really? What ingredients?

JOANNE Oh you know, just some brown sugar, honey, some butter . . . a little hemlock and a dash of arsenic.

CHARLES You spoil me my love.

JOANNE Naturally. Only the best for you, dear husband.

CHARLES Those biscuits do sound "to die for" but sadly I'd prefer a crepe.

JOANNE Well, guess I have no choice. [*Beat.*] I'll kill you one day.

CHARLES Oh I do hope it's in the foyer with the candlestick.

JOANNE Beg your pardon?

CHARLES I've always dreamed of dying in a foyer with a candlestick.

JOANNE Why the foyer?!

CHARLES Because the blood would accent the decor.

JOANNE But of course.

CHARLES Naturally.

JOANNE Well, I'll go make your crepes. I'm all out of hemlock though. Would you settle for strawberries?

CHARLES Sounds exquisite.

JOANNE Good . . . Well I'm off. I'll leave these biscuits here in case you change your mind.

CHARLES Please do, darling, you never know what will happen. Life is funny that way.

[*She places the tray of cookies at the center of the table.*]

JOANNE Is it?

CHARLES Of course.

JOANNE Well I always thought the biggest joke in life was death.

CHARLES How so?

JOANNE You spend all of that time living to accomplish something, and then often die before you do. Death always gets the last laugh.

CHARLES Sounds dismal.

JOANNE Such is the sad truth of life . . . and death I do suppose.

CHARLES Well I do suppose you are right.

JOANNE Oh well. I'll make you a crepe now. Yell if you need me. Unless you try a biscuit, then die a peaceful, agonizing death.

CHARLES Oh, darling, I don't know what I would do without you.

JOANNE I am still trying to figure out what to do with you.

[Lacrimosa *at the fourth beat starts playing at :45 as she exits. It plays for five seconds in the blackout.*]

[*She gives him a devilish smile. He still doesn't look up from his paper. She exits.*]

[*Lights fade.*]

Day 3

[Lacrimosa *plays softly in the background. Lights come up.* CHARLES *is flipping through his newspaper, and drinking his tea. Joanne comes out with a teapot. He sits the cup down and she pours him a cup. He continues to look at his newspaper without looking at her.*]

[*Music pauses when she puts teapot down.*]

CHARLES   Good morning, dear!

JOANNE   Hello, dear.

[*She starts to walk back toward the kitchen.* CHARLES *grabs his chest and winces in pain.*]

CHARLES   Oh my . . .

JOANNE   [*Excited.*] Something the matter?

CHARLES   Looks like the weather will be terribly hot today.

JOANNE   [*Disappointed.*] Will it?

[*She walks over to a fruit bowl with a slasher knife in it. Picks up a piece of fruit and starts to cut it. She stops and has a bright idea.*]

CHARLES   Undoubtedly.

JOANNE   Well then make sure you are prepared.

CHARLES   For what?

JOANNE   [*Feigning innocence.*] The weather of course.

CHARLES   I needn't worry about the weather. I don't plan on going out at all today.

JOANNE   Not at all?

CHARLES   No. I'll be here with you all day.

JOANNE   [*Strained.*] All day, you say?

CHARLES   Yes dear. All day. Here with you all day long.

JOANNE   Wonderful . . .

[Lacrimosa *continues playing while* JOANNE *is doing her business.*]

[JOANNE *quietly and purposefully retreats back to the kitchen as he continues to read his newspaper. She comes out with kindling and firewood. She drops it around his chair. She returns to the kitchen and comes back with more kindling. She pulls out a book of matches or flint and steel. He continues to read the paper, not paying attention to her at all. She tries to strike it, but it won't light. She tries again; nothing. In a fit of desperation, she repeatedly strikes it over and over, and then springs up and turns away from him.*]

JOANNE   Damn it!

[*Music abruptly cuts.*]

CHARLES   [*Still looking in the newspaper.*] Better luck next time, dear.

JOANNE   Thank you, dear. You always know how to make me feel better.

CHARLES   Anything for you, darling.

JOANNE   It warms my heart to know that I have your support.

CHARLES   A warm heart is always better than a cold one.

JOANNE   Certainly.

[*She grabs the teapot and tops off his tea.*]

CHARLES   Thank you, darling.

JOANNE   You're more than welcome dear.

[Lacrimosa *starts again. Plays five seconds into the blackout.*]

Day 4

[Lacrimosa *plays well into the second or third measure.*]

[Lacrimosa *plays.* CHARLES *is sitting at the table drinking tea and looking at his newspaper.* JOANNE *walks in staring at him with a bit of a grimace. There is more ferociousness in her expression.*]

CHARLES Good morning, dear.

[*Music pauses when he speaks.*]

[*She points a gun that she is concealing in her upstage hand at him. She pauses for a moment waiting for some reaction from him, but he doesn't look up from his newspaper. She pulls the trigger four or five times but the gun is empty. She throws a bit of a tantrum as the music fades.*]

JOANNE UGGGGHHHHHHHHH!!!!!

CHARLES I do apologize, dear. We're completely out of bullets. I used them all at the range last week. Forgot to replace them.

[*Beat.* JOANNE *composes herself after her breakdown. She softens and gives him a heartfelt smile.*]

JOANNE It's quite alright, dear. One can't expect to shoot a gun, when one is out of bullets.

CHARLES Indubitably!

JOANNE Do let me know when we get some more.

CHARLES I'll make sure it's the first thing I do.

JOANNE Wonderful. I'll get you some more tea, dear.

CHARLES Thank you, darling.

[*Music continues through to the next scene.*]

[*She exits. Blackout.*]

Day 5

[Lacrimosa *is playing softly in the dark. Lights come up with* CHARLES *sitting at the dining room table looking through his newspaper and drinking tea.*]

CHARLES Good morn—

[*Music pauses*]

[*Before he could finish his sentence, a tomahawk, arrow, or an ax flies by him to the other side of the stage.* JOANNE *appears in some separate part of the stage or audience as if she's in another room.*]

JOANNE [*Voiceover.*] I am terribly sorry about that, dear.

CHARLES [*Still looking in his paper.*] That's quite alright!

JOANNE Are you still alive?

CHARLES As lively as can be.

JOANNE That's rather unfortunate . . .

CHARLES Next time, dear. Next time.

JOANNE Yes, dear. I'll go on and get started on your breakfast.

CHARLES Excellent.

[*Music continues.*]

[*Blackout.*]

Day 6

[*Music continues.*]

[*Day opens the same as others.* JOANNE *comes in with the teapot. She's at the point of breaking. She's finally hit her emotional tipping point.*]

CHARLES Good morning, dear!

[JOANNE *screams.*]

[*Music stops when she screams.*]

CHARLES Quite a peculiar response.

JOANNE I can't do it.

CHARLES Do what, dear?

JOANNE This! I cannot do this anymore.

CHARLES I'm sorry but you've lost me a bit.

[*He looks up from the newspaper for the first time.*]

CHARLES   Are you alright? You sound a bit flustered at the moment.

JOANNE   Flustered!? You want flustered? I'll show you flustered.

[JOANNE *runs to the kitchen.* CHARLES *puts the newspaper down and gets up from his seat and stares at her offstage. She runs back with a knife or sword in hand.*]

CHARLES   Ah choosing the direct approach I see?

JOANNE   VERY MUCH SO!

CHARLES   Naturally.

JOANNE   I am going to murder you.

CHARLES   Splendid! When you're done can you give me a bit more tea.

JOANNE   Here's your tea!

[*She screams and runs at him. She rams the knife into him. He finally shows some emotion when looking at her. He looks at the blade that is still inside of him, then looks at her with fear.*]

CHARLES   Oh dear!

[*He takes forever to die. Being as physically dramatic as possible. After every dramatic choice, he stops moaning and coughing to look and see if she's looking at him. After checking in, he continues back in his dying fit. Eventually, he sits on the floor, still going on and on with his death. She gets annoyed and pushes him down or stabs him again. He dies.* JOANNE *begins a giggle that grows into a maniacal laugh. She stares at* CHARLES' *lifeless body.*]

JOANNE   Free . . . I'm free of you. I am finally free of you for good. Who's getting your tea now, you no good bastard? You don't need this newspaper do you. No. Not where you're going. You made my life a living Hell, but at least I can find solace in your death.

   [*She sits in his chair with a sense of triumph, and she neatly closes his newspaper. She stares at it for a moment. Then she starts laughing.*]

   I did it! I finally did it.

[*She grabs one of the biscuits from earlier and takes a bite. With a breath of triumph, she exits offstage back to the kitchen.*]

[*Lights fade when she's exiting.*]

Day 7

[Lacrimosa *begins where they are singing on the track.*]

[*Day opens with* Lacrimosa *playing in the background.* CHARLES *is seated in his chair again and looking through his newspaper drinking his tea.* JOANNE *walks in the room in a trance-like state holding her teapot in hand. She notices* CHARLES.]

[*Music cuts abruptly. She comes to her senses, confused and bewildered.*]

CHARLES   Good morning, dear!

JOANNE   . . . But . . . but . . . but . . . How could this?—

CHARLES   Are you feeling alright?

[*She looks at him afraid and confused.*]

JOANNE   How is this . . . How could this . . . I killed you.

CHARLES   Yes you did, dear, and it was quite splendid. Quite splendid indeed.

JOANNE   But . . . I KILLED YOU!

CHARLES   Don't let it bother you, dear. There's always next time.

JOANNE   No . . . this isn't possible. HOW IS THIS POSSIBLE?

[*She starts frantically pacing around the room adlibbing and miming the events of her murdering him.* CHARLES *puts down the newspaper and out of nowhere gives her an evil sneer.*]

CHARLES   *Dies illa. Judicandus homo reus.* Latin is quite the lovely language. Lovely language indeed. Do you know what it means, dear?

JOANNE   [*Angry.*] I don't speak Latin!

CHARLES   It's quite alright, dear. It's a passage from Mozart's requiem. It translates to "On that day, the guilty one is judged."

JOANNE   But . . . but I was finally free of you.

CHARLES   You'll never be free of me HERE, darling.

JOANNE   WHAT THE HELL IS GOING ON HERE!

[Projection of hell fire comes on the screen behind them.]

[CHARLES*'s visage morphs into a dark and demonic grin.*]

CHARLES   *What the . . .HELL indeed.*

[CHARLES *starts reading the newspaper again.*]

CHARLES   [*Continued.*] It's terribly hot today . . . terribly hot indeed.

[Lacrimosa *"AMEN" section plays until the end.*]

[CHARLES *does a continuous demonic laugh.* JOANNE *collapses to the floor crying*]

JOANNE   NOOOOOOOOOOOOOOOOOO . . . !

[*Lights fade.*]

• • •

Be Yourself

Daniel Guyton

Be Yourself by Daniel Guyton. Copyright © 2018 by Daniel Guyton. All rights reserved. Reprinted by permission of the author.

CAUTION/ADVICE: Professionals and amateurs are hereby warned that performance of *Be Yourself* is subject to a royalty. It is fully protected under the copyright laws of the United States of America, and of all countries covered by the International Copyright Union (including the Dominion of Canada and the rest of the British Commonwealth), and of all countries covered by the Pan-American Copyright Convention and the Universal Copyright Convention, the Berne Convention, and of all countries with which the United States has reciprocal copyright relations. All rights, including professional and amateur stage performing rights, motion picture, recitation, lecturing, public reading, radio broadcasting, television, video or sound recording, all other forms of mechanical or electronic reproduction, such as CD-ROM, DVD-ROM, information storage and retrieval systems, and photocopying, and the rights of translation into foreign languages, are strictly reserved. Particular emphasis is placed upon the matter of readings, permission for which must be secured from Daniel Guyton in writing in advance. Inquiries concerning rights should be addressed to Daniel Guyton at dguyton21@ gmail.com.

Daniel Guyton

DANIEL GUYTON is an award-winning playwright and screenwriter from Atlanta, GA. His stage plays have been produced over five hundred times around the world, and he has been published in over forty-five anthologies and solo publications, including several of the *Best American Short Plays* collections. His play *Three Ladies of Orpington* recently won seven awards from the Metropolitan Atlanta Theatre Awards. He is a theater professor at Georgia State University and Georgia Military College and is a member of the Dramatists Guild and the Writers Guild of America East. In addition, he is Vice Chair of the Fayette County Public Arts Committee, and Chair of the Professional Division of the Georgia Theater Conference. For more info, please visit: www.danguyton.com.

···production history···

Be Yourself premiered at Allen High School (CA Taylor, teacher) in Allen, TX, in December 2018. It was directed by Stephanie Scarano and Thomas Schnaible. The stage manager was Emma Chumley, and the crew was Grayson Schnaible. The cast was as follows:

ASHLEY COWEN / CARMEN, Lauren Secrest

MRS. COWEN / MRS. HIGHTOWER, Aurora Field

BERNARD, Nick Merritt

GREG / GNA / MR. HIGHTOWER, Colin Champman

BIG PHARMA / MR. WHITTAKER / DR. RENAUD, Brock Jones

COSMO / JESSICA HIGHTOWER, Leah Hudler

Be Yourself was subsequently produced by Winder-Barrow High School (Sherelle Patisaul, Drama Teacher) in Winder, GA, in April 2019. It was directed by John Thomas. The assistant director was Kirsti Garrett. The costumes were designed by Lauren Harper and Addison Loebl. The cast was as follows:

ASHLEY, Hailey Brodie

GREG, Sidney Hall

MR. WHITAKER, John Thomas

BIG PHARMA, Ezekiel Harrell

COSMO, Madison Hughes

MRS. COWEN, Zoe Demos

BERNARD, Crews Proctor

CARMEN, Evie Shelton

G&A, Alexus Kelley

JESSICA, Elise Taylor

MR. HIGHTOWER, Bo Robinson

MRS. HIGHTOWER, Abby Mangham

DR. RENAUD, Justin Sharp

characters

ASHLEY, a teenage girl.

GREG, a teenage boy.

MR. WHITTAKER, a math teacher.

BIG PHARMA, a walking pharmaceutical commercial.

COSMO, a walking *Cosmopolitan* magazine.

MRS. COWEN, Ashley's mom.

BERNARD, a teenage boy.

CARMEN, a teenage girl.

G&A, a walking *Guns and Ammo* magazine.

JESSICA, a teenage dancer.

MRS. HIGHTOWER, Jessica's mother.

MR. HIGHTOWER, Jessica's father.

DR. RENAUD, a therapist.

note

Please double as needed. Characters can be any race or ethnicity. Some characters may be any gender, unless specified.

• • •

scene 1

[ASHLEY *talks directly to the audience.*]

ASHLEY You know, people always tell me, "Be yourself." "Be yourself," they say, as if that's going to make everything better.

GREG [*Entering.*] Hey, um . . . Ashley?

ASHLEY Yeah?

[*He winks and clicks two finger guns at her.*]

GREG Be yourself.

[GREG *exits.*]

ASHLEY But then it's like . . . when I *am* myself . . . [*She falls to the ground melodramatically and weeps.*] Oh god! It's so horrible, I just wanna die!

MR. WHITTAKER [*Entering, nervously.*] Hey, um . . . Ashley?

ASHLEY [*Still weeping.*] What?

MR. WHITTAKER Please don't do that, OK? [*He looks around, nervously.*] No . . . nobody wants to see that.

ASHLEY [*Wiping her eyes.*] But I'm just being myself.

MR. WHITTAKER Yeah, but not like that, OK? Be yourself like . . . you know, like the way everybody else is doing it.

ASHLEY And what way is that, Mr. Whittaker?

MR. WHITTAKER You know, like . . . happy?

ASHLEY But I'm not—

MR. WHITTAKER [*Cutting her off.*] Hey, I'm glad we had this talk. [*He winks and clicks two finger guns at her.*] Feel better, OK?

[*He exits.* ASHLEY *turns to the audience.*]

ASHLEY But what if I don't want to feel better? What if I *like* my depression, huh? What if I enjoy—

[BIG PHARMA *enters as if he/she were driving an ambulance, making the sounds with his/her mouth.* COSMO *also enters and stands prim-and-properly at one side of the stage*]

BIG PHARMA Whee-oo! Whee-oo! Whee-oo! Big Pharma here, making sure that no one ever feels sad and blue! Here kid, take one of these and you'll feel good as new!

[BIG PHARMA *offers her a gigantic blue pill, ideally half the size of her body.* ASHLEY *holds it, confused.*]

ASHLEY What *is* this?

COSMO Ladies, if you want to meet a man, it's imperative that you stay happy and glad, 100% of the time!

ASHLEY Yeah, but what if I don't want—

COSMO [*Dropping the pretense into a scary growl.*] Even if you feel like dying. [*Forcing herself into a smile again.*] You must smile through and pretend. For their sake.

ASHLEY For whose sake?

BIG PHARMA You wouldn't want to make your friends unhappy, now would you? Drag them down into your depression?

ASHLEY Well, no. I . . .

BIG PHARMA Then, take the pill!

COSMO All the hottest celebrities are doing it. Why, just last week . . .

ASHLEY [*Dropping the pill.*] No! Now look, I understand that some people really need this medication, all right? And if it helps people, then that's great, and I'm not knocking it in any way, shape, or form. But why do *I* have to take this pill if I'm happy just the way I am?!?

BIG PHARMA [*Really pushing it.*] But are you? I mean, are you *really* happy?

ASHLEY Well, yeah. I mean . . .

BIG PHARMA But you were just crying a minute ago.

ASHLEY So? People get sad sometimes.

COSMO Not if they want to meet a man, they don't.

ASHLEY What? But, I don't want to meet . . .

[GREG *enters into a halo of light, as angelic music plays. He pauses in a superhero gesture for a moment, then looks at her.*]

GREG Hey Ash. You know, you look really . . . cute. When your eyes aren't all puffy and you're . . . actually smiling for once.

[ASHLEY *looks at* COSMO.]

ASHLEY Yeah, no. That's not gonna do it for me. I've known Greg my entire life. He's like a brother to me.

GREG   Ooh, friendzoned! Ouch, man. That really hurts my feelings a
bit.

[BIG PHARMA *sidles on up to him.*]

BIG PHARMA   Well hey, big guy. Feelin' a little down in the dumps
there, are ya?

GREG   Yeah. I guess. Maybe a little.

BIG PHARMA   Well, have I got a treat for you!

[BIG PHARMA *puts his arm around* GREG *and leads him offstage.* ASHLEY *crosses to* COSMO, *and tries to confide in her.*]

ASHLEY   Look. The reason I'm depressed is . . .

[MRS. COWEN *enters. She is extremely fashion conscious, and very well put together.*]

MRS. COWEN   Ashley, dear. Are you ready for school yet?

ASHLEY   Oh. Coming, mom!

MRS. COWEN   Will you stop reading my magazines, dear, and let's go! I
have a spa appointment at nine and I still have to drop you off. I
swear, the sacrifices I make for you kids.

[MRS. COWEN *exits.*]

COSMO   [*Conspiratorially.*] I think I understand. Overbearing mother,
yes?

ASHLEY   Well . . . sort of. You don't know the half of it.

COSMO   Oh goodie! On page twenty-four, there's a terrific article on
how to deal with an overbearing mother-in-law.

ASHLEY   What? I'm only seventeen! I don't have a mother-in-law.

COSMO   Yet! But you will, my dear, if you simply follow my advice.

ASHLEY   Look, there's more to life than just . . .

MRS. COWEN   [*Offstage.*] ASHLEY!!!

ASHLEY   OK, coming, Mom! [*To* COSMO.] Look, I gotta go. I'll check in with you later, OK?

COSMO   OK, sweetie. But remember . . . a happy wife is a happy life.

[ASHLEY *stares at her, confused, then shakes her head and exits.* COSMO *smiles pleasantly as the lights fade.*]

scene 2

[BERNARD *talks to the audience*]

BERNARD   People always tell you to be yourself. Yeah, like it's so easy. But what do you do when you hate yourself, you know? It's like . . . Why would I want to subject other people to *this*?

[CARMEN *enters.*]

CARMEN   Hey, Bernard. [BERNARD *nods, but doesn't speak.*] What'cha up to? [BERNARD *shrugs.*] Yeah, you know. Me too. Just . . . you know, gettin' ready for that math test today. You know, Mr. Whittaker's really difficult.

[*Long awkward pause.*]

BERNARD   [*To the audience.*] Look, it's bad enough I have to live with myself, but . . . to subject other people to *this* piece of garbage? [*He points to his own body.*] I mean, that's just cruel. To *them*.

[*He looks at* CARMEN.]

CARMEN   OK, well um . . . I'm gonna go . . . I guess. [*She lingers.*] See ya around.

BERNARD   Yeah. See ya. [CARMEN *exits. He turns to the audience.*] Trust me, I am doing her a favor. The last thing the world needs is for me to be myself. Around anyone.

[G&A *enters, wearing camouflage and some sporting equipment.*]

G&A   [*Proudly.*] Well hey there, fella. "Guns and Ammo" magazine here. Wait'll you see the new line of Smith & Wessons we got in stock just for you.

BERNARD   Sweet!

G&A   Check out this beauty on page six!

[BERNARD *looks at the audience.*]

BERNARD   Look, I know what you're thinking—but... it's not that kind of play, all right? I just like looking at them.

G&A   Hey pal, check it out!

BERNARD   What?

G&A   [*Rolling up his sleeve and flexing.*] Two tickets for the gun show! YEAH!

[G&A *exits.*]

BERNARD   [*To the audience.*] They say you should just be yourself at all times, but . . . sometimes being yourself is really scary. And not just for myself, either. For . . . society at large. [*Pause.*] I don't think I'm ready to be myself.

[*He exits. Lights out.*]

scene 3

[JESSICA, *a ballerina, dances across the stage.*]

JESSICA   My parents always encouraged me to be myself.

[MR. *and* MRS. HIGHTOWER *enter, holding hands.*]

MRS. HIGHTOWER   You're such a brave and beautiful girl, Jessica. I'm so proud of you.

MR. HIGHTOWER   I know you'll be the best at whatever you want to be.

JESSICA   And I've always found it easy to be myself. [*Still dancing.*] It sounds egotistical, but . . . when you're comfortable in your own skin, and you have a wonderful childhood, and parents who adore you, and you really feel passionate about something in your life . . . It's very easy to be yourself . . . when you love yourself.

[*She ends her dance in a beautiful, freeing pose, but suddenly her parents look very sad. They stop holding hands.* MR. HIGHTOWER *crosses to* JESSICA.]

MR. HIGHTOWER Jessica, darling, I'm so sorry. But Daddy has to go away for awhile.

JESSICA What? Where?

[*He looks back at his wife.*]

MR. HIGHTOWER Well, your mother and I, we . . . We've decided to spend some time apart, you see. And . . . and so I'm moving to Minneapolis.

JESSICA What? Will I ever see you again?

MR. HIGHTOWER Yes, of course, my darling! Absolutely! I just . . . can't see you for a little while, that's all. Not until I get myself settled in Minneapolis.

JESSICA And when will that be?

MR. HIGHTOWER Oh, just a few weeks, I'm sure! And then I'll send for you, I promise. [*He backs away.*] I'll send for you. [*He backs away further, like a shadow.*] I'll send for you.

[*He exits.*]

JESSICA Except he never sent for me. He moved to Minneapolis and . . . then he died about seven months later. I never danced again after that. It's just difficult to be yourself when . . . when you blame yourself for . . .

MRS. HIGHTOWER Oh honey, it isn't your fault! He . . . Your daddy loved you.

JESSICA And I know she said it isn't my fault, but . . . but when you're eleven years old, and your parents split up. And your father takes his own life, it's . . . really difficult to not blame yourself. And it's really difficult to love yourself. When you have all of that guilt.

MRS. HIGHTOWER I love you, my darling. So much.

JESSICA I know you do, Mom. I know.

MRS. HIGHTOWER   And I really wish you would dance again. You were so pretty when you danced.

JESSICA   I know, Mom. And I love to dance. I do. But . . . in order for me to dance, I would have to love myself again. And I'm . . . I'm just not ready for that kind of commitment.

[JESSICA *exits.*]

MRS. HIGHTOWER   [*Distraught.*] Oh, Jessica! Wait!

[MRS. HIGHTOWER *does not run after her. Instead, she hugs her chest as the lights fade*]

scene 4

[BIG PHARMA *stands onstage, trying to sell prescription drugs to people in the audience.*]

BIG PHARMA   Hey there! You! Yes, you. Do you ever get a runny nose? Itchy eyes? Really stinky armpits even after you bathe? Well, have I got the drug for you! Only four-ninety-nine with an insurance plan! [*Beat.*] Oh, no. Not four dollars and ninety-nine cents. Four hundred and ninety-nine dollars, with an insurance plan. [*Beat.*] Oh, I know. It's expensive. But I can smell your armpits from here, sir! Trust me, it's a worthwhile investment. [*Beat.*] Oh. You don't have an insurance plan? Yeah, you don't even wanna *know* what the price is, then.

[MR. HIGHTOWER *enters. He looks like a ghost. He stares at* BIG PHARMA.]

MR. HIGHTOWER   You know, I really could have used you back in Minneapolis.

BIG PHARMA   Oh! Why? Did you have stinky armpits?

MR. HIGHTOWER   No. I had serious depression. It was hard for me to look in the mirror sometimes. Until . . . one night . . . I ended it all.

BIG PHARMA   Oh. Were you . . . having a fight with your wife, perhaps?

MR. HIGHTOWER   No.

BIG PHARMA   Lose your job, sir?

MR. HIGHTOWER Nope.

BIG PHARMA Drug addiction?

MR. HIGHTOWER No. Sometimes depression just . . . makes you think terrible things about yourself. For no reason at all.

BIG PHARMA Well, we have medication for . . .

MR. HIGHTOWER Yes, I know. And I talked to you three years ago about that medication, but I couldn't afford it then.

BIG PHARMA Well, I have to make a profit too, you know.

MR. HIGHTOWER Yes, I know. But now my baby girl doesn't have a father.

BIG PHARMA And you blame me?

MR. HIGHTOWER No, I blame depression. But you could have helped me.

BIG PHARMA Oh, I can help everyone, Mr. Hightower. For a fee, of course.

MR. HIGHTOWER Yes, for a fee. I know. Everything for a fee.

BIG PHARMA Hey, I'm just being myself, Mr. Hightower. I find it very easy to be *myself*.

MR. HIGHTOWER Well, I wish you could be *me* for just a day. Maybe you'd feel differently about it.

BIG PHARMA Yes, maybe I would. [MR. HIGHTOWER *exits.*] I'm sorry for your loss, sir. [*After* MR. HIGHTOWER *is completely gone, he turns to the audience.*] Hello! You there! Yes, miss. Do you ever feel your skin itch on the back of your knee? I'm not sure what they call that. It's not an elbow. It's like . . . a knee-bow? I dunno. Anyway, does that ever itch? Because if so, have I got the cream for you!

[*Lights out. End of scene.*]

scene 5

[DR. RENAUD *talks to the audience as though they are patients in a group session. She is dressed professionally, like a therapist.*]

DR. RENAUD The problem with being yourself is this: We, as human beings, can be very judgmental. We all do it. We try not to. But we look at someone and think, "Oh, that person has their whole life together," or we look at someone else and think, "Oh, that poor person. Thank God I'm not them." But in actuality, the person who looks like they have everything together may be dealing with some very emotional things deep down. Meanwhile, the person who looks disheveled may be happier than you deep down. You never know until you get to know them. As they say, you shouldn't judge a book by its cover. But, even if you know this, other people will judge you anyway. That's part of the privilege, and the scariness, of living in society. Knowing that anywhere you go, people will judge you. It's impossible to find a society that doesn't do this. From Europe to Africa and Asia to the United States. We are a judgmental species, human beings. So you have a choice in your life: You can either be someone that *they* want you to be, and let other people judge you for not being yourself. OR you can be the person *you* want to be, and let other people judge you for not being whom *they* want you to be. Which one do you think will make you happier in the long run?

[*Lights up on* ASHLEY, *raising her hand.*]

ASHLEY Being myself.

DR. RENAUD That's good. But why?

ASHLEY Because I'm being judged either way, so I might as well be happy in what I'm doing.

DR. RENAUD That's good, Ashley. Very good.

[*Lights up on BERNARD. Lights out on ASHLEY.*]

BERNARD But what if I want to hurt people?

DR. RENAUD What?

BERNARD What if . . . Now listen, everything I say to you is confidential, right?

DR. RENAUD Well, yes, Bernard. Of course. Unless you make a direct threat. You should know this upfront, that if you threaten someone— or even yourself—I have to report it. I am obligated by law.

BERNARD I understand.

DR. RENAUD But I want you to be honest with me. So . . . I will tell you what. You just tell me what you want to say, and if anything sounds like something I have to report, then I will tell you. I want you to be upfront with me, Bernard, so I will be upfront with you. Is that a deal?

BERNARD [*Shrugging.*] I guess.

DR. RENAUD So, what's on your mind?

BERNARD Well . . . it's like this . . .

[*Lights up on* JESSICA, *lights out on* BERNARD.]

JESSICA I want to dance! [DR. RENAUD *turns to face her.*] I want more than anything to be a dancer, Dr. Renaud. It's just . . . the last time I danced, my father was there. He watched me the entire time. It's like . . . if I dance, I feel like I'm moving on without him. It feels like . . . he's really gone.

DR. RENAUD Do you believe he's watching you, Jessica? I mean, right now? In Heaven?

[MR. HIGHTOWER *enters, watching her.*]

JESSICA I guess? I'm not sure.

DR. RENAUD Well, if he's watching you, then what's the problem?

JESSICA See, that's . . . [*Beat.*] I don't know that he is.

DR. RENAUD Oh.

JESSICA In my church, we . . . Well, the pastor says that suicide . . .

[*She grows quiet.*]

DR. RENAUD I see. He says that suicide will keep you out of Heaven? [JESSICA *nods.*] I understand. So you believe your father is . . . suffering. In agony. Somewhere down below.

JESSICA I don't know.

DR. RENAUD Well, I don't know either, Jessica. I don't. I don't know what happens to us after we die. But I know this. My daughter, Melanie. She is a painter. She paints beautiful landscapes of oceans and beaches, with the sun on the horizon. I absolutely love the way she paints. And I love the joy it brings her to paint. And I know that if she ever stopped painting—because of something I did—I would be devastated. *That* would be agony for me. For her to stop doing something she loved because of me. Did your father enjoy watching you dance?

JESSICA He cried. He said it was the most beautiful thing he had ever seen in his life.

DR. RENAUD Well. I can tell you something I know about suicide, Jessica. [MR. HIGHTOWER *looks at* DR. RENAUD.] I've worked with many patients over the years that were struggling with these thoughts. And this may surprise you, but not a single one of those patients wanted to die. Not one of them. They just didn't want to live the way that they were living now, and they didn't know how to fix it. Most were in pain. Physical, or emotional, it all feels the same when you're living in it. But through therapy, and communication, and sometimes even medicine, there is usually hope. But, I promise you this, Jessica: for your father to do what he did, he was already in agony before he died. But even in his pain, there was one thing that made him smile. [MR. HIGHTOWER *holds out his hand for* JESSICA.] One thing that made him feel good. And do you know what that was?

[*Somehow,* JESSICA *sees* MR. HIGHTOWER. *She reaches up and takes his hand.*]

JESSICA My dancing?

[MR. HIGHTOWER *pulls her to her feet.*]

DR. RENAUD That's right. So, I don't know where he is right now, Jessica. But, if he's suffering . . . and if he can see you, then don't you think you owe it to him to . . . maybe ease that suffering just a little bit?

[MR. HIGHTOWER *twirls* JESSICA.]

JESSICA So, you're saying I should dance?

DR. RENAUD Oh yeah, kid. You should dance like his soul depends on it.

[MR. HIGHTOWER *and* JESSICA *share a smile. Lights fade.*]

scene 6

[MRS. COWEN *is applying makeup.* COSMO *is offering her advice.*]

COSMO Now, the key to eliminating wrinkles, Mrs. Cowen, is to sanitize, moisturize and revitalize. Keeping the face clean and moist at all times is crucial—

[ASHLEY *enters, in a rush.*]

ASHLEY Mom, I have to tell you something!

MRS. COWEN What? Ashley, I'm putting on my makeup. I have a fundraiser in less than an hour.

ASHLEY I'm gay.

[MRS. COWEN *stares at her, then resumes.*]

MRS. COWEN I am not in the mood for your jokes, Ashley. Now go finish the setting the table for you and your brother.

ASHLEY No. I'm serious. I've known for a while now. But . . . I was afraid to say anything, because . . . because I was afraid you'd be mad at me.

MRS. COWEN Ashley, I don't have time for this!

COSMO I have to say, *that* is no way to meet a man, young lady.

ASHLEY No, I'm serious! I have been depressed for so long because . . . because I had a secret that I didn't want to tell you! Because I was afraid you would be mad at me.

MRS. COWEN Mad at you! Ashley, I am the vice president of the Washington County Country Club! What do you think the ladies there will say about me if they knew . . .

ASHLEY If they knew what?! That your daughter was gay?

MRS. COWEN Oh god, I think I'm having a heart attack.

ASHLEY That's what you said when I got a C on my math final.

MRS. COWEN Well, all the other girls got B's and A's!

COSMO The key signs that you might be having a heart attack are shortness of breath . . .

ASHLEY [*Shutting* COSMO *up.*] So what? This isn't about the other girls! This is about me! And by the way, I know for a fact that Margaret Kenner's daughter is gay also.

MRS. COWEN What?!? How do you know this? No, never mind. Don't tell me. I have to leave. I have to leave immediately. And when I return . . . Well, we'll just pretend this never happened, then, won't we?

ASHLEY No! I won't pr—

MRS. COWEN Goodbye.

[*She starts to leave.*]

ASHLEY Mom!

MRS. COWEN What?!

[*Beat.*]

ASHLEY I love you.

MRS. COWEN No, you don't!

[MRS. COWEN *exits.* ASHLEY *looks at* COSMO.]

COSMO We have a . . . Well, you know, we have an LGBT section now. As of . . . as of 2014.

ASHLEY I know. That's usually the section I read.

COSMO Oh. I thought you were just an avid reader, reading *all* the sections.

ASHLEY Yes. But I also like the pictures.

[ASHLEY smiles *at* COSMO.]

COSMO Oh! Well, when taking a photograph, dear, it's important to have good lighting. And always make sure the background is clear of any embarrassing items.

[*Lights out. End of scene.*]

scene 7

[BERNARD *is holding* G&A *over a garbage pail.*]

BERNARD I have to get rid of you, G&A. I'm sorry.

G&A But whaddya mean? We're buddies.

BERNARD No. I'm a human being and you're a magazine. We're not buddies.

G&A Yes, but you've been a *Guns & Ammo* subscriber for years now, man! You can't just get rid of me like this!

BERNARD I have a problem. OK? I have a . . . borderline personality disorder. And keeping you around is just not a good idea for me.

G&A Why not?

BERNARD Because . . . I get these ideas in my head sometimes. Like . . . I wanna hurt people. But then, after a while, they go away. And with proper medication, I can . . . minimize the amount of times I have these feelings.

G&A But shouldn't you be yourself? Isn't that what EVERYBODY says?

BERNARD   Yes, but part of being myself means admitting when I have a problem! And I do have a problem. And if I don't deal with my problem, then I'm gonna end up in jail or dead. And I might take out some people with me, and I don't want to do that. Because I know . . . that as soon as that feeling passes, and those ideas go away, I start to regret everything. I regret the thoughts, even . . . Even if I haven't acted on them yet. And if I ever did act on those thoughts, then . . . oh god. I already hate myself as it is, and that's just for *having* those thoughts. But when I talked to Dr. Renaud, she said:

[*Lights up on* DR. RENAUD.]

DR. RENAUD   Do you see yourself as a villain, Bernard? [BERNARD *nods.*] But you haven't done anything, yes? [BERNARD *shakes his head no.*] And yet, you've wanted to? [BERNARD *nods.*] And that makes you feel terribly guilty, doesn't it? [BERNARD *nods.*] But do you know what I see, Bernard? When I look at you? [*He looks up at her.*] I see a superhero. I see someone who has saved so many lives, and who has helped so many people just by fighting against those urges. You're like Superman, Bernard. Or like Wolverine.

BERNARD   I am?

DR. RENAUD   You have a battle going on inside your brain, and it's a painful one, I can tell. But you didn't choose for that battle to be in there, did you?

BERNARD   No.

DR. RENAUD   But, like a hero, you've been fighting it anyway. How many lives have you saved by fighting that battle, Bernard? Be honest. How many people are alive today because you kept that battle in here? [*She points to her brain.*] Instead of out there?

[*She points out the window.*]

BERNARD   Seven.

DR. RENAUD   Seven people. Are alive today because you fought that battle in here [*she points to her brain again*] instead of out there. You deserve a medal of honor.

BERNARD I've . . . never looked at it that way before.

DR. RENAUD Of course not. Because you're a modest person. But did you ever see those people on TV who save a child from a burning building, or who tackle a criminal that's running away from a crime? What's one thing they always say to the reporters? [*He shrugs.*] "I'm not a hero. I just did it because it was the right thing to do." But those people are always heroes, Bernard. Every one of them. Even if they don't see it yet.

BERNARD Yeah. Yeah, I like that.

DR. RENAUD So, let me ask you, Bernard. Do you want to keep being the hero? Or do you want to be the villain?

BERNARD I want to be the hero.

DR. RENAUD Good. Then, there's a few steps we need to take, so that we can make sure that you stay the hero. [*She sits near him.*] First, you *must* get rid of all the weapons in your home.

BERNARD What? I . . .

DR. RENAUD It's not that I don't trust you, Bernard. I do. But do you think Superman keeps Kryptonite in his home? Do you think Wolverine has adamantium bullets lying around? Those weapons are a temptation, Bernard. They are not your friend. Now, I don't tell many of my patients this, but . . . my father was an alcoholic. For my entire life growing up, he would drink bottle after bottle after bottle after bottle. Day after day after day. It was destroying him inside and out. Now, he covered it up well. Most people didn't know he had a problem. But we knew. My sisters and I. We knew. Then, one day, he just . . . quit. He stood up and just . . . dumped out every liquor bottle he owned. Never touched another drop until the day he died. When they say "Be yourself" . . . my father wasn't himself until the day he took charge of his own life, and stopped letting the alcohol control him. Now, you are fighting a battle of your own, Bernard, and those weapons belong to the enemy, not you. If you don't get rid of them, you will lose the battle eventually. Maybe not today or tomorrow, but eventually. Now, I need you to understand something. You are not a villain. You are a good man and you are a hero, but if you ever use those weapons incorrectly, then you will become a villain. Do you understand me?

BERNARD [*Nodding.*] Yes.

DR. RENAUD Good. Now, let's talk about medication—which is another tool that can help you win this battle.

[BIG PHARMA *enters and smiles. Lights fade on* BIG PHARMA *and* DR. RENAUD. BERNARD *turns to* G&A.]

BERNARD So that's why I have to get rid of you.

G&A But I'm not a weapon! I'm a magazine!

BERNARD But you're a trigger. And not in the literal sense either.

[*He is about throw* G&A *in the trash.*]

G&A Wait wait wait! Does it have to be in the garbage pail? Can't you . . . sell me on eBay or something?

BERNARD No. I'm sorry. It has to be this way.

[*He throws* G&A *in the trash, then exits.* G&A *calls out from inside the trash can.*]

G&A Oh god, it's so disgusting in here! Is that an old shoe?!

[*Lights out. End of scene.*]

scene 8

[JESSICA *is dancing, as* MR. HIGHTOWER *watches. He cries happily.* ASHLEY *enters, and watches her for a moment.* MR. HIGHTOWER *sees* ASHLEY, *then smiles at* JESSICA, *and exits. Suddenly,* JESSICA *notices* ASHLEY.]

JESSICA Oh, hey Ashley. Sorry. I just got lost there for a little bit.

ASHLEY Wow, you're really good.

JESSICA Yeah, it feels amazing. I had forgotten what it feels like to be myself, for a long, long time.

ASHLEY I know what you mean.

JESSICA Oh yeah?

ASHLEY Yeah. It's . . . It's a long story.

JESSICA Do you believe in ghosts?

ASHLEY What? Why?

JESSICA Well, it's just . . . weird. I feel like my dad was just watching me.

[ASHLEY *looks around.*]

ASHLEY I don't see anybody.

JESSICA Yeah, I don't feel him now either. But . . . I could swear, he was right there.

ASHLEY What was he like?

JESSICA Funny. Sweet. He worked a lot, but . . . the times I got to see him were . . . [*Beat.*] You know, he hid a lot of things from us. I never knew he was depressed. Mom knew, but she kept it secret from us.

ASHLEY I'm sorry.

JESSICA It's all right.

ASHLEY Say. You . . . wouldn't want to go grab a bite to eat with me sometime, would you?

JESSICA You mean like . . . as friends? Or . . . ?

ASHLEY Wow. Um . . . I don't know. Are you . . . ?

JESSICA Maybe.

ASHLEY Wow! Really?!

JESSICA Yeah. Are you?

ASHLEY I don't know. Maybe . . .

JESSICA What are you doing now?

[*They talk as lights fade. Lights up on* CARMEN, *about to eat lunch.* BERNARD *enters and sits next to her.*]

BERNARD Hi.

CARMEN Oh. H—hi.

BERNARD Do you mind if I sit here?

CARMEN [*Clearing room for him.*] No, of course not. I'll . . . I'll be honest with you, Bernard. I . . . thought you hated me.

BERNARD No! Never. I . . . [*Pause.*] The fact of the matter is that I hate myself.

CARMEN [*Pulling away.*] Oh.

BERNARD But, I'm seeing a specialist. A . . . doctor. I . . . Well . . . I have some health issues that are pretty severe. And . . . I know that you probably think I'm a freak, or something, for . . . telling you this, and I don't blame you. But . . . part of being yourself is being true to yourself. And I'm trying. To be true to myself. So this is who I am. And if . . . you want me to sit somewhere else, then I will understand. I . . .

CARMEN I suffer from depression.

BERNARD What?

CARMEN I understand. I'm . . . I'm on medication myself. I have anxiety, depression, bipolar disorder, you name it.

BERNARD Wow. I never would have guessed.

CARMEN I've been on medication since I was nine. It's pretty well controlled.

BERNARD Wow.

CARMEN See, I thought you would think I was a freak.

BERNARD Never.

CARMEN I'm really sorry that you hate yourself.

BERNARD Yeah. Well . . . I'm getting better. I guess. You know what my doctor told me?

CARMEN What?

BERNARD That I'm a hero.

CARMEN [*Taking his hand.*] You are a hero, Bernard. Everyone that fights these battles is a hero. And if you need my help in any way? I'd . . . Well, I'd kinda like to be your sidekick.

BERNARD The Deadpool to my Wolverine?

CARMEN Haha, yeah, I like that!

[*They laugh together as the lights fade. Lights up on* MRS. COWEN, *rushing in.*]

MRS. COWEN OK, hon, I have great news! Listen. I talked to the ladies at the country club, and they said it's totally fine that you're gay! In fact, you were right about Margaret Kenner's daughter! You know, she got accepted to Yale next year?

[*Lights up on* ASHLEY.]

ASHLEY Mom. You needed permission from your country club friends for me to be true to myself?

MRS. COWEN Well . . . yeah. Hello? Those ladies know everyone in town. If we want to *be* someone in this town, we have to win them over!

ASHLEY But why can't we just be ourselves?

[*MRS. COWEN laughs, way louder than is necessary.*]

MRS. COWEN Oh, please. You kids today and your funny ideas. [*She turns to exit.*] Well, I'm heading to bed, darling. Love you.

[*She exits.* ASHLEY *shakes her head.* GREG *enters.*]

GREG Hey um . . . Ashley?

ASHLEY Yeah?

[*He winks and clicks two finger guns at her.*]

GREG Be yourself.

[*She repeats the gesture back at him.*]

ASHLEY Yeah, you too, Greg.

[*Lights up on* COSMO.]

COSMO   Ah. I always love a happy ending.

ASHLEY   Ending? We're just getting started.

[*Lights up on* JESSICA, *dancing—being herself once again. Lights up on* BERNARD *and* CARMEN *talking and laughing together. Lights up on* DR. RENAUD *and* MR. WHITTAKER *talking. Lights up on* MR. HIGHTOWER, *breathing peacefully. Lights up on* MRS. HIGHTOWER, *speaking to* BIG PHARMA.]

MRS. HIGHTOWER   [*Sadly.*] Do you think you could help me, Mr. Pharmacy? I could really use your help.

[BIG PHARMA *takes her hand and smiles, warmly.*]

BIG PHARMA   I think I can, Mrs. Hightower. Yes.

[MR. HIGHTOWER *and* BIG PHARMA *share a nod.* MR. HIGHTOWER *breathes in peacefully again, then exits. Lights fade on everyone except* ASHLEY.]

ASHLEY   Oh yes. We're just getting started.

[*Lights out.*]

• • •

Blessed Are the Dead at the Department of Life and Longevity

John Yarbrough

Blessed Are the Dead at the Department of Life and Longevity by John Yarbrough. Copyright © 2018 by John Yarbrough. All rights reserved. Reprinted by permission of the author.

CAUTION/ADVICE: Professionals and amateurs are hereby warned that performance of *Blessed Are the Dead at the Department of Life and Longevity* is subject to a royalty. It is fully protected under the copyright laws of the United States of America, and of all countries covered by the International Copyright Union (including the Dominion of Canada and the rest of the British Commonwealth), and of all countries covered by the Pan-American Copyright Convention and the Universal Copyright Convention, the Berne Convention, and of all countries with which the United States has reciprocal copyright relations. All rights, including professional and amateur stage performing rights, motion picture, recitation, lecturing, public reading, radio broadcasting, television, video or sound recording, all other forms of mechanical or electronic reproduction, such as CD-ROM, DVD-ROM, information storage and retrieval systems, and photocopying, and the rights of translation into foreign languages, are strictly reserved. Particular emphasis is placed upon the matter of readings, permission for which must be secured from John Yarbrough in writing in advance. Inquiries concerning rights should be addressed to John Yarbrough at johnfyarbrough@gmail.com.

John Yarbrough

JOHN YARBROUGH's work has been performed in New York, London, Washington, DC, and elsewhere. His play *Petra* was selected for *The Best American Short Plays 2014–2015* anthology, and *The Rose-Red City* won top prize at the British Theatre Challenge.

··· **production history** ···

Blessed Are the Dead at the Department of Life and Longevity was performed in 2019 in the Long Island City One-Act Play Festival with the following cast:

MRS. YATES, JACQUE TEMPLE

MR. BELASCO, MARCOS GABRIEL SANCHEZ

MR. ELLERBROOK, ANGELO ANGRISANI

Directed by Alex Beck

The play previously received a staged reading in 2019 at the Naked Angels Theater Company in New York City with the following cast:

MRS. YATES, STEPHANIE ANUWE

MR. BELASCO, MARK O'BRIEN

MR. ELLERBROOK, LEX DAEMON

Directed by John Yarbrough

characters

MR. BELASCO, male, thirties/forties, a terminally ill man.

MRS. YATES, female, thirties/forties, a government bureaucrat.

MR. ELLERBROOK, male, fifties, corporate CEO, owner of Mr. Belasco's life.

setting

The Department of Life and Longevity.

note

Throughout the play "blessed" is pronounced with two syllables: *Bless-ed.*

···

[*Lights up on a drab government office. Welcome to the Department of Life and Longevity. MRS. YATES, thirties/forties, in a government-issued, police-state outfit, talks on the phone.*]

MRS. YATES Yes, sir! Death rates on the rise! Stage fours everywhere! Fuckers falling like flies! Oh thank you, sir. Yes. Thank you. I have another call coming in, sir. Thank you. Blessed [*two syllables—pronounced "bless-ed"*] are the dead!

[MR. BELASCO, *thirties/forties, frail, walks in carrying a large accordion-style file folder.*]

MR. BELASCO [*In pain, coughing.*] Hello? Hello?

MRS. YATES [*Answers next call.*] Maggie Yates, deputy assistant to the deputy assistant undersecretary of Life and Longevity. Blessed are the dead! Oh. Mr. Ellerbrook. Hi. Yes. I'm seeing him today. So what's it gonna be? Three hundred thousand is your opening bid? Fuck you!

[*Lights up off to the side.* MR. ELLERBROOK, *fifties, suit and tie, frantic, pacing, is on the phone talking to* MRS. YATES.]

MR. ELLERBROOK Fuck me? Fuck you!

MRS. YATES This is a $1.2 million dollar life we're talking about!

MR. BELASCO Mrs. Yates?

MR. ELLERBROOK Don't con me, Mrs. Yates!

MRS. YATES Con *you?*

MR. ELLERBROOK Nobody screws the Dynamic Technology Conglomerate!

MR. BELASCO Mrs. Yates?

MRS. YATES Look, Belasco will be dead by Labor Day.

MR. ELLERBROOK How the fuck do you know?

MRS. YATES Because it says so in his Life Expectancy Report! You'll get the full payout! He's all alone. He wants some money to die on. Paint. Travel. Finish *Moby Dick*, *Ulysses* or whatever the fuck book dying people read. Buy him out!

MR. ELLERBROOK Now you listen to me sweetheart/

MRS. YATES /I told you to diversify, didn't I? We also offered you two stage-four ovarians, three lepers, and a Lou Gehrig. *And* a hairy cell leukemia. These are the people who are meant to die.

MR. BELASCO Hello? Hello!

MRS. YATES Gotta give me more, Mr. Ellerbrook!

MR. ELLERBROOK When are you putting him on the death futures market?

MRS. YATES In twenty minutes. Pull the trigger now!

MR. ELLERBROOK I'll pull the trigger when I'm goddamn ready!

MRS. YATES Once he's dead you'll double your money. You'll be crapping gold!

[MRS. YATES *slams down the phone.*]

MR. ELLERBROOK Goddammit!

[*Lights down on* MR. ELLERBROOK.]

MR. BELASCO Mrs. Yates!

MRS. YATES Mr. Belasco? You're late! But welcome to the Department of Life and Longevity! Blessed are the dead! I'm Mrs. Yates, deputy assistant to the deputy assistant undersecretary. Shit.

[MRS. YATES, *frustrated, puts on a sock puppet. It mimics everything she says.*]

MRS. YATES [*Continued.*] Welcome to the Department of Life and Longevity! Blessed are the dead! I'm Mrs. Yates, deputy assistant to the deputy assistant undersecretary.

MR. BELASCO [*Re: sock puppet.*] What is that?

MRS. YATES We don't talk directly to the soon-to-be dead. For us here on the front lines it's bad for morale. Please. Sit.

[MR. BELASCO *looks for a chair, but there isn't one. He remains standing.*]

MR. BELASCO I heard you could help my situation.

MRS. YATES Yes?

MR. BELASCO The family next to me told me. Before they all died. My medical bills are killing me! I cashed in my pension! And my 401k! I sold off all my wife's possessions! How does this work, exactly?

MRS. YATES   We make dying worth the effort! We sell your life for about half of what it's worth. You get death cash, as we call it. Then— as you're worth more dead than alive—the sooner you die the more money the buyer gets. How much longer do you have anyway?

MR. BELASCO   Six months. [*Re: sock puppet.*] Does he/she/they/it have to be here?

MRS. YATES   Absolutely! So, no beneficiaries? Widower?

MR. BELASCO   Car accident. My wife was on her way to meet me at goat yoga.

MRS. YATES   Wonderful! Single and widowed men die so much sooner! Oh how I love the actuarial tables! And you're so young! It must be thrilling to die young. Fewer regrets, fewer resentments, more mourners, more deathbed visits. We all should be so lucky!

MR. BELASCO   [*Re: Sock puppet.*] Oh for Hell's glory. Please.

MRS. YATES   Ugh. Fine. Margie, take your three o'clock early.

[*The sock puppet stays on* MRS. YATES's *hand, and reluctantly "sleeps."*]

MRS. YATES   [*Continued.*] I'll sell your life before the end of the day! Shall we have a gander at your files? Let's see. Lab reports, MRI's, angiograms [*anne-geo-grams*], X-Rays. Excellent!

MR. BELASCO   I did my best.

MRS. YATES   Documentation is key. We can't tell investors you're knocking on heaven's door and leave it at that! Dirty sheeting is a one-way ticket to prison. You don't want to die in prison, do you Mr. Belasco? If you do you'll need to go to floor three.

[MRS. YATES *starts to hand back the accordion file folder to* MR. BELASCO.]

MR. BELASCO   No. I'll stay.

[MR. BELASCO *coughs violently. He falls over onto the floor.*]

MRS. YATES   Mr. Belasco! Pace yourself! Don't die on me yet.

MR. BELASCO   Oh, God.

[MR. BELASCO *gets up.*]

MRS. YATES   Low white cell count! Abnormal cells anaplastic! [*Annaplastic.*] Tumor right next to speech center! Inoperable! It's a home run! Unless you're willing to lose your speech.

MR. BELASCO   Well they said/

MRS. YATES   /But it's right next to the anterior cerebral artery! Fabulous! It would have been a terrible thing to have to choose between being dead or being mute, wouldn't it Mr. Belasco? But you won't have to! Thank goodness for small miracles. Doesn't God just have a way of looking out for us?

MR. BELASCO   How exactly is this legal?

MRS. YATES   Everything's legal now! The free market rules!

MR. BELASCO   [*Holding head in pain.*] My head.

MRS. YATES   You people are all the same. So negative these days.

MR. BELASCO   "You people?"

MRS. YATES   Dying people. You think you'd have a little more appreciation.

MR. BELASCO   Coming here was a mistake! Why prolong the inevitable!

[MR. BELASCO *pulls out a gun, puts it to his head. The sock puppet perks up, shaking its head "no."*]

MRS. YATES   You'll be no good to me then! How did you get that in here?

MR. BELASCO   My life has been one long Belasco fiasco! I carry this around everywhere! I put it to my head, in my mouth, under my chin! If only I had the guts to do me in!

MRS. YATES   But you have so much to live for!

MR. BELASCO   I don't!

MRS. YATES But you do! As we say here, "Impending death brings clarity! Happiness like never before! Your big pay day is here!"

[MRS. YATES *gives* MR. BELASCO *a pamphlet. He slowly lowers his gun to his side.*]

MR. BELASCO Really?

MRS. YATES You will become what we call a Super X4372C. Catchy, huh? You want to Super X4372C your life. Once we decide to Super X4372C then we are Super X4372C-ing, and when we are done Super X4372C-ing you are Super X4372C'ed. [*X4372-seed.*] From the noun to the infinitive to the present participle to the past participle. Simple enough?

MR. BELASCO Yes. But/

MRS. YATES You should be happy you are sick! The sicker you are the more you get! Inoperable tumors are like champagne on Christmas morning!

MR. BELASCO But/

[*A call comes in to* MRS. YATES.]

MRS. YATES /Hold on. Dammit.

[MRS. YATES *takes the incoming call. Lights go up on* MR. ELLERBROOK.]

MRS. YATES [*Continued.*] Maggie Yates, deputy assistant/

MR. ELLERBROOK /Four hundred thousand.

MRS. YATES No, Mr. Ellerbrook!

MR. ELLERBROOK Four twenty and you give me first crack at some pulmonary edemas.

MRS. YATES Higher! I'm putting him on the markets in ten minutes.

MR. ELLERBROOK Four twenty-five plus two colorectals.

MRS. YATES Not a chance.

MR. ELLERBROOK Four-fifty and three soft tissue sarcomas.

MRS. YATES Mr. Ellerbrook/

MR. ELLERBROOK /*And* we'll talk measles junk bonds.

MRS. YATES More! Mr. Belasco is dying!

MR. ELLERBROOK Like every other "breathing-last-breath" fuck you've been pushing on me? Everyone you touch lives. How can you live with yourself! I swear to God. Fine. Four-seventy-five/

[MRS. YATES *ends the call.*]

MR. ELLERBROOK [*Continued.*] Goddammit!

[*Lights down on* MR.ELLERBROOK.]

MRS. YATES Mr. Belasco, do you want to die destitute or just sort of destitute? Well? Well!

MR. BELASCO Damn. Fuck. Fine. Sure. Whatever. Okay. I'll do it.

MRS. YATES One more time, with energy.

MR. BELASCO I'll do it. Yes. I'll do it.

MRS. YATES Come on! You're on death's door! Carpe diem!

MR. BELASCO I'll do it! I'll do it! I'll do it to be done with it!

MRS. YATES Excellent! Let's get started!

[MRS. YATES *types on a laptop, the sock puppet jumps.*]

MRS. YATES [*Continued.*] Sorry. Stage four, untreatable, six months to live. Send!

MR. BELASCO Whad'ya just do?

MRS. YATES You're now on the death futures market! This is just preliminary. Later we'll bring in the medical underwriters, sign contracts, blah blah blah. Hopefully the buyer will only want medical exams once a month.

MR. BELASCO Once a month?!

MRS. YATES Could be every week. For the rest of your short life.

MR. BELASCO Why?

MRS. YATES Investors want to keep tabs on their investment. Do a mortality check in. Kick the floorboards, so to speak.

[*The phone rings,* MRS. YATES *answers.*]

MRS. YATES [*Continued.*] Maggie Yates, deputy assistant/

MR. ELLERBROOK /Four-seventy-five and three anals!

MRS. YATES Not enough!

MR. ELLERBROOK And two bile ducts!

MRS. YATES He's on the markets right now. Time to nut up!

MR. ELLERBROOK Four-seventy-five and three early-onset diabetes! No—three cranial fractures and/

[MRS. YATES *slams down the phone.*]

MR. ELLERBROOK [*Continued.*] Goddammit!

MRS. YATES Sorry, Mr. Belasco. Let's see. Ping! There's one.

[*The sock puppet dances with each "ping."*]

MRS. YATES [*Continued.*] Ping! Ping! Ping! Yes! Let's see. Equity Financial of Munich offers four hundred thousand. Lame. Eurasian Energy Solutions—425. The Womens' Investment Club of Highland Park, Texas—450. Cheap bastards. Stop lowballing, people! With your policy we want nothing less than five hundred thousand!

MR. BELASCO Just make it happen. Please!

MRS. YATES Ping! The Royal Bank of China! Five hundred! Wait.

MR. BELASCO What?

MRS. YATES They'll only take you as part of an IDF. American lives aren't worth what they used to be, unfortunately.

MR. BELASCO IDF?

MRS. YATES Imminent Death Fund. With a nun with ovarian cancer in Chicago, a postman with Parkinson's in Montreal, and a retired lounge singer in Rio de Janeiro. Pneumonia-induced fecal vomiting.

MR. BELASCO Holy crap.

MRS. YATES Ping! Bingo! Yes! The Dynamic Technology
Conglomerate of Boise! 550! Fabulous! Mr. Ellerbrook came through!
The Gem State! The Potato State! Esto Perpetua! Birthplace of blue
Astroturf! Hallelujah! Death doesn't get any better than this, Mr.
Belasco!

[*The sock puppet dances in ecstasy.*]

[*The same office, a year later.* MRS. YATES *stands at a table next to* MR. ELLER-
BROOK, *in a suit.* ELLERBROOK, *pacing, frantically goes through* MR. BELAS-
CO'*s files.*]

MR. ELLERBROOK He was supposed to be dead in six months! It's
been a year! No astrocytoma! [*Astro-sigh-toma.*] No goddamn pituitary
tumors! No glioblastoma [*gleo-blast-oma*] blowing away his spinal
cord! There's no good news here! I wanted to leave here with a hard
on for days!

MRS. YATES Mr. Ellerbrook, please!

MR. ELLERBROOK No Li-Fraumeni [*lee-fro-main-ee*] syndrome, no
von Hippel–Lindau disease, no neurofibromatosis [*neuro-fibro-matosis*]
type 1 or neurofibromatosis type 2. He's not hitting his benchmarks!

MRS. YATES He's still a solid investment.

MR. ELLERBROOK Where is this turd curd! Our investments aren't
dying off quick enough! He's one of thousands of failed investments!
We're bleeding! We want these people dead! As you said, these are the
people who are meant to die!

[MR. BELASCO *walks into the office. He looks virtually the same as before.*]

MR. BELASCO Dead?

MRS. YATES Mr. Belasco! Thanks for coming! Blessed are the dead!
Shit.

[MRS. YATES *puts on the sock puppet.*]

MR. ELLERBROOK [*Re: sock puppet.*] What the fuck is it with this place?

MRS. YATES Mr. Belasco! Blessed are the dead! This is Mr. Ellerbrook of the Dynamic Technology Conglomerate. They own you. Because of your recovery, he is considering selling you to the Cottonseed Oil Producers of America.

MR. ELLERBROOK How bloody is your urine now, Belasco! Any puss cascading from your ears? Eyes? Ass? Loss of bladder control? Shareholders must know every time you vomit, cough, and crap!

MR. BELASCO You're not my doctor!

MR. ELLERBROOK You should be seizing all the time now. And it says here your parietal lobe is deteriorating. So are your nipples more sensitive now? Considering your heightened levels of prolactin, are you lactating yet?

MR. BELASCO You're not my doctor!

MR. ELLERBROOK Your doctor's a fraud! Six months to live, three months to live. Oh no! I'm sorry! Now he has a full year to live! Mrs. Yates, can't I just kill him and get my money?

MR. BELASCO They said my tumor flipped.

MR. ELLERBROOK They'll say anything!

MR. BELASCO It could flip back again and I'll get worse. I promise!

MRS. YATES Mr. Ellerbrook, please! He's doing the best he can.

MR. ELLERBROOK Whose side are you on? You don't get paid until I get paid, Yates. And don't you forget that!

MRS. YATES Yes. But/

[MR. BELASCO *coughs violently.*]

MR. ELLERBROOK That's it! Cough away!

MR. BELASCO I just want to die.

MR. ELLERBROOK Yes! Think positive, you goddamn miscreant!

MR. BELASCO Miscreant? Miscreant?

[MR. BELASCO, *struggling, pulls out a gun, puts it to his head.*]

MR. BELASCO [*Continued.*] This time I'm really going to do it, Mrs. Yates!

MRS. YATES No, Mr. Belasco!

[MRS. YATES *tosses aside the sock puppet.*]

MR. ELLERBROOK Yes, Mr. Belasco!

MRS. YATES The sale doesn't cover suicide!

MR. ELLERBROOK No, Mr. Belasco!

MRS. YATES They'll say it's collusion! We'll all go to jail! Well, maybe not me. Mutually-agreed-upon suicide, gross negligent manslaughter, and criminal infringement on bodily sovereignty!

MR. BELASCO A trifecta! [*Sighs.*] But you're right. Today's not the day.

[MR. BELASCO *turns the gun on* MR. ELLERBROOK.]

MR. BELASCO [*Continued.*] How much blood is in your stool today, Corner Office!

MR. ELLERBROOK You don't have the guts to do it. You're weak. You're all weak! Weak weasels, weak pigs, weak worms. Do it!

[MR. ELLERBROOK *puts his mouth around the gun barrel.*]

MR. ELLERBROOK [*Continued.*] [*Muffled, mouth still on barrel.*] Do it! Do it!

MR. BELASCO How much are those annuities going to be worth as worms slide through your eye sockets? How much market leverage will you have as your organs digest themselves?

[MR. ELLERBROOK *takes his mouth off the barrel.*]

MR. ELLERBROOK Coward!

MRS. YATES Stop!

MR. BELASCO [*To* MRS. YATES.] Maybe I'll do you instead!

MRS. YATES No!

MR. ELLERBROOK That's it! Kill her!

[MR. BELASCO *points the gun back and forth between* MRS. YATES *and* MR. ELLERBROOK.]

MR. BELASCO Eenie, meenie, miny, mo, catch a tiger/

MRS. YATES /Please, no! I don't want to die!

MR. BELASCO Don't interrupt me! Eenie, meenie, miny, mo, catch a tiger by his toe. If he hollers make him pay . . .

[MR. BELASCO *holds the gun on* MRS. YATES.]

MRS. YATES What about "fifty dollars every day"?

MR. ELLERBROOK Coward!

[MR. BELASCO *kills* MR. ELLERBROOK.]

MR. BELASCO [*To* MRS. YATES.] So whad'ya say?

MRS. YATES What?

[MR. BELASCO *struggles as he moves closer to* MRS. YATES, *turns the gun on her.*]

MR. BELASCO What was it? The sicker you are the better price you get?

[MR. BELASCO *picks up the puppet, puts it on his hand. It is now on his side.*]

MR. BELASCO [*Continued.*] "A cerebral tumor is like champagne on Christmas morning, Mr. Belasco!" "Blessed are the dead, Mr. Belasco!"

MRS. YATES Mr. Belasco, I beg you!

MR. BELASCO Shut up. I'm the only one handing out death today! Exactly how much is your life worth to you, Mrs. Yates?

MRS. YATES Please, no.

MR. BELASCO Let's go through it. You will be the, what was it? Super X4 something?

MRS. YATES The/

MR. BELASCO   /Fuck it. You are about to Super die. As you Super die you are Super dying, and when you are done Super dying you are Super dead. From the noun to the infinitive to the present participle to the past participle. Simple enough?

MRS. YATES   But/

MR. BELASCO   /How much is your life worth to you!

MRS. YATES   No!

MR. BELASCO   Clock's ticking! Clock's ticking for all of you!

MRS. YATES   Oh, God.

MR. BELASCO   Yes. Oh, God.

[MR. BELASCO *cocks the gun.*]

MR. BELASCO   [*Continued.*] He just has a way of looking out for us. Doesn't He, Mrs. Yates!

[*Lights out.*]

• • •

SEEN

Crystal Skillman

SEEN by Crystal Skillmam. Copyright © 2019 by Crystal Skillman. All rights reserved. Reprinted by permission of the author.

CAUTION/ADVICE: Professionals and amateurs are hereby warned that performance of *SEEN* is subject to a royalty. It is fully protected under the copyright laws of the United States of America, and all of countries covered by the International Copyright Union (including the Dominion of Canada and the rest of the British Commonwealth), and of all countries covered by the Pan-American Copyright Convention and the United States Copyright Convention, the Berne Convention, and all of the countries with which the United States has reciprocal copyright relations. All rights, including professional and amateur stage performing rights, motion picture, recitation, lecturing, public reading, radio broadcasting, television, video or sound picture recording, all other forms of mechanical or electronic reproduction, such as CD-ROM, DVD-ROM, information storage and retrieval systems, and photocopying, and the rights of translation into foreign language are strictly reserved. Particular emphasis is placed upon the matter of readings, permission for which must be secured by the playwright in advance in writing in advance. Inquiries concerning all rights should be addressed to the author. You can reach Crystal Skillman at: crystalskillman@me.com or crystallouiseskillman@gmail.com. Her website is: https://www.crystalskillman.com/.

Crystal Skillman

CRYSTAL SKILLMAN is an award-wining dramatist. She is a NY Innovative Theatre Award winner, an alumni of Youngblood, the WP and Soho Rep Writer/ Director Lab, and an EST member. Plays include NY Times Critics' Pick *Open* (The Tank), *King Kirby* (The Brick), *Geek* (Vampire Cowboys), and *Cut* (Theatre Under St. Marks), as well as *Another Kind of Love* (Chopin Theatre) and *Wild* (Lucille Lortel MCC Reading, IRT). New plays include *Pulp Vérité* (Kilroys List Honorable Mention) and *Rain And Zoe Save The World* (EMOS Prize). She was selected for the Civilians R&D Group to write her new piece, *This Show Is Money* (Music/ Lyrics Gaby Alter). Crystal is the book writer of the musical *Mary And Max* (Composer/Lyricist Bobby Cronin), winner of the MUT Award Critics Prize. *Mary and Max* premiered at Theatre Calgary, and has just had its European Premiere. TV/ Comic Books include: *Eat Fighter* (WebToon), *Adventure Time* (Boom! Studios), and original pilots *Overnight Success* and *Paper Heroes* (Finalist for Big Break and Launch Pad). https://www.crystalskillman.com/.

···production history···

SEEN was first presented on February 1st, 2019, at Marathon Music Works by End Slavery Tennessee. It was directed by Janet Jones, stage management was by R. Preston Perrin, and the assistant stage manager was Jacob Heinz, with Jacqueline Graham as dramaturg. The cast was as follows:

WOMAN, Rebekah Alexander

character

WOMAN

time and place

Now, backwards, and forward.

note

SEEN is a play for one person. The play is written to be performed by a female-identifying actress.

For more about End Slavery Tennessee please visit: https://www.endslaverytn.org/

• • •

[*A light appears. A woman steps into it. She looks up, and at us.*]

WOMAN   When I look in the mirror, there is a light.
Not all gas stations have a light above their mirrors. This one does.

When I look in the mirror, I talk to myself to remind myself I'm there. But when I talk to myself, I pretend I'm talking to my mother. You. You can hear me.

You look different every time.
Here, time goes in any direction.
I don't tell you about where I'm hit, or the parts of my face where I don't feel anymore.

[*She touches her forehead.*]

Here was because the nice woman pretending to be my friend told them first.

That was the first time I tried to run.

What they did feels empty to me, like the word friend.

We're in a city now.

I tell you my age, Nineteen.
Hotel.

There are so many mirrors in so many places.

But there are all sorts of mirrors.

In the fairy tales, a mirror can speak back to you and tell you the things you want. "Fairest of the land." "Bring me back her heart."

The mirror draws you in, because it can see you.
You are seen.
Everyone deserves to be seen.
What people say tells you this.
What people do tells you this.
How people treat you tells you this.

And then you define yourself.
This is you. This is you.
I step outside.
Words.
Seventeen.

[*She imitates Bobby, a pimp, speaking to her:*]

"*You piece of shit. You're worthless. That is you. You see those girls. That's why I brought you here. That's you.*"

I loved Bobby so much since, I don't know. Fourteen? He was the first I loved, after I lived with the husband and wife who found me at the diner. I slept in their bed a whole year.

But I found Bobby. Bobby wasn't like that. He took me out to eat. We went home together. The other girls lived there. But he only had eyes for me. I loved to clean. I loved to cook. Going to the grocery store, I could live there, in those aisles. I'd get anything in a box. I'd follow the instructions, I was really good at it.

He took me to the zoo once. We watched when they feed the baby animals. He held my hand. It was only me. He asked how I was feeling.

You heard this before? Momma?
Yeah, you did.
You did. You'd say, "Baby, baby, it wasn't always like this."

Did you drink to forget me or am I drinking to forget you?

Step outside.

One day I was sleeping and I woke up in a car. Bobby was taking me to someone else. I cried. I cried like you did when it was late. I love him.

I looked outside the window and everything was going by fast.

You remember when we went to Radnor lake, Momma?

The trees. They stood tall.

One of the other girls, she told me later, you cut open the trees later, you count the rings. She learned it in school when she went there. Time goes both ways. Back and forward, you just follow.

You told me about your garden, when you first moved here, before you had me, you had the flowers—the kind hummingbirds come to.

The water was still, and we could see ourselves. I was too young to remember, but parts of me remember, parts of me remember everything. And I made up what I wanted to see.

Your eyes were blue and bright. You stood up straight. You held my hand.

And there was wind that smelled clean, that could rip through your heart.

When the cousins came over, when I was real small, they played a game where we'd hide and we'd find one another.

Why would anyone want to hide?

You don't have to hide for people not to see you. I walk down the street every day and no one sees me.

I know a better game. I look in the windows of all the houses. Do you know them Momma. The houses? You didn't go outside for a long, long time, but where I go. We go past the houses. There are lights in the windows. There are pictures on the walls. Christmas trees or decorations. They are boys and girls inside.

Sometimes it looks beautiful like a shining star. Sometimes it looks the same, but shinier.

But they have lights on inside. Until it's time to go to bed and they turn them off.

But if you go down the road, you see so many lights. Some houses are falling down. Some are built right, but do you ever see the people?

Do you ever look in their eyes and see if they shine back?

Like shining windows?

Do you ever wonder if they can see you?

Step outside.

[*She imitates the judgmental outside world dismissing her.*]

"*Whore.*"
"*Slut.*"
"*You'll never be anything else.*"
"*You want this.*"
"*You deserve to be raped.*"

We don't say that word. But I know what is it. I know it is happening to me, but I don't want to tell you the bad things.

This mirror, I'm holding in my hand. I found it. Broken from the hand mirror Bobby got me. A sliver. It was outside. It must have broken when they dragged me.

[*She imitates her pimp.*]

"You can't talk to anyone outside of this life."

I tried to hide the money, but Kevin found it. What he does to me I don't feel anything but pain, but I don't want to leave.

He said this is what his daddy and his mommy did.
I asked him if he knew what he was doing to me.
When your jaw gets broken, it's like your face is split in two. When you look in the mirror in the club, it's like there's two of you.
You step outside. Up and down in the aisles. You see who you have to see.

[Imitates different pimps/Kevin.]

"You're going to work here for me." "You know I didn't mean to hit you that hard."

"Daddy's sorry."

I jumped from a car once.
Once I hid.
I hid for at least an hour in the backyard.

Twelve. But I looked older.

That was Peter. And his girlfriend.

Step outside.

The eyes of the families on the street, the mothers in the store, the ladies behind counters, the men at the cash registers, the waiters, the attendants, the police.

[The police stating why they won't report what is happening to her.]

"You already work at the club."
"This is what you want."
*"Obviously you made a **choice**."*

Choices are what characters in a fairytale do. They decide. But it was already decided. Where they were born. Their family. Who stayed. Who died. Who hurt. Who sells. Who loses. Who wins. Who is seen.

To be seen, you have to take away the bruises, you can't limp, you have to be young and clean.

You need money. And every time when they give it.

"It's a shame. You should be in school. You should have a home. You should be loved."

They know what they're doing, but they never say "I". You look at me, you pass me, I don't talk this way. I say "Yeah" and look away.

"Poor, dumb, and worthless. Has no value." When a run away from foster care, asks a stranger for a job, they say that is what she becomes. They say that is her story.

But the mirror in front of me now.

It is oak and wood and carved, and it is growing.

Time goes in all directions.

Twenty.

Twenty-one.

Twenty-two.

"I know what you want. A house, a garden, a family. I'm your family, baby. We're your family, baby. Stand in the middle of the circle. You've got to be hurt now. Because you disrespected my friends."

A tree doesn't break. A tree cracks.

OPEN.

[As herself, very young—a wish about her mother.]

"One day she'll treat me different.
One day we'll be a real family."

I love you.

Until all the mirrors are one. One inside the other and the longer you look you are swallowed inside, and there is the light, you are a sliver, there is the growing branches, and the water is still and YOU FALL IN.

Today.

Twenty-three.

Today. Out of my mouth. LOUD.

"I'm here."
And there was one woman, and her eyes were shining like those windows. She looked through her window. And she'd seen me before. So many times. And then all of a sudden. She saw me. And I believe. Someone is coming.

I believe I will see you.

This is you.
This is you.
This is you.
Cut me open, count the years.

I want them back.

Do you see—a light?

• • •

The Bottle

George Sapio

The Bottle by George Sapio. Copyright © 2019 by George Sapio. All rights reserved. Reprinted by permission of the author.

CAUTION/ADVICE: Professionals and amateurs are hereby warned that performance of *The Bottle* is subject to a royalty. It is fully protected under the copyright laws of the United States of America, and all of countries covered by the International Copyright Union (including the Dominion of Canada and the rest of the British Commonwealth), and of all countries covered by the Pan-American Copyright Convention and the United States Copyright Convention, the Berne Convention, and all of the countries with which the United States has reciprocal copyright relations. All rights, including professional and amateur stage performing rights, motion picture, recitation, lecturing, public reading, radio broadcasting, television, video or sound picture recording, all other forms of mechanical or electronic reproduction, such as CD-ROM, DVD-ROM, information storage and retrieval systems, and photocopying, and the rights of translation into foreign language are strictly reserved. Particular emphasis is placed upon the matter of readings, permission for which must be secured by George Sapio in writing in advance. Inquiries concerning rights should be addressed to George Sapio at: sapio@gsapio.com.

George Sapio

GEORGE SAPIO is a playwright/director/producer/dramaturg whose work has been commissioned by the Kitchen Theatre and Actors Workshop of Ithaca. His play *Ghosts* won the 2001 Mildred and Albert Panowski Award; *Oatmeal and a Cigarette* is published by Broadway Play Publishing. He produces and hosts the podcast *Onstage/Offstage*, now in its tenth year, featuring interviews with theatre professionals from around the world. His book *Workshopping the New Play: A Guide for Playwrights, Directors, and Dramaturgs* is published by Applause Books. He was the founder and artistic director of the Ithaca Fringe Festival and is also a photojournalist whose book *Collateral Damage* features his pictures from two trips to Iraq in 2003. Websites: gsapio.com, onstageoffstage.org, workshoppingthenewplay.com.

···production history···

The Bottle was originally produced at the Warner Theatre International Playwrights Festival, Saturday, October 12, 2019:

Director, Katherine Ray

SAGE, Amanda Kim Friedman

MAN, Joshua Newey

characters

MAN, male. No specific age/ethnicity.

SAGE, female. No specific age/ethnicity. She is terminally ill.

setting

Alleyway, coffee shop. A city.

···

1—Alley

[At rise: MAN dashes in, clutching woman's bag. He looks to see if he's being followed, then crouches on ground. MAN opens bag and begins rifling through it. He empties items on the ground, then pauses. His hand dips into the bag and pulls out a bottle filled with dark liquid. He stares at it for a second then opens it and smells it. He grimaces. SAGE explodes onto the stage.]

SAGE Don't drink that!

MAN Back off!

SAGE Be careful with that!

MAN Back *off*!!

SAGE No. Please. Don't. Please. Don't spill it. Please. I need that.

[MAN *sniffs it again.*]

MAN Smells like shit.

SAGE Please. You can have everything else. Everything. Just. Don't. Please give that back.

MAN What is this?

SAGE It's my medicine.

MAN Bullshit.

SAGE I swear! It's my medicine. My life depends on that.

MAN Oh please!

SAGE Asshole!

MAN What!

SAGE Asshole! Stupid asshole!

MAN You don't talk to me like that.

SAGE You're right. I'm sorry. I should address my mugger with more respect. Please. Just let me have that bottle back. You can have everything else.

MAN Are you nuts?

SAGE I need it.

MAN So?

SAGE I need it. I really need it.

MAN What kind of medicine is this?

SAGE It's vitamins.

MAN Lady, I don't know what your problem is, but this is not medicine.

SAGE Yes it is. It is. Please. I'll do anything.

MAN Lady, get out / of my way!!

SAGE My life depends on that!! I have no way of getting another one. Please, please, please. I need it. Please. I'm begging you.

[MAN *picks up her bag, and starts to walk around her. She jumps in his way.*]

MAN Get out of my way or I'm gonna hurt you.

SAGE   I can't.

[SAGE *flings herself at* MAN, *who dodges and tries to run around her. She turns and tries to tackle him. Struggle ends with* SAGE *on her knees grabbing his leg, refusing to let go.*]

MAN   I warned you!

[MAN *grabs her hair; it's a wig, which comes off in his hand. He yells at the sudden surprise and drops the wig, backing away.* SAGE, *quite bald, grabs for the wig and begins to cry in earnest.*]

2—Coffee shop

MAN   My mother had cancer.

SAGE   I'm sorry.

MAN   No insurance neither. [*Beat.*] I didn't have to do this, ya know. It's a favor. [*Beat.*] I felt sorry for you. [*Beat.*] Bald head an' all.

[SAGE *removes her wig.*]

MAN   [*Continued.*] Don't do that. Put that thing back on.

SAGE   Give me my bottle.

MAN   Why? I wanna know what's so special about this bottle. [*He unscrews the cap.*] What kind of medicine is this?

SAGE   Don't. Don't drink that.

MAN   Why not? Why is it so special?

SAGE   It's made specifically for me. It's part of my cancer treatment.

MAN   In this? This is a used soda bottle. Just tell me what this is and I'll give it back.

SAGE   I told you. It's—

MAN   Medicine, yeah. Look. I'm leaving. I'm sorry about your cancer and all, but I got things to do. You get in my way, I'll hit you.

SAGE   No you won't.

MAN Why the hell not?

SAGE I have cancer.

MAN S'what?

SAGE Fine then. You hit me, they'll catch you.

MAN You are just messed up, lady. What's to stop me from walkin' outta here?

SAGE Me. Wrapped around your leg. Screaming that you said you have a gun and tried to rape me. This coffee shop is a cop hangout.

MAN Bullshit. Is not.

SAGE I used to work here. I was the night manager. Believe me, it's protected. They'll take you down first and then ask questions.

[*Beat.*]

MAN Oh man. What is it with this goddamn bottle?

SAGE My business.

MAN Put the wig back on.

SAGE Give me my bottle.

MAN Your head's freakin' me out.

SAGE I apologize. Guess I shouldn't have got cancer.

MAN Why do you want the bottle so bad?

SAGE My business.

MAN I never seen anybody want a bottle so bad except my Uncle Dutch. Used to cry when when we hid his whiskey.

SAGE Okay! Look at me. Look at me. I'm sick. Chemo ain't gonna do it. I don't have that long.

MAN So?

SAGE So why would I want that bottle?

MAN How should I know?

SAGE Think, Tesla. Does it look like I have any decent insurance? The health care I have doesn't cover "pre-existing conditions," which is what this was determined to be. The mountain of red tape and paperwork I have to go through will outlast me. Literally.

MAN Jesus Christ. So what kind of medicine comes in a soda bottle?

SAGE The kind you make yourself.

MAN Oh. I get it. This is your painkiller. Jesus.

SAGE Brilliant. Top of your class, you are.

MAN I wanna try it.

SAGE No!

[MAN *opens caps, takes a small sip, grimaces, then smacks lips, considering.*]

MAN Doesn't taste too bad, actually. Kinda sweet.

SAGE Please. Believe me. You don't want to drink any more of that. Now I'm not begging, I'm warning. Just give me the bottle and I'll tell you why I really need it. *And* I'll put the wig back on.

[MAN *seals the bottle and passes it to* SAGE.]

MAN Happy?

[SAGE *puts her wig back on.*]

SAGE Yes. It's my suicide cocktail.

MAN You were sittin' in a Greenwich Village playhouse. Watching some awful piece of shit. With a suicide cocktail in your bag.

SAGE Which you stole.

MAN Well, yeah. You know how easy it is to take shit from people when they're distracted?

SAGE You steal from theatregoers?

MAN With these prices, the people that go to theatre, they have money. It's an easy score if you can get it. Wallets, purses.

SAGE That's not bad, actually.

MAN   You weren't holding on to your bag. I took it.

SAGE   And I noticed.

MAN   Yeah. So. Again. What's with the suicide cocktail?

SAGE   I have drugs to keep me going for a short while, then it's all going to start crashing down. Everything from my breathing to my stool to my . . .

MAN   I get it.

SAGE   It's either me in a hospital, which won't happen in any way, shape, or form because my mandated pay-up-or-we-fine-you insurance won't cover it, thank you US corporate government. Or me taking the fast way out.

MAN   Ferchrissakes.

SAGE   Yeah. But you don't know how I'm going to do it.

MAN   Ain't too many choices. Drink. Drink. Or drink.

SAGE   That's not what I mean. It's what I do right before that matters.

MAN   Like what?

SAGE   I'm going to make the world a slightly better place.

MAN   Yeah, good luck with that.

SAGE   You found me tonight in that theatre, correct?

MAN   Uh-huh. By the way, that play sucked. Really sucked. You keep seeing crap like that, that'll make you drink that thing . . .

[SAGE *grins*.]

MAN   No. Nooooo!

SAGE   Yes.

MAN   You're gonna . . . ? You're gonna *take them with you*?

SAGE   What?

MAN   You were gonna take those actors with you??

SAGE Are you out of your mind? *No.*

MAN Then what? I don't get it.

SAGE What I'm planning to do is find the worst show imaginable.

MAN Well, that piece of shit tonight sure qualifies. Am I really supposed to believe that chick had a seagull in her . . . you know.

SAGE In her what?

MAN Seriously. Don't play games. What kind of sick mind has a woman hide a bird . . . never mind.

SAGE Pfft. You'd be amazed at what's considered "art." "Avant-garde." "Experimental." If it's shocking *and* defies reasonable explanation, then it's considered "groundbreaking."

MAN Okay, okay. So if you ain't gonna make the actors drink it, then what?

SAGE I was going to . . . I *am* going to . . . find the worst show I can. A play. Performance art. Whatever. Poetry slam if I get really desperate. And when I'm convinced that it's something that the world should be excused—no, *saved*—from, then I will stand up and start screaming at the performers to stop for godsakes stop, to please end this utterly worthless disaster, to just stop it and I can't take it anymore and that's when I bring out the bottle and kill myself.

[*Long beat.*]

MAN Oh my god.

SAGE What do you think?

MAN I have heard some unbelievable shit in my time.

SAGE Didn't I tell you?

MAN You're gonna scar them people for life.

SAGE Better than them inflicting their self-indulgent artistic crap on an unsuspecting public.

MAN That is just *cold.*

SAGE Oh, please.

MAN No. Seriously. That's wrong.

SAGE Wait. What? You're telling me *I*'m wrong? *You* steal from people!

MAN I steal from people who can afford it. I don't steal from people who can't.

SAGE What does that mean? I should only commit suicide in front of people who can afford decent counseling?

MAN If I'd known you were gonna do that I never would have given you the bottle back.

SAGE You have a very weird set of ethics.

MAN Why would you do something that twisted? Cuz that is twisted.

SAGE I have my reasons.

MAN What reasons?

SAGE I have my reasons.

MAN No. You tell me.

SAGE Why?

MAN Because . . . you owe me an explanation.

SAGE I don't owe you anything.

MAN Then I would like an explanation. Come on. You can't just say I'm gonna commit suicide by poison and scar an entire theatre company and its audience for life without telling me why. This is not something private like jumping off a bridge or driving your car into a tree. This is *public*. Particular. This is specific. This is the product of a seriously warped mentality that took the time to concoct a truly diabolical particularly warped public incident.

SAGE That's the nicest compliment I've gotten all week. Okay. What the hell. Let's just posit that it will balance out the karma. My ex-husband is a playwright. He wrote all this high-falutin horse shit about shallow, self-absorbed yuppies having midlife crises, wallowing in affairs, and doing stupid things to each other out of selfishness and stupidity. When he wasn't doing that he was creating these ephemeral psychoscapes—those are his words—of movement and sound that made no sense whatsoever.

MAN   Holy shit. A real loser.

SAGE   He won four Obies.

MAN   This is not a good world.

SAGE   I finally had enough of him one year and we divorced. I lost my job two years later because of cutbacks and there went my benefits. My new job—if you can call it that—provides no insurance and now I'm on the public lottery. In three months I went from a beautiful apartment on 85th and First to a shelter and outpatient clinic on Grand St.

MAN   The ex don't help? I mean, you guys were married. That's gotta mean something.

SAGE   Wouldn't even take my phone calls.

MAN   This is not a good world.

SAGE   So I looked at what lay ahead, and the choices were disturbingly few. I didn't want to slowly waste away, in great pain and not sure I could even get morphine. I decided that I will pick the time when I want to go. That's my right and my choice. Nobody's going to tell me how and when. This is my life; this will be my death.

MAN   Yeah. Good for you.

SAGE   So you're not going to tell me I don't have the right to end my life prematurely? That it's a sin? That it's morally reprehensible?

MAN   Lady, I steal purses. I sell pot. I wipe windshields when there ain't nothin' else. Your life is your business. Your body is your business. You ain't getting' a lecture on morality from me.

SAGE   So since I decided to go my way, I had to decide what my way was. I was sitting in the library watching cat videos when the woman next to me was reading the news online and there was an article about assisted suicide. A woman took her own way out with a cocktail of sedatives. I figure the universe was helping me out. That was part one. Part two was determining the ingredients because I want to go peacefully. Some of them were hard to get. I had to pay big-time for two of the things in this bottle.

MAN   Therefore your panic about getting the bottle back.

SAGE   Exactly. The next bit was where and when. I had the choice, understand?

MAN   Helluva decision. Why bad theatre? Wait . . . the ex.

SAGE   Precisely. I have spent so much time looking at really awful, self-indulgent crap theatre that I decided that I would give something back. Reviews might come out and say this is awful, that's bad, but it doesn't really do anything to stop the flow of what I call script-arhea, and save the unsuspecting public. So I decided my gesture might.

MAN   Lady, you are somethin' else. So did I stop you from killin' yourself today?

SAGE   No. I'm not ready yet.

MAN   Cuz that would have been the perfect show to do it at. That was awful.

SAGE   I know. And unfortunately it closes tomorrow. If it was supposed to run for another month I'd be golden.

MAN   That's what you're thinking of? A month?

SAGE   Look. In every case I've researched where a doctor says, "You have X months to live," they've been wrong by approximately thirty-six percent. They overestimate.

MAN   How do you know this?

SAGE   My uncle Dave was told he had eight months. He went in five.

MAN   Poor Dave.

SAGE   Yeah. I liked him.

MAN   Cancer?

SAGE Well, sort of.

MAN Sort of?

SAGE He had cancer, yes. But what actually killed him was a heart attack. The paramedics had to pry the bacon strips out of his hand.

MAN Who knew?

SAGE My cousin Dakota was told she had a year. Went in four months.

MAN Bacon?

SAGE Hit by a bus.

MAN Come on. Those ain't valid.

SAGE My mom. Given three months. Went in one.

MAN Eating bacon on a bus?

SAGE Advanced stomach cancer. So much for doctors' estimations.

MAN So you have no chance?

SAGE Nope. Done deal. So I figured I'd go when it got bad enough. It may be selfish, but I have always done things my way, and I will most certainly not stop doing them my way now.

MAN Good luck with that.

SAGE If I had good luck I wouldn't be dying of cancer.

MAN I read somewhere that more and more people are dying of that. Not just that we're hearing about it more, but that actually more people are gettin' it. That all the stuff in our food that ain't right but been okayed by the EPA is what's killin' us.

SAGE Microwaves.

MAN Wifi.

SAGE Shit in the water. Companies dump their toxic effluent everywhere. Nobody stops them.

MAN Anyway. I'm sorry for you. It's a rough deal.

SAGE   You get philosophical about this. Like life is finite. That everybody will go, sooner or later. Some way too soon. Others stay much too long. It's okay. I mean it's not really. But knowing what's what, I'm okay with it. You hate my plan.

MAN   You kiddin'? I fucking love it.

SAGE   Thanks.

MAN   What's yer name?

SAGE   Sage.

MAN   I'm sorry, Sage.

SAGE   Thank you for returning my bottle.

MAN   You're welcome. [*Stands.*] I guess I'd better move on. Good luck to ya.

SAGE   Sit. I have a better idea.

MAN   What?

SAGE   You like the takings at theatres?

MAN   Pretty good most nights.

SAGE   We partner up. I can be a beard for your activities, provide legit cover, so to speak.

MAN   In trade for?

SAGE   I wouldn't mind a theatre buddy.

MAN   You want me to go see lousy theatre with you?

SAGE   Broadway. Off-Broadway. Better venues have more well-heeled patrons. We get ourselves dressed up a bit better and we hit the market.

MAN   I ain't gonna help you kill yourself.

SAGE   Deal.

MAN   Or watch. Or be any kind of a party to it.

SAGE   Let's find a newspaper.

3—Three weeks later

[MAN *reading paper.* SAGE, *noticeably less energetic, reads with him.*]

MAN   This one. "*The Gibbets of Judgment.* A hilarious, rollicking revue of song and dance based on the legendary tragedy of Arthur Miller's *The Crucible.*"

SAGE   Ewww. Put it on the list.

MAN   Mmmmm . . . maybe . . . ?

SAGE   "*So What If I Married My High School Math Teacher?* Sock puppets tell the engrossing story of a young girl on the brink of womanhood . . . Blah, blah, blah . . .

MAN   It's been done. This one. *Of Mice and Menopause.*

SAGE   Certainly rates at the top of the icky scale, but I'm still running with *The Crucible* knockoff.

MAN   *Idaho Housewives in Prison.*

SAGE   No.

MAN   *Kinky Sex, Alcoholism, Six Kinds of Venereal Disease, Lobbyists, and Transgender Shenanigans: My Rise to the Top of the Political Food Chain By an Anonymous Retired Hooker Turned Congress Member.*

SAGE   That's the title?

MAN   Make a helluva marquee. You know if we don't go for the Arthur Miller it might be time for the emergency poetry slam.

SAGE   Keep looking. I'm not committing suicide at a poetry slam. I deserve better than that.

MAN   Just sayin'.

SAGE   Here. This one.

[MAN *reads.*]

MAN   Wow.

SAGE   Right?

MAN You sure?

SAGE Yes. This has to be it.

MAN [*Looks closely.*] Jeezus. You may need to share that bottle.

4—Later That Night

[MAN *hobbles onstage, carrying* SAGE.]

MAN What the hell??? You told me you were gonna drink that yourself! You ain't supposed to jump on stage and attack the *actor*! You lied to me!

SAGE I didn't mean to.

MAN You didn't mean to? What? You made a mistake? The actors are the ones on the stage, and you are in the audience. It's a simple thing to not fuck up!

SAGE I'm sorry.

MAN Anyway, I think we're safe. Nobody followed us. I thought you were ready. You took out the bottle and . . .

SAGE You stayed. And held my hand. Thank you.

MAN Hey. I've grown attached to you. Been three weeks already. You're okay.

SAGE You aren't a bad guy either. Thank you.

MAN So what happened back there? I mean, that was unbelievably awful. What was that piece of shit called?

SAGE "*Man-Gina.*"

MAN Omigod. [*Dramatic voice.*] "Greg Sampson awoke one dark, cold, apocalyptic morning to find his nature-bestowed manliness had been replaced with that glorious chamber of miracles, a vagina."

SAGE [*Bass voice.*] "Omigod. I have a vagina!"

MAN And that fuckin' chorus: "Hoo-HAHHH!"

TOGETHER "Hoo-HAAHHH! Hoo-HAAAHHHH!"

MAN   What the hell kinda music was that?

SAGE   A didgeridoo.

MAN   A what?

SAGE   Didgeridoo. It's a long tube they use in Australia.

MAN   Yeaahhh. I got nothing for that.

SAGE   Probably best.

MAN   How you doing? I'm sorry I couldn't carry you all that way.

SAGE   Ahhh. You know? I think . . . I'm not going to go anywhere again. It took everything I had just to go to that play. I'm just weaker every day. I blew my shot back there.

MAN   Why did you attack that guy? You were supposed to drink it yourself.

SAGE   Ah. Well, that. That was my ex-husband.

MAN   That guy? Was your ex? Mr. Omigod-I-have-a-vagina?

SAGE   In the lady-flesh.

MAN   No wonder you're angry.

SAGE   Four Obies. Four.

MAN   This is not a good world. Hey. Listen. We can go back tomorrow.

SAGE   No.

MAN   I'll get you there. I'll carry you if I have to.

SAGE   No.

MAN   One day. This would be perfect. This would be the thing. The thing!

SAGE   No.

MAN   Look. Instead of attacking him next time, just wait and do it at the same time. Right when he has his "joyous life-affirming orgasm" and the blood starts leaking out of his crotch. And he yells "I'm now a woman! I'm now a woman! Hear me roar!" Come on!

SAGE No.

MAN Okay.

[MAN *adjusts himself to sit on the ground against the wall. He pulls* SAGE *onto his lap, holds her. They stay like this for a bit.*]

SAGE Thank you.

MAN You're welcome.

SAGE Strange. It's so quiet here. No noise at all. Kind of like the city stopped out there. What will you do now? Keep stealing from theatre patrons? Sell pot?

MAN Probably. Maybe I'll become a theatre critic. We could use a new John Simon.

SAGE You'd be perfect.

[SAGE *pulls the bottle from her bag, opens it.*]

SAGE Here's looking at you, kid.

[*Drinks. Settles back into* MAN's *arms. He takes bottle from her hand, seals it. Sets it aside. Holds her until she is still.*]

MAN "And flights of angels sing thee to thy rest."

[*Kisses her forehead. After a bit he rises. He carries her offstage into the noisy city.*]

• • •

Saving Grace

Bara Swain

Saving Grace by Bara Swain. Copyright © 2019 by Bara Swain. All rights reserved. Reprinted by permission of the author.

CAUTION/ADVICE: Professionals and amateurs are hereby warned that performance of *Saving Grace* is subject to a royalty. It is fully protected under the copyright laws of the United States of America, and all of countries covered by the International Copyright Union (including the Dominion of Canada and the rest of the British Commonwealth), and of all countries covered by the Pan-American Copyright Convention and the United States Copyright Convention, the Berne Convention, and all of the countries with which the United States has reciprocal copyright relations. All rights, including professional and amateur stage performing rights, motion picture, recitation, lecturing, public reading, radio broadcasting, television, video or sound picture recording, all other forms of mechanical or electronic reproduction, such as CD-ROM, DVD-ROM, information storage and retrieval systems, and photocopying, and the rights of translation into foreign language are strictly reserved. Particular emphasis is placed upon the matter of readings, permission for which must be secured by Bara Swain in writing in advance. Inquiries concerning rights should be addressed to Bara Swain at: bcswain4@aol.com.

Bara Swain

BARA SWAIN's plays have been staged in 125+ venues in 25 states and abroad. NYC theatres include Urban Stages, Abingdon, Barrow Group, Symphony Space, Sam French, NY Madness, Westside Theatre, Artistic New Directions, and T.A.R.T.E. Other venues include NJ Rep Theatre (NJ), Open Fist (CA), Theatre-Works (TN), Lyric Theatre (FL), Old Opera House (WV), Potluck Productions (MO), OnStage Atlanta (GA), Birdhouse Theatre (GA), and Warner Theatre (CT). Recent: *Turn! Turn! Turn!* (Tom Mann Theatre, Sydney), *Responsible* (The Junction, Dubai), *Pandemonium* (Open Fist Theatre, LA), *The Wonder of You* (Barn Theatre, NJ and FAB @ Barrow Group, NYC), *Choose* (Theatre Workshop of Owensboro, KY), *Yearning for Peace* (Articulate Theatre, NYC). Recent awards: Standing Ovation Award for *I Love Lucy* and *Can You Hear Me Now?* and City Theatre 2019 National Award Finalist for Short Playwriting for *Extraordinary* (FL). Bara serves as the Creative Consultant at Urban Stages. www.BaraSwain.com.

··· production history ···

Saving Grace was produced by Hand to Mouth Players in Montrose, New York in August 2018. The production was directed by Frank Rakas and featured the following cast:

GRACE, Jacqueline Smith

DOROTHY, Anne Rodgers Pearl

characters

GRACE, mid-twenties to early thirties, free-spirited, caring, jack of all trades, independent, underemployed.

DOROTHY, her mother. Fifties to sixties, energetic, opinionated, personable.

time

Midday, the present.

setting

Small one-room studio apartment, East Village, NY.

• • •

[*At rise:* GRACE *is sitting at the table in front of her laptop, multitasking. She is on her cell phone and, simultaneously, balancing a tennis racket on her forefinger. The racket falls to the floor. She tries again. The racquet falls again.*]

GRACE   [*Impatiently.*] . . . I couldn't pick up my phone because I'm working on my curriculum vitae. [*Raising her voice.*] A resume, Mom! For a job query! . . . Well, if I sound impatient, it's because I left my phone charger at Starbucks and I have to babysit at 3:30. [*The racket falls again. When* GRACE *picks it up, She finds a lifesaver on the floor, dusts it off, and pops it into her mouth.*] . . . Ma! Mom! Mother!! I didn't say that I'm not concerned about Uncle Lenny. It's just that I'm also concerned about paying my rent . . . I'm not mumbling. I'm eating lunch, that's all . . . Well, thank you. I'm sorry, too. [*Patiently.*] Now why don't you start over again from "It's not a heart attack." . . . Right,

I got that part . . . So Uncle Lenny's blood culture came back positive for a bacterial infection . . . Uh huh. And that's good or bad? . . . Fungal is bad. Streptococcus is good. So now what? . . . I can't understand you, Mom. Just take a deep breath and speak slower and louder . . . And Uncle Lenny was just sent down for a—what kind of echocardiogram? [*Plugging her ear.*] . . . What?

DOROTHY [*Offstage.*] A TRANSESOPHAGEAL ECHOCARDIOGRAM.

GRACE Why?

DOROTHY [*Offstage.*] THE TRANSESOPHAGEAL ECHOCARDIOGRAM WILL GIVE THEM A BETTER LOOK AT THE INFECTED TISSUE AROUND HIS HEART!

[GRACE *looks up from her cell phone and listens. She returns to the cell.*]

GRACE Mom, where are you?

DOROTHY [*Offstage.*] I'M AT THE DOOR!

GRACE What're you doing in Manhattan?

[GRACE *stares at her laptop. Then, frantically, she begins turning her papers over, tossing some into the garbage, and closing out her document.*]

DOROTHY [*Offstage.*] UNCLE LENNY WAS MEETING A DATE AT THE HOLOCAUST MUSEUM WHEN THE CHEST PAIN STARTED. HER BOSOM IS LARGER THAN SUFFOLK COUNTY *AND* NASSAU COUNTY. ALL THREE OF THEM WENT HOME. OPEN THE DOOR, GRACE!

GRACE I'M COMING!

DOROTHY [*Offstage.*] YOUR INTERCOM IS BROKEN BUT A YOUNG MAN WITH HOLES IN HIS FACE LET ME IN. YOUR MAILBOX IS BROKEN, TOO.

[GRACE *takes another glance around the room, then opens the door. DOROTHY enters, carrying a large tote bag. She walks right past GRACE and drops bag on chair.*]

DOROTHY I'm going to join a bereavement group.

GRACE What!?

DOROTHY A bereavement group. A group for widows and widowers. They talk. They grieve. They date. They're available. Your uncle's last girlfriend taught him kickboxing, can you imagine? He said that grabbling is better than foreplay.

GRACE [*Correcting her.*]—Grappling.

DOROTHY And she did his laundry twice a week, too. With eco-friendly starch.

GRACE But, Ma. Mom! MOTHER! You're not widowed.

DOROTHY Your father lives in Florida. What's the difference? [*Collapsing into a chair.*] Oh, Gracie, I'm not good at these things.

GRACE [*Gently.*] You've been divorced for seven years, Ma.

DOROTHY Get me an aspirin.

GRACE And Dad was open to a reconciliation.

[DOROTHY *bolts upright. She outstretches her hands, palms up.*]

DOROTHY [*Lowers left hand.*] Boca Raton. [*Raises right hand.*] Huntington. [*Lowers further.*] Boca Raton. [*Raises higher.*] Huntington. [*Lower.*] Boca Raton. [*Higher.*] Huntington. [*She lowers her hands.*] Grandma Lillian always said, "Never move somewhere that isn't close to a hospital." Your father didn't give me a real choice.

GRACE There are hospitals in Boca Raton.

DOROTHY Do you know the quickest way to find a doctor in Florida? [*She answers.*] Go to the airport.

GRACE I don't get it.

DOROTHY And that's one less thing for you to worry about, Gracie. Beth Israel is only ten blocks away! When I was your age, I walked to Huntington Hospital to give birth to your sister. Thank God Long Island is flat. Even flatter than Aunt Julie before she went from cherries to grapefruit.

GRACE It's called a breast augmentation, Mom. Do you need one aspirin or two.

DOROTHY I need a facelift. What do you call that?

GRACE A facelift. [*Hands her the aspirin.*] Can I get you some water?

DOROTHY No, but you can serve me some lunch. [*She looks around.*] Where's your lunch?

[GRACE *opens her mouth wide, and sticks out her tongue, revealing the lifesaver.*]

DOROTHY Oh, for God's sake. Did you eat anything today? [GRACE *sticks out her tongue again.*] Then you can share a quarter of a corned beef sandwich with me. And half a pickle, courtesy of your uncle's buxom girlfriend.

GRACE I don't get it.

DOROTHY WHY DOESN'T ANYONE UNDERSTAND ME? [*Pouting.*] Now I've lost my appetite.

GRACE There's no . . . look at me, Ma. There's no logical progression.

DOROTHY Well, la-de-da. There's no mustard, either. End of discussion.

[*Silence.* DOROTHY *sulks.*]

GRACE [*Reasonably.*] Don't be like this. I'm not a mind reader. Sometimes you talk in riddles, you know that? Your thoughts are nonsequential, Ma. [*Patiently explaining.*] What that means is—

[DOROTHY *raises her hand.*]

DOROTHY You want a sequence? I'll give you a sequence: Harry Potter, Star Trek, Rocky . . .

DOROTHY . . . Superman, Fifty Shades of Grey. "What has no beginning, middle or end?

A doughnut." "At what time of day was Adam created? A little before Eve."

GRACE You're upset, Ma. Don't be mad at me. I'm not the enemy.

Please don't work yourself up like this.

GRACE It's called a transference, Ma.

DOROTHY I'm not listening.

GRACE You're not mad at me. You're upset that Uncle Lenny is sick, and Dad is—I don't know what part of the equation Dad is. [*Pulling at straws.*] Are you . . . having regrets? Now?

DOROTHY Sure, I have regrets. I regret that I didn't divorce him sooner. *You* were the saving grace in our marriage, Gracie. If I didn't have you, I would've sent him packing when he had his gall bladder surgery. Also at Huntington Hospital.

DOROTHY I could walk there! **GRACE** [*Mumbling.*] You could walk there, right.

DOROTHY [*Energized.*] NUMBER ONE: he hit on the head nurse. And all I'm going to say is that it involved a thermometer, several times. Number two: I'm not good with illness. It's so . . . unpleasant. I don't even like cutting my toenails, Gracie. It sets off my gag reflex watching those bits of . . . bits of —

GRACE The nail plate? Keratin?

DOROTHY STOP IT! STOP IT! MY TURKEY BACON IS REPEATING. Please, let's change the subject! [*Changing her tone completely.*] So, how's your writing?

[GRACE *stares at her blankly. She is caught off guard by the rapid shift in tone and subject.* DOROTHY *smiles serenely.*]

DOROTHY Did you hear from any graduate school programs?

GRACE I don't want to talk about it.

DOROTHY Oh! I met with my accountant—he always smells like garlic knots, Gracie—and he said I can get a home equity loan to pay for your tuition—

GRACE You won't need to, Ma!

DOROTHY —Or I could pawn my wedding ring. Your father asked for it back, can you imagine? I said, "Sure, Larry. *You* give me back my virginity and I'll give you back my three-stone ten carat diamond ring with a cluster setting."

GRACE —Mom. Mom! MOTHER! Not now.

DOROTHY [*Raising her hand.*] I'm just saying! I'm just saying!

[GRACE *ignores her. Silence.* DOROTHY *looks around the apartment and spies the tennis racket.*]

Well, I'm glad to see that you're making time for some extracurricular activities! Uncle Lenny still has a membership at the Cold Spring Country Club. You should come out and stay with me next weekend, Gracie, and I'll reserve you an alley.

GRACE A court. Tennis is played on a court.

DOROTHY I know! Maybe I'll take a car service in tomorrow, visit your uncle, and you can come home with me for some baked halibut and a movie. [*Temptingly.*] I've got "On Demand." It doesn't listen to me, but nobody does.

GRACE I have to work, you know that. I can run over to Beth Israel and see Uncle Lenny before my shift tomorrow.

DOROTHY Fine fine fine. [*After a moment.*] You know . . . there are plenty of Starbucks on Long Island.

GRACE Oh, so I can have a Bean Specialist Career in Huntington? That's what you tell everyone, don't you?

DOROTHY [*Shrugs.*] Not exactly.

GRACE Then say what you mean, Mom. For once in your life, say what you mean.

DOROTHY I didn't mean anything by it! Okay, so maybe I did. Maybe it's time you moved back home. Not forever! Just for a while, Gracie. Until you figure out what to do next. You won't have to pay rent, you can write your stories, you can eat anything in my refrigerator except for my Skinny Cow vanilla and caramel ice cream cones. And you can play tennis!

GRACE I DON'T KNOW HOW TO PLAY TENNIS!

[GRACE *looks away. She is, indeed, on the verge of tears.* DOROTHY *sees her distress.*]

DOROTHY   Of course you do, honey. You and your father played every summer, over on Oakwood Road. Behind Huntington High School, remember? Every weekend!—until you got your friend.

[GRACE *swings around and stares at her.*]

DOROTHY   [*Lowers her voice.*] Your period.

GRACE   I don't play well, Ma! I don't do anything well.

DOROTHY   Now who's being ridiculous.

GRACE   I've been working on my resume for two hours, two hours! —and I can't think of a single special skill to write down. [*Miserably.*] Do you know what I do with my tennis racket? I use it to drain macaroni.

DOROTHY   [*In awe.*] You've always been so creative, Gracie.

GRACE   [*Exasperated.*] Ohhhhhh!

DOROTHY   That's what I tell everyone. Look at me, sweetheart. Look at me.

[*Reluctantly,* GRACE *looks at her mother.*]

DOROTHY   You're a writer, Gracie! That's what I tell everyone. I say—exactly this, I say, "My youngest daughter Grace is kind and hardworking and thoughtful.

GRACE   Those are attributes, not skills.

DOROTHY   [*Ignoring her.*] And independent and stubborn. Sometimes she can be too serious but that's because she's always been such a responsible girl. And now she's grown into a capable young woman and the most talented writer that I've ever had the privilege to know! . . . and even read. [*Motioning to her.*] Come here, honey. Don't you know how special you are?

GRACE   I'm not sitting on your lap, if that's what you're trying to make me do.

DOROTHY I wouldn't try to make you do anything you didn't want to do.

GRACE Good.

DOROTHY Well . . . [*She shrugs.*] . . . almost anything.

GRACE Ma-a-a-a? Say what you mean. I dare you.

DOROTHY [*Shaking head.*] I'm not good at these things.

GRACE What things.

DOROTHY Thing, things! I don't have your skills, Gracie. I don't know how to express myself the way you do, or string words together the way you do. I can't write—

GRACE —Yes you can.

DOROTHY Sure, if you count grocery lists and heartfelt thank you notes! I can't balance my checkbook or watch a movie with subtitles. I'd rather change my hair color than a light bulb, and I can't read a newspaper that doesn't carry a daily horoscope.

GRACE [*Softly.*]—Mom.

DOROTHY I failed at penmanship, my written driver's test, and I failed at my marriage. And then there's my vocabulary. Do you know the biggest word I use on a daily basis? "Kardashian."

GRACE You're selling yourself short. You've got plenty of skills!

DOROTHY Right, I can consistently make babies laugh! I'll share pizza with any kind of topping except anchovies, and I'm always up for dessert. I don't know how to pick up my voicemail or keep my cactus alive, and I certainly know that I can't take care of Uncle Lenny by myself. Oh, Gracie, please come home. Just for a little while. Will you think about it?

GRACE Yes.

DOROTHY I mean, really think about it? It's a win-win situation.

GRACE I said, yes.

DOROTHY   How long will you have to think about it, Gracie? Uncle Lenny will probably be discharged on Friday.

GRACE   Yes! I'll come home for awhile.

DOROTHY   Thank you, thank you, thank you. Mwah!Mwah! Mwah!

GRACE   I can reassess my plans and help you take care of him. Like you took special care of me, Mom. You're a good mother.

DOROTHY   I didn't hear you. Can you repeat that, please?

GRACE   [*Sighs.*] I said, you're a good mother.

DOROTHY   Yes, I am! [*Kisses her own shoulder.*] I am a good mother! Thank you, sweetheart, thank you. You are the best daughter. Numero uno! And I am a good mother. Maybe even a great mother!

GRACE   Don't push it, Ma.

DOROTHY   Oh, I am so relieved. I am so relieved! And I need to use your bathroom. [*After a moment.*] Honey, what's a metaphor?— because I think I just used one.

GRACE   I don't get it.

DOROTHY   [*Pleased.*] I'm relieved. I have to relieve myself.

GRACE   It's called a homonym, Ma.

DOROTHY   I LOVE homonyms! And I love you. Do you have a coupla' plates? And a bathroom?

GRACE   You know where the bathroom is, and I've got paper plates, but I don't have any food in the fridge.

[DOROTHY *exits quickly, calling out behind her.*]

DOROTHY   LOOK IN MY BAG. I'VE GOT A QUARTER OF A LEFTOVER CORNED BEEF SANDWICH FROM KATZ'S DELI. [*Offstage.*] YOUR UNCLE LENNY WAS HAVING LUNCH THERE WHEN HIS DATE CALLED 911. THANK GOD!

GRACE UNCLE LENNY WILL BE FINE.

DOROTHY [*Offstage.*] OTHERWISE HE'D BE AT NEW YORK
DOWNTOWN HOSPITAL. THIS IS SO MUCH MORE
CONVENIENT! ONLY THERE'S NO MUSTARD ON IT. DO
YOU HAVE MUSTARD?

GRACE I HAVE MUSTARD PACKETS.

DOROTHY [*Offstage.*] OH, AND THERE'S A PACKET FOR YOU,
TOO! IT'S IN MY BAG! YOU KNOW, YOU SHOULD ASK
THE SUPER TO FIX YOUR MAILBOX, GRACIE! WHO DO
YOU KNOW FROM SOUTH AMERICA!

[GRACE *takes out the sandwich and the large package.*]

DOROTHY [*Offstage.*] THE RETURN ADDRESS IS FROM SOUTH
AMERICA!

[GRACE *looks at the package. She turns it over several times. Then she rips it open,
removes the letter and reads. Silence.*]

GRACE MOM! IT'S FROM COLUMBIA!

DOROTHY [*Offstage.*] THAT'S MY FAVORITE COFFEE! WHO DO
YOU KNOW FROM COLOMBIA?! MY HOUSEKEEPER IS
FROM MEXICO. I'VE BEEN PICKING UP A LITTLE
SPANISH. BUENOS DIAS! UN MOMENTO! MUCHAS
GRACIAS!

[DOROTHY *reenters.*]

DOROTHY HOLA!

GRACE [*Hushed.*] I got in, Mom. I got into the writing program at
Columbia.

[DOROTHY'*s face drops.*]

DOROTHY Oh. Umm . . . *salud.*

GRACE Columbia <u>University</u>. It's on 116th Street. Near Columbia
Presbyterian Hospital. Oh, my God, I don't believe it. I don't believe
it! Do you believe it?

[GRACE *looks at her mother expectantly.* DOROTHY *is brimming with pride.*]

DOROTHY I believe that you can do anything you want to do, Gracie.

GRACE Then I'm going to do this.

[GRACE *crosses to her mother and sits on her lap. She wraps her arms around* DOROTHY'*s neck.* DOROTHY *kisses her daughter on top of the head several times.* GRACE *looks up.*]

GRACE Are you proud of me, Ma?

DOROTHY I'm always proud of you, sweetheart.

GRACE Can I call Uncle Lenny?

DOROTHY Why don't you tell him yourself tomorrow. In person.

GRACE We can celebrate next weekend. If I want to get my rent deposit back, then I have to move out by Thursday. Is that okay with you? [*She repeats.*] Ma?

DOROTHY No.

GRACE What do you mean, no.

[DOROTHY *extends her arms, palms up.*]

DOROTHY [*Lowers left hand.*] Huntington. [*Raises right hand.*] Manhattan. [*Lowers further.*] Huntington. [*Raises higher.*] Manhattan. [*Lowers left hand.*] Huntington. [*Raises right hand.*] Manhattan. [*Lowers her hands.*] I mean no, Grace, it's not okay with me. This is what's going to happen. You're going to stay here—in this . . . palace!—and I will pay your rent and you will go to school and study hard and make a life for yourself. I can manage without you. Barely, but I will.

GRACE But I don't mind—

DOROTHY End of discussion.

GRACE But, Ma, it's—

DOROTHY End of discussion! It's my turn to save you, Grace. It's my turn. [*Suddenly.*] Now—do you have any leftover macaroni? [GRACE *nods her head.*] Mayonnaise packets?

GRACE   Uh huh.

DOROTHY   I think a little macaroni salad will compliment a quarter corned beef sandwich and half a pickle, don't you?

GRACE   Yes, I do. You amaze me, Mom.

DOROTHY   I have an obscure quote that I'd like to share with you today. [*She recites.*]

"I love when people underestimate me and then become pleasantly surprised." [*She beams at her daughter.*] Do you know who said that?

GRACE   Hillary Clinton? Margaret Thatcher?

DOROTHY   Kim Kardashian.

GRACE   I love you, Ma.

DOROTHY   Of course you do!

[*Lights to black.*]

• • •

Amulets for Garthenon

Jake Hunsbusher

Amulets for Garthenon by Jake Hunsbusher. Copyright © 2018 by Crystal Skillman. All rights reserved. Reprinted by permission of the author.

CAUTION/ADVICE: Professionals and amateurs are hereby warned that performance of *Amulets for Garthenon* is subject to a royalty. It is fully protected under the copyright laws of the United States of America, and all of countries covered by the International Copyright Union (including the Dominion of Canada and the rest of the British Commonwealth), and of all countries covered by the Pan-American Copyright Convention and the United States Copyright Convention, the Berne Convention, and all of the countries with which the United States has reciprocal copyright relations. All rights, including professional and amateur stage performing rights, motion picture, recitation, lecturing, public reading, radio broadcasting, television, video or sound picture recording, all other forms of mechanical or electronic reproduction, such as CD-ROM, DVD-ROM, information storage and retrieval systems, and photocopying, and the rights of translation into foreign language are strictly reserved. Particular emphasis is placed upon the matter of readings, permission for which must be secured by Jake Hunsbusher, in writing in advance. Inquiries concerning rights should be addressed to Jake Hunsbusher at jakehunsbusher@gmail.com.

Jake Hunsbusher

JAKE HUNSBUSHER received his MFA in Dramatic Media from the University of Georgia and is an instructor at Brenau University. His short play *Oh Brother Where Aren't Thou?* was selected for the KCACTF Region VI Festival in 2018, and his full length *Everybody's Movin'* was commissioned by the Theatre Department at Gardner-Webb University. Jake developed *Amulets for Garthenon* into a television pilot concept which retains the core of the piece but adapts it to work as an episodic series. Jake loves pushing and pulling the fantasy genre to new extremes and creating wild genre mix-ups. However, no matter the genre Jake always makes sure to keep the "spirit of strangeness" alive in all his work.

···production history···

Amulets for Garthenon was produced by JAM productions as part of the Spring 2018 One Act Play Festival at The Manhattan Repertory Theatre. It premiered April 5, 2018, and was directed by Jake Hunsbusher with the following cast:

AVERY MANN / GARTHENON, Jake Hunsbusher

BROOKYLN ACCENT / AERITHIN, Matthew Suwalski

CUE CARD HOLDER, Anna Corbould

characters

AVERY MAN / GARTHENON, a man in his mid-twenties, a quiet reserved sort.

BROOKLYN ACCENT / AERITHIN, a man in his early twenties, a lighthearted drifter. He has a Brooklyn accent. Called BROOK for short.

CUE CARD HOLDER, a person with the ability to hold cue cards.

setting

Living room of an apartment.

notes

This play incorporates the live audience element from televised sitcoms. Therefore it is important to have a method of goading the audience into making various responses such as "Applause," "Laughs," "Hoots and Hollers," "Awww." This can be done simply by having a stagehand off to one side with cards indicating the desired audience response or with an elaborate panel system with the responses lighting up when appropriate. If using the lit panel system, disregard the lines spoken by the Cue Card Holder in the beginning and treat all related cues as corresponding with the panel system.

In a similar vein, actors should treat this as a sitcom with a live audience. So, if the audience decides to respond without the cue cards, as they become more comfortable, the actors should stop and wait until the audience is finished before continuing. Whether it is a timed response specifically noted in the script, or one that is naturally occurring.

• • •

[*Lights up.* CUE CARD HOLDER *comes out.*]

CUE CARD HOLDER   Welcome! Is everyone excited? Well, you should
be because tonight you're going to be part of a very unique
experience. We are in the early production phases of producing a new
sitcom and we need a live audience to help gauge consumer interest.
Hey, you're a live audience, right? Well, most of you seem alive.
Would you mind helping us out?

[*Pause for audience response. Repeat question if response is unsatisfactory.*]

CUE CARD HOLDER   Alright! Now, you're smart people, I'm sure you
understand how cue cards work. Actually, we should probably do a
quick practice run.

[CUE CARD HOLDER *holds up all the different cards and teaches the audience
about effective cue card response.*]

CUE CARD HOLDER   Have you considered pursuing a career as a live
studio audience? Because you've got a natural talent for this. Let's
hope you can keep it up because we're rolling in Five! Four! Three!

[CUE CARD HOLDER *mouths the word "two" and then the word "one" while
pointing to the camera.*]

[*Blackout.*]

[*Lights up.* CUE CARD HOLDER *stands to the side with cue cards in hand.*
AVERY MANN *anxiously waits for his girlfriend to show up. He dials her number
and gets the voicemail.*]

AVERY   [*To the voicemail.*] Hey, sweetie, it's me again. I know you said
you'd be a little late but you're not picking up and it's kind of freaking
me out. I don't mean to be that clingy boyfriend but I'm just
concerned abou—

[*There is a loud knock on the front door.* AVERY *is initially startled but lights up
thinking that his girlfriend has arrived.*]

AVERY [*Continued, as he opens the door.*] Took you long enough, you
nearly gave me a hear—

[AVERY *realizes that the person at the door is not his girlfriend but rather a man
with a large duffel bag slung over his shoulder and a gaudy pendant hanging around
his neck.*]

BROOK Well, I'm here, ain't I?

[*This is* BROOK's *catchphrase and it comes with its own set of movements which are
at the actor's discretion.*]

[*The applause cue for the audience comes on.*]

AVERY Oh, Lord—I'm sorry. I thought you were someone else. Who
are you, exactly—

BROOK [*Interrupting.*] That's alright, not the first time I've been
confused with someone else. Prolly 'cause of the wanted poster they
got of me at the police station.

AVERY What!?

[*Laughs cue.*]

[BROOK *walks past* AVERY *into the living room and sets his bag down.*]

BROOK Hah! I'm only messing with you, friend. Ah . . . I can already
tell we're gonna have a unique chemistry you and I.

[*Laughs cue.*]

AVERY Oh, hah, you certainly fooled me. Speaking of you would you
mind telling me why—

BROOK Dynamic differences. That's what makes a great relationship,
and not just in love or friendship either. I mean, take my butcher,
Frank, for example—

AVERY Who are you!?

[*Laughs cue.*]

BROOK Oh jeez, I've done it again. I've come all the way into your
house without even introducing myself. I guess I just assumed the

email was introduction enough. But as my Ma always used to say, "Electronic manners don't equate to real life manners. No matter how many emojis you got." Good on you for standing up for your values, I respect that.

AVERY   Can I have your name, please?

[*Laughs cue.*]

BROOK   Oh! I'm Brooklyn Accent.

[*A beat and laughs cue.*]

BROOK   But my friends call me Brook for short.

AVERY   Alright, Brooklyn. I'm Avery, Avery Mann. Now that we're properly acquainted . . . what are you doing in my apartment?!

[*Laughs cue.*]

BROOK   Hah! I'm here about the vacancy of course!

AVERY   The vacancy? Oh! My ad! Wait, you said you sent an email?

BROOK   You didn't get the email? Oh, so that's why you were being such a rude jerk. That's a great relief. I didn't know how long I'd be able to put up with such overt rudeness.

[*Laughs cue.*]

BROOK   It's probably for the best, though. That email had way too many emojis. I usually save that for the ladies. You know what I'm saying?

[*Hoots and hollers cue.*]

AVERY   Okay. Well, Mr. Accent normally I'd show you around but I'm not exactly ready to give a tour and also someone is supposed to be meeting me here soon so—

BROOK   You don't need to make any fuss on account of me, and please call me Brook. I don't care if the place is a little 'lived in' right now. Just gives me realistic expectations.

AVERY   Alright. Well, I'll really only be free until my friend gets here. You'd be okay with a short tour?

BROOK Well, I'm here, ain't I?

[*Applause cue.*]

AVERY Cool, then I'll show you to the bedroom.

BROOK Why?

[*Laughs cue.*]

AVERY I thought you wanted to see?

BROOK There's no need to show me every little detail.

[BROOK *sits down on the sofa and gets comfortable.*]

BROOK This is just fine.

[*Laughs cue.*]

AVERY Right. Well, if you saw my ad then you'll know that the price is $350 a month firm. Now, I know that may seem like a lot for a room in the suburbs, but you do have your own bathroom and complete access to the living room—

BROOK Wait wait wait, hold on a second. I get my own room?!

[*Laughs cue.*]

AVERY Well, yeah? What did you think you were renting?

BROOK The couch!

[*Laughs cue.*]

AVERY You wanted to rent the couch?

BROOK Well, I'm here, ain't I?

[*Applause cue.*]

AVERY You thought you were paying $350 dollars a month for a couch?

BROOK Oh, I knew I must have read that wrong. I mean only $350 for a couch as nice as this one? I thought this might be some sort of scam with the price being so low but I figured you were probably knocking a couple hundred off because it didn't pull out.

[*Laughs cue.*]

AVERY   Oh no, it pulls out.

[BROOK *gasps loudly. Laughs cue.*]

AVERY   But the vacancy isn't for the couch. It's for my spare room.

BROOK   Well, if the couch is $350 a month then the room has gotta be outta my price range.

[*Laughs cue.*]

AVERY   I'm not renting out the couch!

[*Laughs cue.*]

BROOK   So what you're saying is?

AVERY   I'm renting out the room for $350.

[*BROOK gasps even louder.*]

BROOK   No!

[*Laughs cue.*]

AVERY   Yes.

[*Laughs cue.*]

AVERY   Now, I don't really have any more time to spare, on account of my plans with my friend, so if you want a full tour you'll have to come back another time.

BROOK   Well, they ain't here, are they?

[BROOK *does a toned down version of his catchphrase movements.*]

[*Applause cue.*]

AVERY   No, they're not but—

BROOK   Then let's get on with this tour!

[*Laughs cue.*]

AVERY   Listen, Brook, I'd really rather do this another time.

BROOK   Oh, I see what's going on here!

[*Laughs cue.*]

AVERY You do?

BROOK This "friend" you're waiting on isn't really your friend, are they?

AVERY Well, I guess technically they're more than a friend.

BROOK I knew it! You've got another potential roommate coming in right after me!

[*Laughs cue.*]

AVERY What?

BROOK Look, I'm not judging. You're just trying to get a good deal here.

Play the field. See who wants the room the most. Well, I want that room the most and I'm willing to pay the $350 for the first month right now to reserve my spot!

[BROOK *takes out his wallet. Laughs cue.*]

AVERY No, no, you've got it all wrong.

BROOK What, is the other guy offering you more? I knew $350 was too low. How much is this guy offering? Whatever it is I'll match it. $400? $450?

AVERY I haven't been offered anything!

[*Laughs cue.*]

BROOK I know how this works. Listen, I'll go as high as five hundred dollars a month but I'm not going any higher no matter what that other guy is willing to shell out!

AVERY Done.

[*Laughs cue.*]

[*They shake hands. AVERY's phone begins to ring. He walks toward the door and answers it. It's his girlfriend.*]

AVERY Hey! Finally you call back! Where are you? No, look, its fine. It's not even that big of a deal. Everyone is late now and again. Just come over as soon as you can and we'll talk about it.

[*A beat.*]

AVERY What do you mean? How could you say that I—Hello? Hello?

[AVERY *puts his phone away and sits on the couch.*]

BROOK So, your friend isn't coming?

AVERY No.

BROOK Was it because of the couch?

[*Laughs cue.*]

AVERY [*Sarcastically.*] Yes, Brook, it was because of the couch.

[*Laughs cue.*]

BROOK I'm sure if you pulled it out they'd give you another chance.

[*Laughs cue.*]

AVERY No, it's not really about the—

BROOK Just, pull it out, show them how big it is, and I'm sure they'll want to sit right on it. I mean, hey, I'm here, ain't I?

[*Hoots and hollers cue.*]

AVERY It wasn't anyone answering the ad. It was my girlfriend. She was supposed to meet me for our date but she just dumped me. Way to go, Avery. You drove another one away!

[*Laughs cue.*]

[AVERY *puts his head in his hands.* BROOK *leans* AVERY *onto his shoulder and tries to comfort him.*]

BROOK Hey, buddy, hey. It's not your fault. You're the one who got stood up. Not her. If anyone should'a been dumping anyone it should'a been you dumping on her.

[*Laughs cue.*]

AVERY   No. No. She was great. I'm just a loser.

BROOK   No way! You're great! I've only known you for a few minutes, but you've got a great apartment. And you're probably a really great guy too.

[*Laughs cue.*]

AVERY   You mean it?

BROOK   Yeah, I mean, probably!

[*Laughs cue.*]

AVERY   Thanks, Brooklyn.

[AVERY *lifts his head off of* BROOK's *shoulder.*]

AVERY   You're being nice, and I appreciate it, but I'll be okay. You don't have to hang around here to comfort me . . . if you don't want to.

BROOK   [*In a genuine tone.*] Well, I'm here, ain't I?

[*Aww cue.*]

BROOK   Listen, I've been through this kinda heartache before. There was a time when the girl of my dreams just up and dumped me. And I didn't even get a phone call! All I got was a poorly worded text message. Not a single emoji.

AVERY   Not even a crying one?

BROOK   Nope. The only crying face I saw was the one in my mirror.

[*Laughs cue.*]

BROOK   Yeah, I was so broken up about it I was crying for days. Eventually my uncle Tony busted into my room, slapped me cross the face, and told me . . . a little story about love. Then he gave me this.

[BROOK *points to his pendant.*]

BROOK   He was planning on giving this ugly old necklace to his girl but she dumped him before he could. He was so obsessed with the girl that he started wearing the thing around town. Embarrassing. But after only six months he met aunt Gina. He figured it must'a been a good luck charm all along.

[*Laughs cue.*]

AVERY [*Indicating the pendant.*] So, this was a gift from your uncle?

BROOK Yeah? What?

AVERY Well, why did he give it to you instead of your aunt? Did he keep wearing it even after they got married?

[*Laughs cue.*]

BROOK You're missing the point. The necklace is a reminder that good luck will always find you. Sometimes you just gotta look for it. This thing helped me through some tough times in my life. But it seems like there's someone here who needs it even more.

[BROOK *puts the necklace on* AVERY.]

AVERY You're giving this to me?

BROOK Yeah, but only until you're outta this funk. I ain't married yet. So I'm gonna need that back.

[*Laughs cue.*]

[AVERY MANN *stands up holding the pendant and walks away from* BROOK *while examining it.*]

AVERY Wow, Brook you're . . . A COMPLETE FOOL! MWEHEHEHEE!

BROOK [*Without a Brooklyn accent.*] No! No, it can't be!

[BROOK *stands in shock.* AVERY MANN *removes his beanie to reveal a mystical looking pattern tattooed on his forehead.*]

BROOK It is!

AVERY The great and powerful GARTHENON!

[BROOK *recovers from his shock and tries to rush* GARTHENON *and take back the pendant but* GARTHENON *holds it up and uses its power to command* BROOK.]

GARTHENON FREEZE!

[BROOK *freezes in his tracks.*]

GARTHENON Now go sit on that couch you proclaim to love so much.

[BROOK *complies.*]

GARTHENON There, aren't we more comfortable now? Aerithin?!

AERITHIN Do you really think you'll get away with this?

GARTHENON Funny. I was planning to ask the same of you. Did you really think there was a place in the multi-verse where I would not find you? Did you think there was a limit to my thirst for the power of the amulet of Taromesh? There is no black hole dark enough nor gravity well deep enough to keep me from my birthright!

AERITHIN The elder council revoked your claim to the throne!

GARTHENON The elder council. Pah! They are mere children compared to my intellect! My ambition!

AERITHIN What you were doing was wrong!

GARTHENON You dare question the ethics of Garthenon!? I find you far in the deepest recesses of the universe and what are you doing? Living under an assumed name, trying to master the powers of the amulet, just as I was.

AERITHIN I'm nothing like you! I was learning how to control the amulet so it could be used for good!

GARTHENON Hypocrisy! You can change your name, Aerithin, but I know you now as I knew you then. Young and foolish! With a thirst for power to rival my own. Why else would you be harnessing the sheer potency of the comedic duo ritual? Gaining strength from the catchphrase incantation?

AERITHIN I should have known. The energy signature emanating from this apartment was too good to be true. What kind of straight man warms up that quickly? There's no dramatic longevity.

GARTHENON Yet, you still attempted to charge the Amulet of Taromesh with the Audiencial power.

AERITHIN   The romantic subplot rune was almost visible. I thought if I placed it directly on the source . . .

[AERITHIN *is overcome with regret.* GARTHENON *sits down on the couch and leans* AERITHIN's *head onto his shoulder.* AERITHIN *has no choice but to comply.*]

GARTHENON   Don't be too hard on yourself, Aerithin. The Audiencial force was coursing through your veins. No one can resist its wiles.

AERITHIN   Avery Mann? How could I have missed *Avery Mann*?

GARTHENON   It's quite simple really. Your lust for power blinded you to archetypes . . .

[AERITHIN *subtly tries to grab the amulet but* GARTHENON *is aware of the attempt and moves away.*]

GARTHENON   Just as my trust in you blinded me to your impending treachery all those years ago.

AERITHIN   It's true; I was young and foolish so I followed a man with nothing but the promise of strength on his lips. But I now know what that power can do and that's why it must be kept from the likes of you! You're a monster!

GARTHENON   Pity. I had thought we might have worked together again. But, perhaps I am growing sentimental in my old age.

[GARTHENON *points the amulet at* AERITHIN.]

GARTHENON   I won't make the same mistake twice. Any last words, Aerithin?

AERITHIN   [*With a Brooklyn accent.*] Well, I'm here, ain't I?

[*Applause cue. The ground quakes.*]

GARTHENON   That doesn't even really make sense!

[*Laughs cue.*]

AERITHIN   Regardless, it seems to have been enough for the Audencial power. Now give me that amulet, Garthenon.

[GARTHENON, *with obvious strain, takes off the pendant and holds it out to* AERITHIN. *But when* AERITHIN *reaches for it* GARTHENON *closes it in his hand. They are both kinda holding hands.*]

GARTHENON So, I see you're not completely inexperienced. But I know the ins and outs of the Audencial power and more importantly . . .

[GARTHENON, *with some strain, pulls a stereo remote out of his pocket and turns on some funky music.*]

GARTHENON I know what they like.

[GARTHENON *begins dancing to the music. Plants in the audience will begin rhythmically clapping which should hopefully cause the actual audience to do so.*]

GARTHENON [*With the music.*] Oh yeah, that's how daddy does it! Garthy is back! MWEHEHEHEE!

[*Applause cue.*]

AERITHIN I'm sorry Garthenon, I can't let you have this kind of power. No matter the alternative.

GARTHENON [*Still dancing.*] Oh, and I suppose you're going to stop me?

AERITHIN Yes, by invoking the dance battle sacrament.

[GARTHENON *gasps.*]

GARTHENON No.

AERITHIN Yes!

GARTHENON No!

AERITHIN YES!

[*Applause cue.*]

[*The dance battle commences.*]

AERITHIN The Audiencial power shall decide it's ruler!

GARTHENON You know not the forces you trifle with, boy. Have you learned nothing?

AERITHIN Shut up and dance, Garthenon.

[AERITHIN *shows off his moves.*]

GARTHENON You're good. But I can do better.

[GARTHENON *counters with his moves.*]

[*Laughs cue.*]

[AERITHIN *counters the counter with an impressive display.*]

[*Hoots and Hollers cue.*]

GARTHENON No, no! They're turning against me!

[*Applause cue.*]

[GARTHENON *falls to his knees and offers up the amulet.*]

GARTHENON Nooooooo!

[AERITHIN *grabs the amulet and smashes it.*]

[*All the audience cues go up simultaneously and then go out.*]

GARTHENON You fool! You haven't just stopped me! You've stopped this entire dimension! You've doomed us all to an infinite time loop!

AERITHIN Well, then perhaps neither of us were meant to have the amulet.

[*A beat.*]

GARTHENON What?! That's it?! We're going to be doomed to an endless and repeating hell and that's all you have to say?!

AERITHIN Geez, sorry, I thought breaking it would just make it not work.

GARTHENON I'll kill you!

[*Blackout just as* GARTHENON *begins to strangle* AERITHIN.]

[*Lights up.* CUE CARD HOLDER *is gone.*]

[AVERY MANN *anxiously waits for his girlfriend to show up. He dials her number and gets the voicemail.*]

AVERY   [*To the voicemail.*] Hey, sweetie, it's me again. I know you said you'd be a little late but you're not picking up and it's kind of freaking me out. I don't mean to be that clingy boyfriend but I'm just concerned abou—

[*There is a loud knock on the front door. AVERY is startled but lights up thinking that his girlfriend has arrived.*]

AVERY   [*As he opens the door.*] Took you long enough, you nearly gave me a hear—

[AVERY *realizes that the person at the door is not his girlfriend but rather a man with a large duffel bag slung over his shoulder and a gaudy pendant hanging around his neck.*]

BROOK   Well, I'm here, ain't I?

• • •

acknowledgments

This anthology would not be possible if it weren't for the rich community of playwrights living in the United States. My thanks to each and every writer in this anthology, and to those who answered the call for plays but whose scripts were not included at this time. I truly appreciate your giving me the chance to experience your work!

My sincere thanks to Carol Flannery and the rest of the good people at Applause Theatre and Cinema Books and Rowman & Littlefield for having faith in this anthology series. Thank you, also, to my agent, June Clark at Fine Print Literary Management for her continued support. And a personal thank you to my wife, Danielle, and our children for your love, your patience, and for helping me remember what is truly important in this life.